TWENTIETH INTERNATIONAL SEAPOWER SYMPOSIUM

Report of the Proceedings

Twentieth International Seapower Symposium

Report of the Proceedings
18–21 October 2011

Edited by

John B. Hattendorf
Ernest J. King Professor of Maritime History
Naval War College
and
John W. Kennedy

U.S. Naval War College

Newport, Rhode Island

2013

Editor's Note

The editor has made every attempt to establish a clear and accurate record of the symposium proceedings, one that faithfully records the opinions and views of the participants. In establishing the printed text from speaking notes, transcripts, seminar notes, and tape recordings of speakers or of the official English-language simultaneous translators, the editor has silently corrected slips of grammar, spelling, and wording. He has inserted full names and ranks when omitted by the speaker, and occasionally a word or phrase in square brackets to clarify the text.

The editor acknowledges with great appreciation the tremendously valuable support and assistance of John W. Kennedy, in listening to the tapes and helping to prepare the final text for publication, and the assistance of the Naval War College's Visual Communications Department with its Desktop Publishing unit, particularly Jerry Lenihan and Ken DeRouin, for composition and layout, and Shannon Cole and Albert F. Fassbender for copyediting and proofreading.

Newport
July 2012   J.B.H.

CHIEF OF NAVAL OPERATIONS

18 October 2011

It is my pleasure to welcome you to the 20th International Seapower Symposium (ISS-20). We have a broad and diverse group from the International Naval Community. I am assured we will have a robust and energetic meeting of the minds over the next four days. The schedule is the culmination of input from your fellow Heads of Navy and delegates to highlight areas of mutual interest as we build "Security and Prosperity through Maritime Partnerships".

Our frank and open discussions will serve to strengthen our international relationships and rich naval traditions.

Sincerely,

Jonathan W. Greenert

JONATHAN W. GREENERT
Admiral, U.S. Navy

Table of Contents

Editor's Note..v

Welcome Letter to Delegates..vi

Plenary Sessions

Chapter 1   **Welcoming Remarks**

    Rear Admiral John N. Christenson, U.S. Navy
        President, U.S. Naval War College

    Admiral Jonathan W. Greenert, U.S. Navy
        Chief of Naval Operations

    The Honorable Leon E. Panetta
        Secretary of Defense 1

Chapter 2   **Globalization, Security, and Economic Well-Being**

    Mr. Stephen Carmel
        Senior Vice President of Maritime Services,
        Maersk Line, Limited..9

Chapter 3   **Panel Discussion One: Global Perspectives:
The Challenge to Maritime Security**

    Moderated by Admiral Tan Sri Abdul Aziz Jaafar, Malaysia...............23

        Panel Members:

            Admiral Nimal Verma, India
            Admiral Alexander Pama, Philippines
            Staff Brigadier General Ibrahim S. M. Almusharrakh,
            United Arab Emirates
            Vice Admiral Ola Sa'ad Ibrahim, Nigeria

Chapter 4   **An Address**

    Honorable Ray Mabus
        Secretary of the Navy 53

Chapter 5   **Maritime Domain Awareness Operational Game Results**

    Dean Robert C. "Barney" Rubel
        Dean, Center for Naval Warfare Studies,
        U.S. Naval War College..59

Chapter 6 **Panel Discussion Two: Beyond MDA:
Building Responsive Partnerships**

    Moderated by Vice Admiral Johannes Refiloe Mudimu, South Africa... 77

    Panel Members:

        Admiral Bruno Branciforte, Italy
        Admiral Julio Soares de Moura Neto, Brazil
        Vice Admiral Laksdya Marsetio, Indonesia
        Vice Admiral Paul Maddison, Canada

Chapter 7 **The Hattendorf Prize**

    Awarded to Dr. N. A. M. Rodger
        All Souls College, Oxford University 103

Chapter 8 **Regional Breakout Group Reports**

    Moderated by Professor Thomas Culora
        Chairman, Warfare Analysis and Research Department,
        U.S. Naval War College 109

    Atlantic Ocean
        Commander André Panno Beirão, Brazil 109

    Pacific Ocean
        Lieutenant Colonel Saiful Akhmar, Brunei 112

    Indian Ocean
        Captain Saqib Khattak, Pakistan 115

    Mediterranean, Black Sea, and Caspian Sea
        Captain Cihat Yayci, Turkey 118

    Caribbean
        Lieutenant Commander Norman Dindial,
        Trinidad and Tobago 120

    Norwegian, North, and Baltic Seas
        Commodore Henning Amundsen, Norway 122

    Gulf of Guinea and Gulf of Aden
        Rear Admiral Robert Higgs, South Africa 125

    Arabian Gulf and Oman Sea
        Commander Abdulla Sultan Hassan Al Khozaimy,
        United Arab Emirates 129

Chapter 9 **An Address**

    Dr. Nicholas Eberstadt
        American Enterprise Institute for Public Policy
        and Research 133

Chapter 10 **Panel Discussion Three: Maritime Security, Evolving Demands, Adaptive Partnership**

    Moderated by Admiral Edmundo González Robles, Chile 157

        Panel Members:

        Rear Admiral Bernt Grimstvedt, Norway
        Admiral José Santiago Valdés Álvarez, Mexico
        Captain Igor Schvede, Estonia
        Vice Admiral Enrique Larrañaga Martin, Chile
        Admiral Masahiko Sugimoto, Japan

Chapter 11 **Closing Remarks**

    Rear Admiral John N. Christenson and
    Admiral Jonathan W. Greenert 201

                * * *

Appendix **List of Delegates** 205

1

Welcoming Remarks

Rear Admiral John N. Christenson, U.S. Navy
President, U.S. Naval War College

Admiral Jonathan W. Greenert, U.S. Navy
Chief of Naval Operations

Video Remarks: The Honorable Leon E. Panetta
Secretary of Defense

Professor Thomas Culora:

Good morning. Admiral Greenert, Admiral Christenson, distinguished leaders of navies and coast guards from around the world, we are honored by your presence here in Newport. I am Professor Tom Culora, chairman of the Warfare Analysis and Research Department here at the Naval War College.

Now it is my great pleasure to introduce to you the President of the Naval War College, Rear Admiral John Christenson. Admiral Christenson became the fifty-third President of the Naval War College on March 30 of this year. As he likes to point out, he is the fourth of six sons of a U.S. Navy Skyraider pilot and a Navy nurse, so the Navy is in his DNA.

He graduated from the U.S. Naval Academy in 1981 and served in a variety of billets at sea over the years, including, when we first met—I won't say the date—on the USS *Cook*. We had our first deployments together as young ensigns. I'm proud to call him shipmate.

He has had command at sea at every level, including the frigate USS *McClusky*, Destroyer Squadron 21, and Carrier Strike Group 12. Ashore he has led the Navy as Commander of the Surface Warfare Officers School located down the street here in Newport. As a new flag officer, he served as Commander, Naval Mine and Antisubmarine Warfare Command in Corpus Christi, Texas.

He has served at the U.S. Naval Academy, at Headquarters Marine Corps in the Strategic Initiative Group, and on the Joint Staff, in the J5 Directorate and as executive assistant to the assistant chairman. He most recently served as President of the Board of Inspections and Survey before coming here to the Naval War College.

No stranger to this institution, he was first in his class here at the College and graduated with highest distinction. He was also a Navy Federal Executive Fellow at the Fletcher School of Law and Diplomacy up the road in Boston. As you can see,

Admiral Christenson brings a wealth of operational, academic, and leadership experience to his current role as President of the U.S. Naval War College.

We are fortunate to have him here at the College. I'm very pleased this morning to introduce to you the fifty-third President of the Naval War College, Rear Admiral John Christenson.

Rear Admiral John Christenson, United States:

Thank you, Tom. Good morning, leaders of the world's seapower. Welcome to Newport, Rhode Island, and to the Naval War College. We hope that your time here provides you an opportunity to think and to build relationships. My wife Teresa and I really appreciated the opportunity to meet nearly all of you last evening.

In 1969 Admiral Richard G. Colbert was President here at the Naval War College. Forty-two years ago he stood before an impressive group of leaders to welcome them to the very first International Seapower Symposium. Admiral Colbert said, "We are gathered in a truly historic meeting. Never before have so many brilliant and penetrating minds from so many countries gathered in search of a common end."

At that time there were eighty high-ranking navy representatives from thirty-seven different countries, including twenty chiefs of navy or deputy chiefs of navy. Today we gather a new generation of brilliant and penetrating minds, but the numbers have grown. Thirty-seven nations are now 115. Twenty chiefs or deputy chiefs are now seventy-five chiefs of navy and twenty-two heads of coast guard. An additional one hundred flag-level military civilian leaders from the international community are here this week.

We gather to continue that pursuit of a common end that Admiral Colbert spoke of forty-two years ago. This auditorium is named after a great strategic thinker, Admiral Raymond Spruance. Admiral Spruance served here four times, as student, as director of education, as director of tactics, and as President. He was famous for his unparalleled, cool judgment in combat. He was a product of an education designed to develop maritime leaders who think clearly and critically about their profession.

You are the Spruances of today. We are proud to say that many of you are alumni. We admire you and are especially proud of the seventy-two delegates in the audience today who are graduates of the Naval War College. Sixty-one are graduates of our international program courses. Notably, twenty-four of those are heads of their navy or coast guard. To you seventy-two, welcome back to Newport and congratulations on your successes. We are confident that the education you received here made a difference.

Tonight's reception at the Officers' Club is in honor of all our returning alumni as well as the one hundred students representing the sixty-one countries that make up this year's group of international officers. We place great value in our international program. It supports the principles we share: respect and appreciation for the sea, respect for those who serve and sacrifice to create maritime security, and finally, a commitment to work collectively to solve common problems.

As we gather today, many of our senior international students are in seminar with their U.S. classmates working on a capstone exercise, in which they produce an executive-level strategic estimate of the future global security environment. Our intermediate class is in the middle of a joint operational planning exercise focused on maritime warfare in the littoral environment.

While we maritime leaders focus on the challenges of today, be confident that our future leaders are preparing together for the challenges of tomorrow. Again, it is my pleasure and honor to welcome you to Newport and the Naval War College.

It is now my honor to introduce our host for ISS Twenty, the thirtieth Chief of Naval Operations, Admiral Jonathan Greenert. Admiral Greenert is from the hard-working steel town of Butler, Pennsylvania. He graduated from the Naval Academy in Annapolis in 1975. He studied and was qualified in nuclear power and submarines.

He served in USS *Flying Fish* (SSN 673), USS *Tautog* (SSN 639), the submarine *NR-1,* and USS *Michigan* (SSBN 727, Gold crew). He commanded USS *Honolulu* (SSN 718), Submarine Squadron 11, Naval Forces Marianas, the 7th Fleet, and U.S. Fleet Forces Command. Admiral Greenert has worked hard ashore in fleet support and financial management, including as Deputy Chief of Naval Operations for Integration of Capabilities and Resources; Deputy Commander of U.S. Pacific Fleet; Chief of Staff, U.S. 7th Fleet; head, Navy Programming Branch and director, Operations Division Navy Comptroller, and most recently as our thirty-sixth Vice Chief of Naval Operations.

In our Navy, the ultimate aspiration is command at sea. The ultimate recognition for command at sea is the peer-nominated Vice Admiral James B. Stockdale Award for inspirational leadership. Admiral Greenert earned that award in 1992 for his command of USS *Honolulu.* He probably is more proud of all the Battle Es the teams he led consistently won.

Admiral Greenert became the thirtieth Chief of Naval Operations on September 23, 2011. Please join me in welcoming the host of the twentieth International Seapower Symposium, the Chief of Naval Operations, Admiral Jonathan Greenert.

Admiral Jonathan Greenert, United States:

Thank you very much, John. We have obviously a structured program, but it does my heart great good to look out on the video while we were waiting in the greenroom, which is, by the way, white, and see all of you out here doing the networking. That's what really makes the difference. That's a lot of what this conference is about.

John Christenson, thank you very much for what you have done here at the Naval War College. We are truly on a roll with good presidents, great presidents. You are going to be one of the better ones; I can just feel it now.

Thank you to the Naval War College staff. It's a big project, it's a huge effort to get the international program running and going as well as it does, and then of course, to have us come up with this very important symposium. Professor Vince Mocini does just a marvelous job with this, and the behind-the-scenes work is truly impressive. It's running very smoothly.

Distinguished guests; alumni of the Naval War College; and, of course, my colleagues, heads of navy, heads of coast guard, heads of war colleges, and distinguished delegates, welcome to the Naval War College and welcome to the United States. I want to thank all of you. It's not lost on me the effort that you and your nation put forth to bring you here to Newport and the sacrifice of your time and your effort to do what we're going to do.

I want to take a moment to welcome twelve countries who are here for the first time: Comoros, Côte d'Ivoire, Dominica, Grenada, Guinea, Haiti, Panama, St. Lucia, Tonga, Trinidad and Tobago, Tuvalu, and Vanuatu. Thank you all very much for joining us. It is your attendance that will make this that much better. I'd ask our colleagues to welcome our new friends.

I'm honored to be here with maritime colleagues, and I'll tell you that I've had good luck—after the first week in office, I was able to break the suction of Washington, D.C., and get out and travel and see some of you. I look forward to expanding my horizons and seeing so many more of you and learning from you in your environment as well as in our environment.

I'm very honored that you were able to bring your spouses here, many of you. As you and I both know, leading your navy, leading any part of our navy or coast guard is a team effort, taking care of our sailors and our coastguardsmen.

As John said when he introduced us this morning, this symposium is unique, and it's unlike any other in structure and in attendance. It was first held in 1969—think about that. It was last held here in 2009, where we were amazed that we had 102 nations and ninety heads of naval service.

I was here at that time as the Vice Chief of Naval Operations. I was following closely the efforts of my predecessor, Admiral Gary Roughead, who has been a mentor of mine for many years. I find him an amazing visionary. He was a great boss and a mentor. I hope to keep the momentum that he started going as we work together in the challenges.

This year, as John said, we have about 115 nations and ninety-six heads of naval services. We're almost running out of countries in the world, but we're not doing very bad. I love the momentum. Thank you very much. This is the largest meeting of naval leaders in the world. It is the capstone of a seapower conference. It has prospered because all of you are willing to come together, leave your ego and your issues at the door, and sit down and discuss openly the common interests and the common challenges that we have. I'm hopeful that this year will be no different.

Our theme, "Security and Prosperity through Maritime Partnerships," will bear great fruit. We have important collective issues, you and I. We represent our countries' efforts to defend our shores and our maritime interests and to secure the global maritime commons in the world for economic growth.

The stakes are getting higher, in view of the fact that we have emerging worldwide unrest and we have financial challenges out there. The security of the sea lines of communication is even more important, in view of that. Collectively what we need, you and I, is trust and confidence. It can't be surged, and you can't just stand it up. We need understanding among ourselves, and we need cooperation. We need to establish it, and we need to nurture it over time.

Our Secretary of Defense understands this. It's really a first principle of his strategy for our Defense Department. He regrets his inability to be here to personally talk about these topics, but he sent a video for us to watch. I would like to take this opportunity now to have us hear from our Secretary of Defense. Please roll the video.

Secretary of Defense Leon Panetta, United States:

I'm truly honored to be able to address all of you here today at the twentieth International Seapower Symposium. This meeting marks the largest gathering of naval leaders in history. Your efforts to advance mutual interests and collective security are absolutely essential to address the most important challenges we all face together in this very difficult and interconnected world.

Trust and cooperation between the world's maritime services have long been a key enabler of global security, of global stability, and most importantly, of global prosperity. A safe and secure maritime domain is critical to global growth. Lifting all of our nations toward a better future is what this is all about.

International cooperation on issues such as piracy, trafficking, natural disasters, and a range of other potential threats enhances security for all of us and all of our nations. Strengthening maritime partnerships has become even more imperative in today's exceedingly complex operating environment. This symposium provides a valuable opportunity for all of you as maritime leaders to shape the path forward, to increase mutual trust and confidence, and to come up with solutions to current and future challenges.

Sharing your thoughts, sharing your ideas will help every nation, both large and small, rise to meet the challenges that we face at sea. You'll also build the deep and lasting relationships that we need in order to succeed together.

As we've all come to realize, globalization has generated a host of transnational challenges that do not recognize borders, nor do they recognize nation-states. No one nation has the resources or capacity to meet these many complex challenges alone.

As President Obama made clear at the United Nations General Assembly just last month, the need for cooperation among states has never been more urgent. From counterpiracy operations in the Gulf of Aden to many other joint maritime partnerships, you, all of you, have contributed to the robust and expanding international cooperation that we all so vitally need.

On behalf of President Obama, on behalf of the American people, I want to thank you for your service and for your collective efforts to promote a more peaceful, a more stable, and a more prosperous world. Thank you.

Admiral Jonathan Greenert, United States:

This morning, with my remaining time, I would like to leave you with a few thoughts about putting our words into action, about the challenges ahead, and about people, which will really be our legacy. As the secretary highlighted, your efforts are important, and together we've been successful for your nation and for all nations in our endeavors.

Daily today, collectively, our navies and our coast guards are addressing common issues—piracy, illicit trafficking, terrorism, proliferation and smuggling of weapons of mass destruction, and the enforcement of fishery boundaries. These are enduring issues. The operations will probably never really be complete. No one can do it alone.

Success is going to be and has to be collective. Tangible achievements have been made through partnerships. For example, our international counterpiracy efforts in the Strait of Malacca and the Gulf of Aden have reaped benefits. Piracy is down 70 percent in the Gulf of Aden since 2009. The Economic Community of Central African States has been patrolling the waters of mutual interest, and there have been successes.

There are other collective successes out there. The skills that our folks have are built on bilateral and multilateral maritime partnerships and exercises. Through these, we've facilitated important training through our sailors, our coastguardsmen, and our marines. We clearly enhance our interoperability. We enable regional and international disasters to have proper response and have those skills. We provide humanitarian assistance. Examples of our exercises and our operations:

- RIM OF THE PACIFIC exercise is our largest. We enhance the interoperability among the Pacific navies and coast guards and promote stability in the region.
- PACIFIC PARTNERSHIP ACROSS THE PACIFIC is where medical, dental, veterinarian, and engineering assistance skills are brought together in an opportunity to train and practice these humanitarian assistance skills.
- EXERCISE MALABAR, where five nations in the Indian Ocean conduct an annual exercise to develop a wide range of naval skills, from power projection to maritime intercept operations.
- COOPERATION AFLOAT READINESS AND TRAINING IN SOUTHEAST ASIA enhances our regional cooperation and strengthens skills throughout the Southeast Asia region.
- PROUD MANTA involves ten NATO nations working together to hone their ASW [antisubmarine warfare] skills.
- UNITAS is a collection of North and South American and European nations gathering together to focus on supporting stability in the Western Hemisphere.
- PANAMA CANAL EXERCISE involves fifteen to twenty nations gathering to ensure the security of the Panama Canal.
- OBANGAME EXPRESS is in Africa where central African nations and European nations focus on the maritime security of the Gulf of Guinea.
- OPERATION BRIGHT STAR features eleven countries from the Middle East and Europe gathering in an air/ground/naval training exercise process.

There are many others. All are valuable, and all are rewarding.

Of course, real-world humanitarian assistance and disaster relief provide valuable training. Haiti's earthquake recovery effort involved ten thousand sailors, marines, coastguardsmen, and soldiers from ten nations. The great east Japan earthquake and tsunami of 3/11 involved several nations and thousands of sailors, coastguardsmen, airmen, soldiers, and marines.

These exercises and partnerships are really a testament to progress. They are key to improving our ability to respond to our evolving challenge. These examples provide wonderful progress, but we have to welcome new initiatives. We need to be innovative, and we need to keep moving ahead.

Some of our initiatives will be short term, some will be enduring. During your breakout sessions, I really encourage you to instigate discussion about current initiatives that you have in your navy, in your coast guard. What is successful there?

Keep the momentum in our maritime domain awareness, where we're making such great progress. Maybe come up with three regional issues, three issues that we can work on over the next two years, and then reconvene in two years and see how it's going. I encourage you to discuss your specific challenges.

Speaking of challenges, clearly this is a challenging era of time for maritime forces. Most of our nations are experiencing constrained budgets as we look ahead. Others are wrestling with transition from a land focus to a maritime focus. The threats to freedom on the seas are still growing. Criminals are out there in the ungoverned spaces, and we have piracy emerging here and there.

Each country out there has its own perspective, but the challenges are similar. We in the U.S. Navy, our Marine Corps and our Coast Guard examined these challenges five, six years ago. And four years ago, at this very forum, Admiral Roughead came forward, along with Admiral Thad Allen from the Coast Guard and General Conway, Commandant of the Marines Corps, to introduce our maritime strategy, *The Cooperative Strategy for the 21st Century [Seapower]*:

In that document our sea services brought together two major points: preventing wars is as important as winning wars, and global maritime partnerships are absolutely essential to prevent disruptions and to contain conflict. This central idea of global maritime partnerships is enduring. It is just as important as, if not more important now than, it has been before.

We desire to see a cooperative approach to maritime security and the rule of law on the sea. Our *Cooperative Strategy for 21st Century Seapower,* our maritime strategy, has served us well, and I think it will continue to do so. We will need to sharpen its focus here and there as our challenges evolve.

Many of you have developed your own maritime strategy, your own strategic documents. They will help you focus your navies as well and their efforts. They will deal with the unique and demanding challenges of today and the challenges of tomorrow.

Although our strategic documents may be slightly different, there is one underlying theme in all of them—to develop that cooperative relationship with partners, with those of us in this room. It's not an end in and of itself, this cooperation, because the goal is maritime security. We need to prevent these disruptions, and we need to contain conflict out there.

National and international partnerships are essential to maritime security. They allow rapid response in multiple jurisdictions. They provide the capacity to search wide areas and to be able to respond. They build this maritime domain awareness we talk about, where we bring together information from multiple sources.

I would submit that we need to continue to focus these elements at not just the International Seapower Symposium, but the other symposiums around the world that you and I attend from time to time—the Western Pacific Naval Symposium, the International Maritime Defense Exhibit and Conference in Doha, the Inter-American Naval Conference, the Indian Ocean Naval Symposium, and Regional Seapower Symposium, just to name a few out there.

We need to be interoperable, and we need to be able to respond. It's about awareness. It's about communication. It's about the synergy of our navies and coast guards and our ability to respond and to be responsive. We need to have a common understanding of the maritime domain awareness. It is out there.

Our agreements on information sharing will bring us the trust. The Automatic Identification System (AIS) we need to build common operations and the concept of operations of that. The Maritime Safety and Security Information System (MSSIS)— we need to bring a common operational concept to that. Pull it all together, so we're looking toward that common operational picture.

Maritime Domain Awareness and that consolidation will bring us what I would call the speed of trust. If we trust each other, things will move fast. We'll have that speed that is necessary to be able to react. The need to coordinate the actions and the communications will be resolved, of course, by way of hardware that we develop. More properly, it will be brought together by relationships.

Lastly, we need to be able to take effective action. We need to be able to respond. Knowing and talking are one thing. Responding is really where we're going to get it down. We have to have the sufficient capacity through the cooperative agreements that we agree to. We need to have the sustainment whenever things happen. We need to posture ourselves to be able to react. And, of course, we have to trust each other and be willing to cooperate.

Now, a lot of this is going to take time. It's a long-term project. The projects will be implemented by people who understand, the folks that work for you and me, the people who are out there at the international programs here. They'll learn how to work together, how to get past barriers to effectively communicate, bring together the equipment and the organizations that matter, and to develop that military-to-military interaction and relationship.

I look forward to coming to see many of you, throughout my tenure, to talk through what is important to us. We, you and I, we need to build toward the future. We need to nurture the interaction and the engagement of our future leaders, our midshipmen, our officers, and our enlisted people. It's more than just meeting, having punch and cookies or drinks, and talking. It's common training also that will be important. Every opportunity to learn together will be valuable. It's about training programs ashore. In 2011 we've had 1,400 international students attend our courses. That's good. We've had operational gaming, and we've had good attendance. That is good. We need to continue the momentum.

It's also about our training programs at sea—in 2011 we had fifty-six midshipmen under way from sixteen nations out there. We had several midshipmen ourselves out with sixteen foreign navies. Good exchange. I like it. Let's keep the momentum. We've had some of your navies deploy with our carrier strike groups. Good start. Let's keep the momentum. These people will sit where we sit today, these kids of ours, these young officers, these midshipmen, and these enlisted. They will be where we are today. The friendships they develop today will endure for many years. We need to remain committed to this, you and I.

So in the end the successful efforts will be about people willing to get together, respect each other's cultures, beliefs, and find the common solutions.

Let me close by saying thank you to all again for your commitment coming here. We've made remarkable progress. There will be more opportunities. Let's be reminded that the prosperity of the maritime nations is on the sea. We are at a time of unprecedented global interdependence, and we have abundant maritime activity and a lot of disruptions out there. It's a time of budget constraints. We have to innovate. We have to share capabilities, share technologies, and be willing to work together.

Maritime security is impossible for one nation. No one can do it alone. It's a team effort. It's a team sport. On behalf of my Navy, I look forward to forming and continuing the partnerships today and in the future. Thank you very much for your attendance and thank you for listening. Have a great symposium.

2

Globalization, Security, and Economic Well-being

Mr. Stephen Carmel
Senior Vice President of Maritime Services, Maersk Line, Limited

Admiral Jonathan Greenert, United States:

It is now my pleasure to introduce our next speaker, Mr. Stephen Carmel. Mr. Carmel is a senior vice president of maritime services at Maersk Line, Limited. There he is responsible for all technical and operating activity materials within that organization.

He is a graduate of the U.S. Merchant Marine Academy and holds an MA in economics and an MBA from Old Dominion University. Mr. Carmel gained his initial experience in the maritime industry by sailing as a deck officer and later as a master primarily on tankers for Maritime Overseas Cooperation and our own U.S. Military Sealift Command.

He holds membership in an impressive list of associations and organizations, including the Board of Trustees of Old Dominion University and the Research Foundation there, the Marine Board of the National Research Council, the Hydrographic Services Review Panel for the U.S. National Oceanic and Atmospheric Administration, the American Bureau of Shipping, and the Advisory Council of International Maritime Ports and Logistics Management Institute at Old Dominion University. In 2009 Mr. Carmel was senior fellow at the Homeland Security Policy Institute at George Washington University.

Now, I could go on for quite some time. As you can see from this abbreviated list, he has a passion and commitment to maritime trade and to the sea service industry. He also sustains this commitment through his research and publishing interest in the areas of maritime security, trade and conflict, and Arctic regional issues.

Quite impressively, with all he has going on, he is currently pursuing his PhD with an emphasis on international political economy. Mr. Carmel maintains a very strong connection to the U.S. Navy through his service on the Chief of Naval Operations Executive Panel, so he is no stranger to this institution or to the U.S. Navy. We are delighted that he is able to speak to us this morning. Please join me in extending a warm welcome to Mr. Stephen M. Carmel, senior vice president, maritime services, Maersk Line, Limited.

Mr. Stephen Carmel, Maersk Line, Limited:

Thank you.[1] Good morning, Admiral Greenert, heads of sea service, distinguished guests, ladies and gentlemen. Thank you for inviting me to speak to you today about

---

1. A revised version of this address was subsequently published as Stephen Carmel, "Globalization, Security, and Economic Well-Being," Naval War College Review 66, no. 1 (Winter 2013), pp. 41–55.

globalization and interconnected economies. This is, of course, a topic of keen interest to me, both from my academic background and also from my position in international shipping.

The container and advances in information technology, coevolving with advances in business organization, are perhaps more than any other combination of factors responsible for trade as we know it today—characterized by disaggregated supply chains and trade focused on tasks, not goods—a topic explored in detail later. Before going in depth about globalization, security, and economic well-being, a quote from one of my favorite authors will set the stage: "Economies have become so interdependent due to advances in transportation and communication technology that actions in one country produce nearly instantaneous effects in many others. Consequently conflict between states is futile since damage to one economy necessarily translates into damage to others, including that of the aggressor."

You might be tempted to ascribe this argument to Thomas Friedman in *The World Is Flat* (Farrar, Straus, Giroux, 2005) or another from the multitude of gospels of globalization popular today, but in fact it is the argument advanced by the Nobel Prize–winning British economist Norman Angell in his famous *The Great Illusion*, published in 1910. At the time Angell published his book, the world was hurtling toward the catastrophe of World War I, which brought the first great age of globalization to a close. I study Angell's work because he was a perpetual optimist, a brilliant thinker, and a skilled economist, and his story reminds us that even the best and brightest can get something as complex as the global economy drastically wrong. Today when people contemplate globalization and interconnected, interdependent economies, the outsourcing of jobs, trade displacing locally produced goods, access to vital commercial pathways, and the other hallmarks we consider unique to our age, it is important to remember we have been through this before and that leaders of the day badly misunderstood the dynamics then in play.

The first great age of globalization is generally considered to have begun with the repeal of the Corn Laws in Britain in 1846. This was also the height of the Industrial Revolution, with discontinuous advances in methods of production. The huge leaps in transport and communications technology Angell spoke about were the steamship, the railroad, and the telegraph—all every bit as disruptive then as disaggregated supply chains, containerization, and the Internet are today. While today we worry about access to the Strait of Hormuz and the Suez Canal, then it was the Bosporus and Strait of Gibraltar. Then, as now, tensions arose as developing economies were accused of using cheap local resources to invade the distant markets of more advanced countries.

At that time, the roles were somewhat reversed, and it was the flood of cheap agricultural products from a comparatively backward but rapidly developing United States into the more mature and sophisticated markets of England and Europe that was the issue. Among other effects, this trade released local newly surplus labor from agricultural work and triggered rural-to-urban internal labor migrations in those countries, England in particular, which in turn fed the insatiable demand for cheap labor to keep the cogs in the machinery of the Industrial Revolution turning. Social dynamics in those countries were permanently altered, as was the global distribution of power, launching the golden age of the British Empire. Much as is the case today, advances in one facet of economic activity produced unanticipated consequences both within and across borders. Alexander Gerschenkron, in his seminal work *Bread and Democracy in Germany* (Cornell Univ. Press, 1989), lays out how the ways in which countries dealt with those consequences set in motion the train of events that culminated in World War I, even while the most learned men of the day, such as Angell, failed to comprehend the nature of globalization, what it meant, and the effect it was having on society. Consequently the leaders of the day were incapable of correctly responding to the policy and security challenges they faced.

There are those who counter that this time is different from the last in a fundamental way. The last age of globalization was built entirely on advances in technology. This time, the advances in technology are buttressed by a stabilizing institutional structure such as the World Trade Organization (WTO) for trade, a structure that is intended to institutionalize all aspects of global integration, including trade. Anyone placing stock in that view should be greatly concerned over the spectacular failure that is the Doha Round and over the proliferation of bilateral and regional trade agreements in place of broad multilateral advances. Our trading system has become what Jagdish Bhagwati, one of the preeminent trade economists of our time, calls a "spaghetti bowl" in his *Termites in the Trading System* (Oxford Univ. Press, 2008)—a complex, increasingly opaque mass of overlapping, sometimes contradictory, trade relationships that produce consequence pathways difficult to anticipate. Such agreements are also called "preferential trade agreements," for the positive spin, but another view calls them "discriminatory trade agreements," as they are meant to exclude all but the privileged few who are members, contrary to the intent of the WTO and the multilateral trade process. So if the institutional structure of the WTO is what makes some think this time is different, the foundation of that institution is in an advanced state of decay, and every bilateral trade agreement knocks another large chunk out of it.

The first great age of globalization lasted about two-thirds of a century. The second great age of globalization, where we are now, began with the end of World War II. It took a quarter-century to get back to where we had left off at the close of the first in terms of overall economic integration, but in some areas the loss was permanent. The United Kingdom, for example, is still not at the same level of export intensity that it previously was. Since the beginning of this age of globalization, we have witnessed discontinuous changes in the global political economy, driven again by dramatic advances in communications and transport technologies coevolving with advances in methods of production and business organization. We are nearly at the point on the time line of globalization, about two-thirds of a century, where the last age imploded, plunging the world into three decades of darkness. Given that we are approaching the point at which the last age of globalization failed, it is a useful exercise to examine the characteristics of the current one. Given the events we are witnessing around the world, one wonders whether there is some natural age limit for a globalization process after which the strain on society gets to be too much and our ability to manage complexity is overtaken by the complexity we face. The system then demands some sort of reset, and perhaps we are at that point now. Such resets are never graceful.

The U.S. Navy's *Cooperative Strategy for 21st Century Seapower* notes that today's global economies are tightly interconnected but does not explain the meaning of that phrase, something Angell and his contemporaries clearly got wrong in their age. Many understand globalization as cheap sneakers on Walmart shelves made by exploited labor in far-off places. This is a reflection of the general understanding of interdependence, one promoted heavily by some segments in society and all too readily accepted by the public in times of economic turmoil, as we see now. This view focuses on division of labor, some level of exploiting comparative advantage, with all making what they make best and trading what they have for what they need, and in the process becoming mutually and voluntarily dependent on each other, their well-being intertwined—the Ricardian wine-and-cheese-trade relationship from Economics 101. Or, as a just-released report from the Council on Foreign Relations describes it, "Globalization also allows each country to concentrate its scarce resources of people and ideas in those activities with which it is well suited compared with the rest of the world. It can then export these goods and services for imports of other products that can be enjoyed in greater variety and at lower prices."

This is, however, a strikingly narrow view of globalization, and in truth it is a definition more fitting of the last age of globalization than the current one. This age is vastly more complicated than that. We no longer simply trade what we make for what we do not make but need. We now trade in order to get what we need *to make what we make*. Before, we were self-sufficient in some but not all of what we needed, and we could trade the excess of what we made to fill the gaps. Now, we are self-sufficient in nothing but make everything—the trade in tasks mentioned earlier. I belabor the point because this is a major leap in complexity as compared to the last age of globalization. It is apparently not as well appreciated as it should be, as evidenced by the definition the Council on Foreign Relations uses, and it has profound implications across a number of policy areas. It might be appropriate to make a pen-and-ink change to your copy of the new maritime strategy and strike out words like "interdependent economies" and replace them with "interdependent production process across economies."

If the last age was too complex for policy makers to manage competently, imagine how much more so this one is—the tremendous advances in global economic complexity have not been matched by corresponding advances in political or policy skill, evidence of which you can see by simply picking up a newspaper virtually anywhere in the world these days. The current age of globalization is certainly showing signs of stress, buffeted by the same but magnified forces of demographics, politics, change in the global political order, and international instability that disrupted the last. As the last great age showed us, the forward march of globalization is neither inevitable nor reversible: we cannot slide easily backward into a better previous time when the pressure gets to be too much, and when globalization breaks, it does so violently, permanently altering the trajectory of history.

The balance of my article will therefore be spent exploring a few pertinent high-level economic aspects of globalization in an attempt to understand them. (It is important to note that while I view globalization as an economic process, owing to my academic and professional background, many in other disciplines view it as a different set of forces.) Along the way we will dispel some of the common myths surrounding globalization that persist and sadly influence both public opinion and policy. To paraphrase Norman Angell, policy is not driven by facts but by the public's opinion of facts.

The first myth we should address, and perhaps one of the most relevant to readers of this quarterly, is that 90 percent of world trade moves by water. That is simply not true. A more correct rendering of that phrase would be that 90 percent of world trade in physical goods (merchandise trade) as measured by volume moves by water. When measured by value, the number is closer to 65 percent. The first key issue is that of trade in physical goods versus total trade. In 2010, according to the WTO, there was $18.8 trillion in total world trade, of which $3.7 trillion, or about 19.5 percent, was in services. These services are considered very high value and critical (e.g., transportation services, financial services, and communications). Much of this trade moves on fiber-optic backbones, not ships—and in fact, as you will see further on, goods can no longer move on ships without a robust and parallel flow in information. This means that cyber warriors are doing every bit as much to ensure the smooth flow of trade as are those standing watches on the bridges of ships in the Strait of Hormuz.

The second key issue associated with this myth is that given the difference in trade as measured by value versus volume, it is clear that a lot of high-value goods move by means other than water, principally air. The importance to the global economy of aviation supply-chain networks cannot be overemphasized. Such supply chains are responsible for the global movement of such critical items as pharmaceuticals and medical equipment, electronics, automotive parts, and computers. It is also clear that we must pay attention to global supply-chain critical nodes other than the more commonly discussed port system in marine supply chains. The largest air cargo terminal in the world is Nashville, Tennessee, and the third largest is Anchorage, Alaska. These places do not register on the list of critical nodes in the marine supply chain. Air supply chains are faster in cycle times, meaning they fail faster in the event of disruption. They also carry goods with more time sensitivity and lower tolerance for supply-chain disruption.

One example that certainly made the news is the Iceland volcano eruptions of spring 2010. The airspace closure resulting from the ash cloud was hugely disruptive for travel in Europe, but it was also devastating to farmers in Kenya. Europe is the major market for fresh fruits, vegetables, and flowers from Kenyan farms, and such products are delivered via an aviation supply chain that was shut down—meaning rotting product on runways. It is not hard to extrapolate failed farms to social unrest and to the outbreak of conflict in the Horn of Africa due to a volcano in Iceland. I would guess that Kenyan farmers and peace in the Horn of Africa were not high on the list of endangered stakeholders when the potential for an eruption was first contemplated in Iceland, but that is the way causality pathways work now. In the United States, 40 percent of all finished pharmaceuticals, 80 percent of all ingredients for drugs mixed here, and 100 percent of the most common isotopes for nuclear-medicine procedures are imported and delivered via an aviation supply chain and are dispensed within hours of landing. This means that grounding all flights in response to an aviation security threat would rapidly translate into a health-care crisis.

The aviation supply-chain business continues to innovate, as the pharmaceuticals industry shows. In response to soaring demand, drugs are currently the biggest growth segment for air cargo, and service offerings are being refined and specialized ("specialized" being a code word for an increasingly efficient but rigid and unforgiving supply chain). A recent example is the innovation of highly specialized containers with active temperature-control features allowing the transport of pharmaceuticals in temperatures between two and eight degrees Celsius. Clearly this type of cargo is highly perishable, hence time sensitive, and completely intolerant of delays in the supply chain, however induced.

At this point readers in the maritime-security world may be asking themselves, "Why is this guy writing about aviation supply chains? That's not what we do." First, we keep seeing that 90-percent-by-water statistic, but also you can no longer meaningfully separate various supply-chain vectors; in practice these are not stovepiped but are all interdependent processes. You cannot have international trade in physical goods without a robust international trade in services. Aviation supply chains depend on marine supply chains to function properly, and marine supply chains are likewise dependent on aviation supply chains. Both depend on robust truck and train connectors. A friend of mine in the cruise-ship industry tells me of a cruise ship coming into Miami. As usual, a Coast Guard boarding party met it outside the port. But the party decided to review paperwork more extensively than usual, resulting in the ship's being delayed. Airlines in Miami orient their schedules around cruise-ship arrival times; consequently, flights were held, and soon enough the disruption rippled across the entire U.S. air-passenger network. This is just one example of how different transport vectors interact in ways you might not expect.

A critical mistake made in supply-chain security thinking is that sometimes you can break it apart and study individual components to understand the behavior of the overall system. You cannot make that assumption, and decisions made that way will be flawed. Likewise, vulnerability is not about the physical ease or difficulty of attack on any particular node or vector in the supply chain. It is not—instead, vulnerability is a matter of how the system behaves, how it fails, and how quickly it can be made to recover once a particular node or vector has been disrupted. That is a very different view. Some things we may view as tangential must be accommodated, because the system will fail if we do not.

The goods that move by water (to return to them) are no longer simply boxes of manufactured goods made in competition with local labor, and that leads to our next myth, by far the most important—the idea that the "made in" label has any relevance at all in today's version of trade. Unfortunately, much policy is driven by that meaningless anachronism from the first age of globalization. During that age we actually traded goods, and the "made in" label had meaning. But now, as mentioned, we trade in tasks: a specific widget is actually manufactured in a variety of places, the "made in" label denoting only where it received final assembly. Here is the most dramatic effect of the combination of containerization and the Internet. More than 50 percent of containerized trade is now in component-level goods, meaning parts or inputs into factories rather than ready-for-retail goods heading for store shelves. Roughly 45 percent of a Boeing 767 aircraft with a "Made in America" label plate is actually composed of imported parts. In the 787 Dreamliner that figure is more like 70 percent, including such crucial parts as wings and engines; Boeing's role in that airplane has been described as reduced to little more than project management, design, assembly, and test operation.

In the U.S. air-tanker program that was recently in the news, for example, the Boeing plane in question, billed as made in the United States, is actually made in eight countries. The U.S. Congressional Research Service did a study for Congress on the key issues of that airplane program and provided a list of countries where various components are made. The Czech Republic is listed as the source of airframe parts; I am no airplane expert, but my understanding is the airplane will not work well without an airframe. Likewise, the flaps, also critical parts, are made in Indonesia. The avionics are not specifically listed, but of course, we know that the "made in" label is not completely true anyway; they contain components made from rare earths (all avionics do), which are virtually sole-sourced in China, which in turn is not on the list of contributing countries. My guess is that for each of those eight countries listed, if you followed the trails of the components with their respective "made in" labels, they would take you to a multitude of other countries. Clearly, the notion that the production of the air tanker is not subject to events in faraway places is false. A "Made in America" label plate does nothing other than manage a perception.

The fact is, we frequently have no idea where something "made in America"—or anywhere else—is really made. A loaf of bread sold in a local market can have ingredients from up to fourteen different countries. Perhaps the only stage of its production in the United States is the bakery, which puts the "Made in America" label on it. Perhaps the only thing that the American business provides is the heat necessary to bake it—and there is a good chance that those BTUs came from oil from Canada, so even the heat is imported. All we can say for sure is that the last stop on the loaf's production path is in the United States, before being turned over to the customer—and there is nothing wrong with that.

Another facet of trade in tasks is that in many areas positive economies of scale exist, meaning there may be only one or a few plants globally that produce low-value but critical components. The effects of disruption of a single plant in one part of the world that produces some innocuous but critical component, like an electronic power switch, can cascade to disrupt production processes all over the world. It is important to note that the system does not distinguish among disruptions owing to natural disasters, criminals, or bad policy. The system reacts to them all the same way, and that reaction is not good. While criminals get the press, a far greater danger to our collective freedom to leverage global pathways of commerce are the twin "isms" of nationalism and protectionism, with unwarranted fear close behind.

Disruptions to supply chains no longer mean just not having your favorite brand on the shelf; they now mean closed factories, unemployment, and social stress in areas far removed from the initial disruption. The value-added of goods with a "Made in China" label can be as low as 6 percent and usually does not exceed 20 percent, meaning that most of what is in such products comes from someplace other than China. Increasingly that is the United States; China is our largest customer by a very wide margin in terms of containerized exports and a major customer of our agricultural products. The now ubiquitous iPhone has a "Made in China" label on it, but China is actually responsible for a relatively small amount of the production effort for an iPhone—something on the order of 5 percent. Japan is actually responsible for the majority of it, with Germany and Korea as close runners-up.

The United States itself is also a major contributor to that production pattern. A Federal Reserve Bank of Chicago study at the height of the "Great Recession" showed that the proportion of the average value of a typical car sporting a "Made in

America" label actually generated in the United States is only about 75 percent. But that figure is highly contentious, and U.S. domestic content ranges widely. A Toyota Sequoia, a "Japanese" car, was noted to have 80 percent U.S. content (the highest of any car); the Jeep Patriot, an "American" car, had only 66 percent (the irony of its name is amusing). So if you want to buy an American car, you need to buy it from a Japanese company. In addition, in terms of the actual assembly process those cars, "made" in Detroit, probably cross the U.S.-Canadian border five times, meaning not only that the parts are sourced globally but that actual assembly is something of an international activity.

As an indicator of how policy can affect trade, approximately one million dollars of trade crosses the U.S.-Canadian border every minute, twenty-four hours a day, 365 days a year. The thickening of that border as a result of post-9/11 security procedures has erased all cost advantages achieved through the North American Free Trade Agreement, bringing a huge deadweight loss to both the American and Canadian economies.

Overall, the WTO estimates that about 80 percent of the value of goods exported by the United States represents U.S. domestic content, a statistic that excludes such indirect-value components as energy. To compare that with the roughly 20 percent of a typical Chinese export highlights the complexity of today's trade relationships and complicates finger-pointing over who are the offenders in what are perceived as unfair trade relationships.

One implication of all this is that economic sanctions affect not just targeted countries but every country along a sanctioned good's supply chain, often including the country invoking the sanctions to begin with. The fact is that the targeted country is likely to feel directly relatively little of the actual overall effect of the sanction. It also causes some level of discomfort to read articles and news such as of a RAND report recently released offering as a potential cyber-warfare tactic the disruption of a target country's shipping system in order to inflict economic pain—the implication being that such pain would be contained to the target country. As the foregoing demonstrates, it could not be so contained but would in fact amount to an attack on a multitude of countries, widely divergent in economic-versus-security relationships. It is difficult to determine who would be on what side in such circumstances.

The root of the issue is the way we measure things—our methods of accounting have not kept up with global business practices. Since we now trade in tasks—involving a very fine level of supply-chain disaggregation to the activity level, where the distinction between goods and services gets blurry—the old measure of production, gross domestic product (GDP) in real or nominal currency, presents an inaccurate picture of actual economic activity. More importantly from both a policy and public perception standpoint, it gives a distorted picture of actual trade imbalances. This is critically important, because as Alejandro Jara, deputy general of the WTO, puts it, "We know in times of crisis the pressure from public opinion can push in the wrong direction. In the absence of objective statistics demonstrating the interconnectivity of the modern production system, it is to be feared that false and obsolete will remain the panoply of the most popular remedies." Every complex problem has a simple solution, one that is easy to understand, is easy to explain, and fits well in a sound bite but is totally wrong. That is where we are today.

The problem in a nutshell is that the old measure of GDP was based on gross flows, hence double- or triple-counting some aspects of economic activity and failing to take into account trade in intermediate goods. A more informative statistic is the value-added content of trade, whereby the flow of goods is recorded by assigning to each country of origin the value it imbeds in final goods, rather than just attributing all the value to the last places that touch them. The WTO is working on such a system of measurement, but trade tension and poorly designed policy will be the order of the day until policy makers understand, adopt, and communicate it to their respective constituencies. Adoption of such a measure of trade flows would also highlight something that few seem to appreciate fully, because of the distortions induced by current accounting. That is, there is a stark difference now between many countries' security alliances and their economic alliances. With whom a country is allied from a military perspective and on whom its economy depends to function are now frequently completely at odds. Security alliances and high politics are the province of the government elite, but economic alliances are the province of the general population and are where cultural and social, as well as economic, bonds are built. Thus, while virtually all countries say that in a serious crisis the security alliance would prevail, in the end we simply will not know which side a given country will take until that time comes and the internal battle between elites and the populace is waged.

A related myth is the notion that the phrase "owned by" has any meaning when applied to the owners of means of production these days. Frequently now the owners of means both of production and of distribution are international, with the location of "headquarters" being more an accident of history than some current, overt business decision. The roots of ownership and economic beneficiaries of productive activity are no longer easily identifiable. A fascinating recent example of this sort of "globalized ownership" is what has been described as "the battle for the future of copper" that played out in 2012 when Minmetals, a Chinese state-owned mining company, launched a hostile takeover of Equinox Minerals. In itself this was cause for great interest, as hostile takeovers are not the typical strategy for Chinese firms. Equinox is an Australian company that has a nominal office in Toronto and is listed on the Toronto Stock Exchange. One of the world's top twenty copper producers, Equinox has as its main asset a massive copper mine in Zambia and is building a copper-gold mine in Saudi Arabia. At the time Minmetals launched its hostile takeover bid, Equinox itself was in the middle of attempting a hostile takeover of Lundin Mining, a Toronto-listed firm whose primary mining activity is in Sweden and Portugal, with smaller interests in Ireland and Spain.

It is clear how very complicated international ownership structures can get these days and consequently how unpredictable can be the effects of policies like sanctions. In the Equinox example, nine countries were involved. From a security perspective, there were some in Canada who called on the government to block the Minmetal bid as contrary to national security—even though none of Equinox's assets were actually in Canada and beneficial ownership was in Australia, making the national security angle hard to comprehend. In reality, the only thing Canadian about Equinox was a file at the Toronto Stock Exchange.

This is reminiscent of a Chinese National Offshore Oil Company (CNOOC) attempt in 2005 to buy the U.S. oil producer Unocal, a company headquartered in

San Francisco, California, but whose assets were primarily in the Gulf of Thailand. That proposed transaction generated huge amounts of anxiety in the United States and eventually action in Congress to block it, born of a desire not to surrender U.S. oil assets to a foreign company—though none of Unocal's oil assets were actually in the United States. CNOOC went on instead to buy Calgary-based PetroKazakhstan, Inc., a Canadian company whose assets were, as the name suggests, in Kazakhstan. It was in fact the largest private integrated oil firm in that country, although it also owned a stake in Canada's oil sands. So the oil from Canada used to bake that bread mentioned earlier was probably bought from a Chinese oil company.

The Dubai Ports World (DPW) fiasco is also an instructive case. Here a failure to appreciate international linkages in the shipping industry and the political reaction to the proposed takeover of a third-tier terminal in New York by Dubai Ports World, as part of a large acquisition of P&O assets, turned what should have been a nonevent into a potentially serious disruption to U.S. supply chains connecting to the Horn of Africa, Iraq, and Afghanistan. What everyone failed to realize was that DPW controlled Salalah, in Oman, a critical transshipment node in material flowing to Iraq; Port Qasim, Pakistan, a critical supply-chain node for goods flowing to Afghanistan; and Djibouti, the port of entry for goods supporting U.S. activity in the Horn of Africa. So if DPW wanted to disrupt U.S. supply chains, it did not need to buy a third-rate port in the United States (already owned by a foreign company, by the way) to do that—it could, and can, do it at will in the many foreign ports it controls on which the U.S. military is dependent.

By focusing on the local rather than global picture, a serious potential disruption to military supply chains was manufactured where none should have been. Fortunately, the DPW folks reacted with admirable restraint and defused the situation, but that may not happen the next time, when circumstances and actors may be different. As we think through complex ownership structures like Minmetals/Equinox, it is important to remember these are firms engaged in the normal course of business in full compliance with international and relevant domestic laws. If this is what the ownership picture looks like for legitimate firms trying to be transparent, imagine how it would look with illegitimate actors deliberately trying to conceal and deceive. One industry notorious for this is, of course, my own, where ownership is frequently nested in multiple shell companies spanning several countries. The registry, or flag, of the ship is unrelated to wherever ownership really sits, and the ship is operated by a management firm headquartered in yet another country employing crew members from none of the above—and that for a legitimate operation. The number of seams to be exploited for unsavory purposes is obvious, but so also is the potential to disrupt legitimate shipping, acting in conformance with international law, in an effort to close those seams.

The foregoing discussion was meant to point out that we no longer know with any certainty where anything is truly made, hence where supply-chain disruptions might occur or how disruptions might propagate through the global production system. Further, there is no way to know where the effect of deliberate actions, sanctions, cyber attacks, or physical attacks will ultimately be felt, or who will be on what side in the event of conflict. The world is a far more complicated place than you would expect from looking at a "made in" label.

Another topic that needs to be explored is the nature of physical supply chains. It is a fact that in global trade the most efficient method of moving goods from A to B is rarely a straight line. Trade is moved in networks of networks that are themselves interconnected and completely dependent on the smooth flow of information across yet other networks. Disruptions in a rail network ripple out and manifest themselves as disruptions to ship networks. Disruptions in one port propagate out into disruptions into other ports. Ports themselves are not perfect substitutes for each other, owing to advances in ship technology, with attendant implications for resilience. Containers often move through relay ports, entering on one ship and leaving on another, and yet never "leaving" the port—that is, never going through the typical security apparatus found at the gates. The large Asian ports process in excess of eighty thousand containers every day. Individual ships carry fifteen to eighteen thousand containers, enough to fill a train 110 kilometers long if off-loaded at once, carrying cargo for thousands of customers whose identities are just numbers or bar codes on the containers. Prince Rupert, on the west coast of Canada, is a new containerport with enhanced rail infrastructure supported by upgraded roads and highways. Prince Rupert provides direct service to CentrePort, a state-of-the-art intermodal inland port in Winnipeg, Manitoba. This advanced multimodal system is designed to off-load a container directly from the ship in Prince Rupert to a train and have its contents in Chicago within a hundred hours. Prince Rupert is also one of the very few containerports in North America that can handle the largest post-Panamax ships (i.e., too big for the Panama Canal) common in the Asia/Europe trade, a capability in which the United States is woefully lacking.

Container shipping is a step in the manufacturing process, an extension of the factory itself, a conveyor belt between factories linking assembly lines. While speed is important, the critical issues are consistency, reliability, and predictability. Uncertainty is to be avoided at all costs, as uncertainty requires buffer stocks to compensate for it, stocks that are expensive and to be held to the absolute minimum. That means when we say in my company that we will have your box to you Tuesday, we mean Tuesday, because we know if we are late, you may have to shut down a manufacturing line. As in any conveyor belt linking assembly lines, a disruption to any part of the system becomes a disruption to the whole system. The sheer volume of activity can overwhelm even the most robust physical detection system, unless it slows the process down to a crawl, presenting significant disruptions to trade.

Another important issue to consider is that a significant component of the total value imbedded in transportation is information. Today's modern system of trade is completely dependent on the uninterrupted flow of accurate information. Without it, trade simply will not happen. So while we have spent billions hardening ports and thickening borders, the most vulnerable portion of the global system of trade is the information component. Container yards are now fully automated, largely run by robots. In the container yard I see through my office window, if a human is detected inside the yard (by automatic sensors, of course) everything is automatically shut down. This intricate dance is controlled by incredible levels of information and computer technology. A container itself has nothing on it other than a box number and a bar code, and without access to computerized information systems you can have no idea where it came from or where it is going. Consider those eighty thousand containers flowing through a large Asian port every day, or the eighteen thousand on a ship you may be boarding, identified only by numbers, and the critical importance of information should be clear.

The other aspect of information that is increasingly important is the role, hinted at above, of shipping as extensions of the manufacturing process. Like every part of the process, manufacturers need information about what is happening at that particular step in order to control it properly, and that information is an important component of the total value of a shipper's service. You do not need a complex plot, with a bomb on a pier, to disrupt trade; you need a three-hundred-dollar computer and a connection to the Internet. One no longer needs to achieve physical proximity to cause physical damage.

Ship, port, and connecting transportation technology continue to coevolve with production methods and business management practices. The container completely revolutionized world trade and altered balances of power in ways that have not yet completely played out but that draw worrying parallels to the ways the steamship altered balances of power in the last globalization age. One area I think about often is the technology that will make containers obsolete. I do not know what that technology will be, and I doubt it will come from my industry, but it is the technology that the ships you are building today will have to contend with.

To say that the world's economies are interdependent does not adequately, or even remotely, express the true nature of today's global economic activity. Vulnerabilities exist everywhere, the most serious being those obscured by the very complexity of the system. But it is imperative that those charged with regulating and protecting the system of global trade have a good appreciation of what it is they are regulating and protecting. The system will propagate disruptions, and there will be failures as a result of actions taken by those that mean to do us or the system harm, such as transnational actors or terrorist groups. But like any complex, adaptive, self-organizing system, given time and latitude the system will rewire itself and recover from such actions. The global system is far too large and complex for such groups, on their own, to do lasting harm. There is, of course, one set—and only one set—of international actors who really have the capacity and wherewithal to do permanent damage or even destroy the trading system. That group is the states themselves. I reject out of hand the notion that conflict among major powers is no longer possible; I do not make the same mistake Angell did. States will always do what is in their best interest to do, and when they calculate it is in their best interest to fight, they will do so. This means they will calculate first the probability that in fighting they will be better off if they win, and second, the probability that if they fight they *will* win.

Thirty years ago the information needed to make those calculations was relatively clean. That is no longer the case today. As we noted in the GDP discussion, a significant measure of both economic prowess and trade imbalance used today is badly distorted and does not provide accurate information on which to base policies that in the past have led to conflict and in fact directly contributed to the demise of the last age of globalization. The wide and growing gap between security and economic alliances for individual states no longer allows states to gauge accurately which side their bread is truly buttered on or to estimate accurately on which side a potential ally or adversary will judge his own to be buttered. The demise of the meaning of the "made in" label means we can no longer gauge with any accuracy where the incidence of a specific trade sanction will fall or where failures in the global supply chain may manifest themselves. The continued use of a "made in" label that does not convey accurate information may actually make things worse, by giving a false sense of security that we know where critical things we need are made, hence where we can afford to take risks in foreign policy. Trade in tasks means we can no longer accurately predict where and what will be the effects of particular courses of action, an ambiguity that can, among other things, influence the final choice between a security or economic relationship.

The spaghetti bowl of bilateral and regional trade agreements that have replaced multilateral advances has resulted in pathways for trade disruptions that cannot be anticipated with any certainty. When we measure the wrong things and measure them incorrectly, the potential for miscalculation is high. As the last age of globalization showed us, globalization is not inevitable, and it is not reversible, but it is breakable. It also showed us—and it is the one thing Norman Angell got right—that when it breaks, the consequences are catastrophic.

Thank you.

Panel Discussion One
Global Perspectives: Challenges to Maritime Security

Moderated by
Admiral Tan Sri Abdul Aziz Jaafar, Malaysia

Panel Members:
Admiral Nirmal Verma, India
Admiral Alexander Pama, Philippines
Staff Brigadier General Ibrahim S. M. Almusharrakh,
United Arab Emirates
Vice Admiral Ola Sa'ad Ibrahim, Nigeria

Professor Thomas Culora:

The panel we are about to hear this morning is entitled "Global Perspectives: Challenges to Maritime Security." Leading the panel this morning is Admiral Aziz from Malaysia. He will introduce his colleagues on the panel. He is joined by Admiral Verma from India, Vice Admiral Pama from the Philippines, Staff Brigadier General Ibrahim S. M. Almusharrakh from the United Arab Emirates and Vice Admiral Ibrahim from Nigeria. Please join me in welcoming this distinguished panel. Thank you.

Admiral Tan Sri Abdul Aziz, Malaysia:

Thank you, Tom. Admiral Greenert, Chief of Naval Operations, chiefs of navies and coast guards, President of Naval War College, distinguished delegates, ladies and gentlemen, a very good morning to everyone.

First of all, I would like to take this opportunity to thank Admiral Greenert for the kind hospitality extended to us during this Twentieth International Seapower Symposium (ISS XX). I would also like to take this opportunity to thank him for the honor given to me to moderate this ISS XX first panel discussion, entitled "Global Perspectives: Challenges to Maritime Security." This is my second consecutive ISS moderating task. The first one was at the last ISS, in 2009, which I thoroughly enjoyed. Thank you.

Ladies and gentlemen, maritime security is of vital importance to our global economy and prosperity. It is because the seas are and will always remain an important source for living and nonliving resources as well as provide a concurrent medium for transportation, trade, and communication. The importance of the sea is more obvious in today's era of globalization. "The sea" shall refer to the network of sea lines of communications that allows all nations, including landlocked nations, to participate in the seaborne trade which supports a huge chunk of the global economy.

However, the very nature and prosperity of the sea are also attracting negative elements, which pose challenges to the security of the seas. Furthermore, the sea is vast and unregulated. The rise of piracy, maritime terrorism, overfishing, proliferation of weapons of mass destruction, illegal immigration, human trafficking, arms smuggling, and the emergence of new threats will continue to cause challenges for the navies, coast guards, and other maritime agencies. The nature of the contemporary maritime security threats is much different from the conventional and traditional threats of old days. The complexity of the maritime security environment and diversity of stakeholders' interests have also added to the challenges.

Ladies and gentlemen, maritime security is all about ensuring the freedom of the seas, so as to facilitate freedom of navigation and commerce, as well as protecting the ocean resources. In this regard, all nations have a common goal in achieving two main objectives, which are to protect the vibrant maritime commerce that underpins the economic security and to protect against maritime security threats that may hamper the freedom of the legal use of the seas. Though there are numerous challenges to maritime security, there are four specific challenges that elicit our particular attention today. They are piracy, maritime terrorism, critical infrastructure protection, and resource protection. Although these challenges are surely different in terms of nature, scope, and dimension, they, however, pose a common impact in relation to the frequency, scale, and implication toward national and regional as well as global economies.

Ladies and gentlemen, to provide us with a global perspective in relation to the challenges to maritime security, we are fortunate this morning to have four distinguished speakers coming from different parts of the world to discuss, elaborate, and share their experiences and thoughts on the four specific challenges to maritime security which I have just mentioned.

With me on stage is, on my left, Admiral Nirmal Verma, the Chief of Naval Staff of India. Please welcome him. Admiral Verma will talk about maritime piracy, in which he will share with us India's experiences with regard to mitigating the threats of piracy.

On his left we have Vice Admiral Alexander P. Pama, the Flag Officer in Command of the Philippine Navy. Please welcome him. Admiral Pama will speak about the Philippine Navy's experiences and perspectives on maritime terrorism.

On his left is Staff Brigadier General Ibrahim Almusharrakh, the United Arab Emriates (UAE) Naval Forces Commander. Give him a big round of applause. Brigadier General Ibrahim will explore critical infrastructure protection and share with us the challenges faced by the UAE naval forces and the Critical National Infrastructure Authority, or CNIA, in protecting the energy platforms.

Finally, on the far left is Vice Admiral Ola Sa'ad Ibrahim, Nigeria's Chief of Naval Staff. Please give him a big round of applause. Vice Admiral Ibrahim will talk about the Nigerian Navy's perspective on resource protection and challenges to maritime security.

Ladies and gentlemen, before I hand over to the first speaker, allow me to just remind everyone that I have two cards, the yellow and the red card. I think everyone is familiar with soccer's rules. Perhaps for the commander of the Philippine Navy, I will have to use basketball rules. But it's almost similar. I hope I will not have to use these two cards. I request the four speakers to observe the time allocated, as we need to remain on schedule. Once all the four speakers have completed their presentations, the floor will be open for questions and answers.

Ladies and gentlemen, without further ado, I would like to cordially invite Admiral Verma, India's chief of navy, to address the topic of maritime piracy. Before that, I would like to just give a brief introduction of Admiral Verma. I think that it is important for everyone to be highlighted.

Admiral Nirmal Verma took command of the Indian Navy on 31 August 2009, as the twentieth Chief of Naval Staff, and the eighteenth Indian to take over this office. Admiral Nirmal Verma is a specialist in communication and electronic warfare. His nearly forty years of experience spans across various afloat and ashore appointments. His sea tenure includes command of INS *Udaygiri*, a *Leander*-class frigate, INS *Ranvir*, a *Kashin*-class destroyer, and the aircraft carrier INS *Viraat*. In assignments, as the future leader of the Indian Navy, he has commanded the Indian Naval Academy at Goa; has been Head of the Naval Training Team at the Defence Services Staff College, Wellington; and Senior Directing Staff (Navy) at the National Defence College, New Delhi.

Admiral Verma's career is an amalgamation of Indian and global experience. As part of the crew for the first *Kashin*-class destroyer inducted in the Indian Navy in 1980, he trained in the former Soviet Union. He has attended professional mid- and senior-level courses at the Royal Naval College in Greenwich, UK, and Naval Command College Course at the U.S. Naval War College, Rhode Island, graduating with distinction in 1993.

Upon elevation to flag rank as a rear admiral, he has contributed to the consolidation of growth and development of the naval commands, first as the Chief of Staff of Eastern Naval Command, and thereafter as Flag Officer commanding Madarashtra Naval Area. Evolution of the maritime capabilities and policies for future induction were steered by Admiral Verma in his capacity as the Assistant Chief of Naval Staff, Policy and Plans.

After his promotion to vice admiral in November 2005, he guided the human resource development programs for the navy, formulating personnel and service policies as the Chief of Personnel. In his capacity as Vice Chief of the Naval Staff, Admiral Verma structured the framework for the transformation of the navy's combat capabilities and infrastructure development.

Prior to taking over as the Chief of Naval Staff, Admiral Nirmal Verma was Flag Officer Commander in Chief, Eastern Naval Command, and provided impetus to synergize the coastal security infrastructure. The admiral is a recipient of the Param Vishisht Seva Medal and Ati Vishisht Seva Medal for meritorious service, and he is also the honorary Aide-de-Camp to the President of India. Without further ado, I present to you Admiral Verma.

Admiral Nirmal Verma, India:

Admiral Jonathan Greenert, Chief of Naval Operations, United States Navy; chiefs of navy and coast guards present with us this morning; Admiral Christenson, President of the U.S. Naval War College, our gracious host; flag officers; distinguished delegates; and ladies and gentlemen, it is always wonderful to be back at my alma mater.

From what I remember, Newport weather has always had the reputation of a temperamental lover—warm and wonderful, or chillingly cold—most definitely almost always delightfully unpredictable. Today has been that so far. Let us all share the optimism for the rest of the week.

At the outset I would like to thank Admiral Jonathan Greenert and the organizers of the International Seapower Symposium for affording me the opportunity to speak to this august audience on a subject that has affected mariners since time immemorial and yet is very contemporary, maritime piracy.

The difference today is that piracy at sea, which was previously primarily robbery, has now morphed into an elaborate network of operations to extract enormous quantities of ransom. Ransom amounts have increased from an average of 150,000 U.S. dollars per ship to 5.4 million U.S. dollars over the last five years. According to a recent study by One Earth Future, the economic cost of piracy may be as high as $12 billion a year. This translates into increased operating costs; environmental expenses, through rerouting of ships; and most importantly, tremendous human costs. Even as we speak, nine ships with nearly 300 seafarers with a range of nationalities, including fifty-three of my own countrymen, are presently hostages in this contentious conflict. Lethal force and physical abuse are increasingly being used by pirates to leverage ransom negotiations. The roots of piracy are diverse; predominantly political instability has created a void of governance and economic opportunities ashore, resulting in the manifestation of this menace at sea.

Economic Cost of Piracy

Total Costs of Maritime Piracy, 2010

Cost Factor	Value (Dollars)
Ransoms: excess costs	$176 million
Insurance Premiums	$460 million to $3.2 billion
Re-Routing Ships	$2.4 to $3 billion
Security Equipment/ Personnel	$363 million to $2.5 billion
Naval Forces	$2 billion
Prosecutions	$31 million
Piracy Deterrent Organizations	$19.5 million
Cost to Regional Economies	$1.25 billion
TOTAL ESTIMATED COST	**$7 to $12 billion per year**

Source: One Earth Future Foundation

Also worth reflecting upon are the Somalian claims that the origins of piracy can be traced back to illegal fishing by other countries and dumping of toxic waste in

Somalia's exclusive economic zone (EEZ). Given the complications involved, no single response will solve the problem. While there may be some ambiguities about what we can or should do, there is no doubt that the fundamental prerequisite to any solution is a collaborative engagement of a wide range of maritime nations and littoral states to tackle this problem.

Human Cost of Piracy

Sr	Country (In order of number of hostages)	No of Hostages
1.	India	53
2.	Thailand	32
3.	China	27
4.	Syria	18
5.	Indonesia	17
6.	Algeria	17
7.	Others	135
	Total	299

In this context, I would highlight the work of the Contact Group on Piracy off the Coast of Somalia, or CGPCS, under the aegis of the United Nations, which we believe is doing sterling work coordinating international cooperation, particularly information sharing. In a similar vein are the efforts of the Shared Awareness and Deconfliction (SHADE) initiative and those of UK Maritime Trade Operations, or UKMTO, which functions from Dubai. These engagements have facilitated an agreement between independently deployed navies, like China's, Japan's, and India's, to coordinate the antipiracy operations, so that international shipping has more flexible options for escort schedules.

Beyond piracy's complex genesis, it is interesting to highlight the metamorphosis of pirate activities. Despite multinational efforts, the number of incidents and net effects of piracy have all increased, with seasonal variations on account of monsoons and geographic shifts dependent on the presence of naval units. The international efforts in the Gulf of Aden have resulted in piracy spreading to other areas of the Indian Ocean which had not experienced these attacks earlier. Some of these areas have been not too distant from India's Lakshadweep (Laccadive) and Minicoy group of islands, and naturally, therefore, this has been a cause of concern to us. It has become evident that pirates are changing their modus operandi, as they have

Indian Seafarers Held Captive

SER	VESSEL	NO. OF INDIANS
1.	MV ICEBERG	06
2.	MV SAVINA CAYLYN	17
3.	EX MV ASPHALT VENTURE	07
4.	MV FAIRCHEM BOGEY	21
5.	MV ALBEDO	02
	TOTAL	53

GARACAD (01)
- MV ICEBERG 1

EL DANAN (04)
- MV FAIRCHEM BOGEY
- MV OLIB G
- MV BLIDA
- MV ROSALIA D AMATO

GRISBY (04)
- MV SAVINA CAYLYN
- MV ALBEDO
- MV GEMINI
- MV ORNA

been observed to be using highjacked merchant vessels as mother ships. This has given them an extended reach of over a thousand nautical miles from the Somalian coast.

Given the changing tactics and operations, it is, as Clausewitz would tell us, imperative to strike at the pirates' center of gravity, "the hub of all power and movement on which all else depends." To my mind, their center of gravity is an elaborate network of financiers that fund the operations and facilitate revenue collection. A recent United Nations report revealed that of the ransom paid in each incident of piracy, only 30 percent reaches the pirates, while financiers and sponsors hive off 50 percent. The question that begs to be answered is, how do they manage to divert funds in so unfettered a manner? Therefore, there is a need to build a strategy beyond multinational maritime counterpiracy operations to facilitate tracking of the fiscal trail. It is important that our efforts be cultivated before what is at present a relatively benign problem of piracy develops a nexus with radical terrorism, which has a cancerous potential.

Let's move on to what we are doing and some thoughts about what it is that we can collectively achieve. What we have seen today is a hitherto unprecedented full and willing cooperation between a wide range of navies to combat piracy by providing credible deterrence, thereby enhancing commercial confidence and facilitating the freedom of navigation in the global commons. What is required is a collaborative engagement of both maritime powers and the littoral states.

The importance of littoral states moving toward a viable solution was best exemplified by the success of the Southeast Asian countries to combat piracy. While it is obvious to highlight that Somalia is a failed state, in stark contrast to the economically vibrant Southeast Asia, nevertheless, Somalia does have comparatively stable

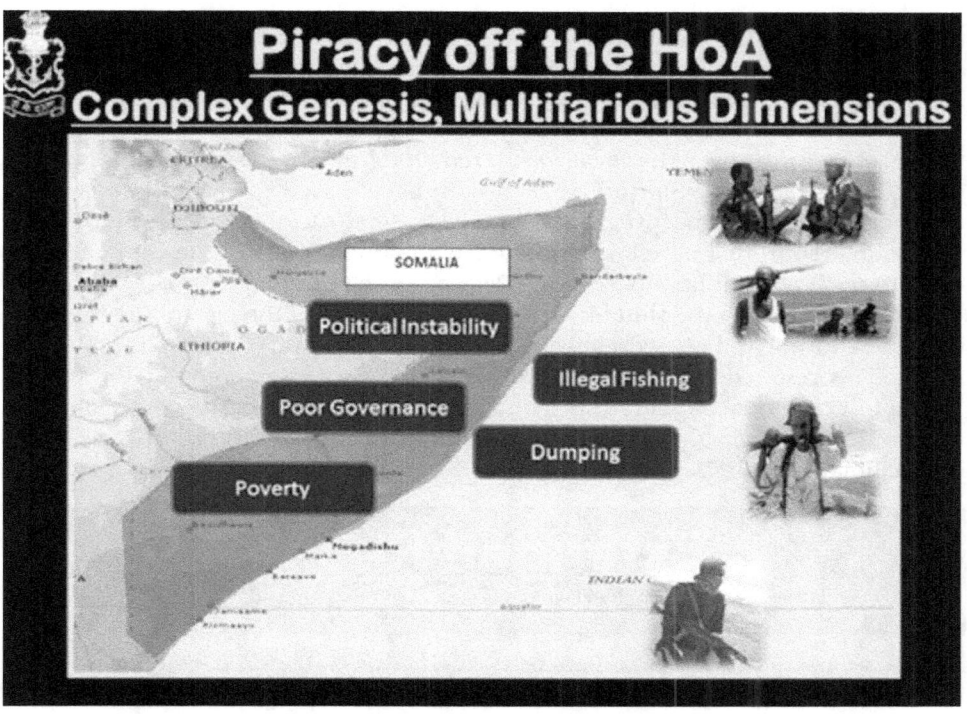
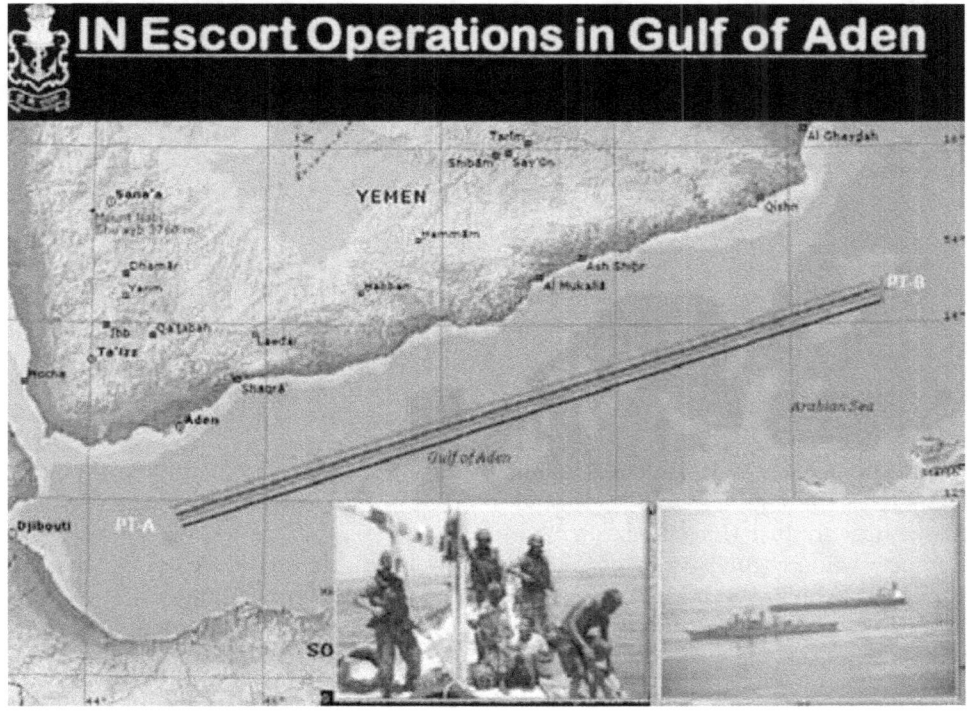

neighbors who could contribute to a regional response, and international efforts could provide impetus to a fledgling Somalian coast guard. Larger maritime forces could facilitate training of local navies and coast guards.

We in India are particulary concerned about the safety of mariners in the Indian Ocean, since we are geographically centered alongside the major shipping routes in the region. Units of the Indian Navy have been tasked to carry out escorts in the Gulf of Aden, irrespective of the nationality, since October 2008. So far, of the nearly 1,800 ships that have been escorted by the Indian Navy in the Gulf of Aden, more than 80 percent have been flying flags other than Indian.

I mentioned about the shift in the areas of operations of the pirates closer to our island territories, and consequently we have had to increase our antipiracy deployments. This resulted in four pirate mother ships being intercepted by the Indian Navy and Coast Guard earlier this year. Consequently, there has been a reduction of piracy incidents in the area, and we intend to maintain this posture to ensure international shipping.

Subsequently, we also noticed a shift in the international sea lanes in the Arabian Sea as merchant vessels attempted to avoid piracy-prone areas. Some of these new routes are just 15 to 20 nautical miles off our coast, and there have now been instances when regular fishermen—Indian fishermen, that is—have been mistaken as pirates. In this cycle of "cause—effect—cause," there is a real danger of innocent casualties on account of mistaken identities. We have, therefore, issued advisories on this aspect.

If piracy is to be deterred, the present "risk-versus-reward quotient" of our ocean must be inverted exponentially by the development of appropriate laws and rules of engagement. These require both national and international consensus, which can be facilitated by an exchange of the firsthand operational experiences of navies presently involved in antipiracy operations, beside ideas from legal and academic circles, as well as expertise and local knowledge of the regional players.

Naval forces have been facing a recent dilemma about apprehending pirates at sea due to inadequacy of or ineffective legal mechanisms to prosecute pirates who have been arrested. It is estimated that nine out of ten apprehended pirates benefit from the "catch and release" policy followed by most navies until now. In India we are presently facing the challenge of prosecuting over one hundred pirates apprehended by the Indian Navy and held in our country. We have moved to make new and effective domestic laws, and we hope to have these in place. I'm sure similar challenges are being experienced by other countries as well, and if you can share experiences in this regard, it will be a positive step in a collective fight against piracy.

While these are policy issues that it may take time to craft consensus on, there are operating procedures that can be adopted immediately. The best management practices that have been published suggest a variety of planning and operational practices for ship operators and masters of ships transiting through high-risk areas. This is a noteworthy initiative that includes suggestions such as having high freeboards, proceeding at high speeds, using barbed wire and water cannons, employing sentries, and establishing citadels or safe rooms on board. One measure that is increasingly getting preference is the use of armed security guards. In this context the maritime community has to be cautious of cases of mistaken identity, which I have alluded to earlier. To mitigate such risk, we have been using acoustic devices that have long-range capability with built-in Phraselators that facilitate passing instructions in the Somali language.

Towards minimizing the possibility of situational escalation, we have resorted to a rather unique measure of using our ship's life rafts. Once the mother ship has been forced to stop, the pirates and crew are made to leave the mother ship and get on to life rafts released by the naval ship. This ensures that the pirates cannot carry arms; after which, they can be brought on board for further investigation. The shipping community could consider installation of mechanisms to disable their ship's engines once it becomes evident that pirates are succeeding in gaining control. This may discourage the attempts to commandeer the vessel, with, of course, the attendant risk of force escalation by the pirates on account of their frustrations. This reemphasizes the importance of establishing a citadel on board.

Finally, I would conclude with a reflection that international efforts towards combating piracy would benefit if there were fewer disparate task forces and independent naval operations. India's relative autonomy of efforts towards combating piracy of Somalia can be traced to its preference for a UN-mandated operation, which, we believe, if adopted, would holistically enhance the efficacy of operations. Our prime minister in his speech at the UN General Assembly last month called on the community of nations to evolve a comprehensive and effective response to the problem of piracy, and has assured the world of India's readiness to work with other nations in this regard. With these thoughts, I conclude my remarks. Thank you.

Admiral Tan Sri Abdul Aziz Jaafar, Malaysia:

Thank you, Admiral Verma. During his fifteen-minute talk, Admiral Verma mentioned a few interesting points. He mentioned piracy, which was previously and predominantly robbery, has now morphed into an elaborate network of operations to effect enormous quantities of ransom, which—unfortunately for him—has fifty-three of his countrymen among the hostages used to leverage ransom negotiations.

He pointed out that the roots of piracy are diverse but it is predominantly political instability that has created a void of governance and economic opportunities ashore, hence, the lure for easy money at sea. He also mentioned the various cooperative and collaborative engagements towards information sharing and to address the piracy in the Gulf of Aden, namely CGPCS, SHADE, and UKMTO, to name a few. He mentioned piracy on the increase, contrary to what Admiral Greenert mentioned earlier. He may have to explain that to everyone later.

He mentioned the envelope expanded to more than 1,100 miles. Admiral Verma came up with some proposals for collaborative engagement between major maritime powers and littoral states. He said that it is most important for littoral states to emulate the success of the Southeast Asian nations. I'm here to share the experiences. If anyone would like to know about our success stories, the Chief of Navy of Singapore and the Vice Chief of Navy of Indonesia are also here. We will be able to explain it and deliberate on that. He also touched on the dilemma of apprehending pirates at sea, due to inadequate or ineffective legal mechanisms to prosecute pirates. Thank you, Admiral Verma.

Ladies and gentlemen, our next speaker will be Admiral Alexander P. Pama, the Flag Officer in Command of the Philippine Navy. Before he goes to the podium, I would like to enlighten you on his background. Vice Admiral Pama is a native of Passi, Iloilo, and graduated from the Philippine Military Academy in 1979. He joined the Philippine Navy after graduating from the PMA and achieved a well-rounded naval career having successfully completed shipboard and shore assignments prior to his appointment as the thirty-second Flag Officer in Command of the Philippine Navy on 4 January this year.

For his shipwork assignments, he has commanded six Philippine Navy vessels. His other sea commands include the Naval Task Groups—61.1 and 61.2—the group operating in Basilan-Sulu and Tawi-Tawi—and the antiterrorism task group called the Naval Task Group "Stingray."

In the course of his naval career, he underwent and excelled in various military and civilian education and training courses, local and foreign, among which were the Naval Command and Staff Course; Naval Command and General Staff Course; Naval Command Course at the U.S. Naval War College, graduating in 2006; the Course in National Security at the Christian-Albrechts University in Kiel, Germany; Strategic Intelligence Course at the Defense Intelligence Agency in Washington, D.C.; and Psychological Operations Course at the U.S. Army Special Warfare School at Fort Bragg, North Carolina.

He is a master in business administration graduate of the Ateneo de Manila University. His decorations include the Philippine Legion of Honor (Degree of Officer), five Distinguished Service Stars, two Distinguished Navy Crosses, and an Outstanding Achievement Medal, the Silver Wing Medal, the Senior Command-at-Sea Badge, and the Honorary Marine Command Badge. He has other military campaign medals and decorations. With that, I'll present to you Admiral Pama.

Admiral Alexander Pama, Philippines:

Thank you very much for that very kind introduction. Admiral Greenert, Admiral Christenson, distinguished chiefs of navies and coast guards from all over the world, participants at today's symposium, good navy morning to all of us. It is nice to be back in Newport. I attended a lot of lectures in this very same hall. I've always wondered how it felt to be up here and not down there. I used to do a lot of dozing when I was down there. Now I know how it feels.

Before I proceed, I would like to thank the organizers for this rare honor and privilege to speak before this very distinguished group. I am here to share our humble experiences with, and perspectives on, maritime terrorism in our area.

Introduction

"MARITIME TERRORISM REFERS TO THE UNDERTAKING OF TERRORIST ACTS AND ACTIVITIES WITHIN THE MARITIME ENVIRONMENT USING OR AGAINST VESSELS OR FIXED PLATFORM AT SEA OR IN PORT, OR AGAINST ANY ONE OF THEIR PASSENGERS OR PERSONNEL OR AGAINST COASTAL FACILITIES OR SETTLEMENTS INCLUDING TOURIST RESORTS, PORT AREAS AND PORT TOWN OR CITIES."

Security Cooperation In The Asia-pacific (CSCAP) Working Group On Maritime Cooperation

❖ Maritime terrorism defined based on int'l and domestic convention

Maritime terrorism is a multifaceted phenomenon that crosses disciplines as freely as it does jurisdictional boundaries. Owing to the ambiguous and unpredictable character of terrorism itself, maritime terrorism is considered an enigma as compared to other maritime security threats, like piracy.

Drawing from the Philippine Navy's experience, we posit that the key to combat maritime terrorism lies in understanding and addressing the root causes of the problem. An accurate and comprehensive understanding of the nature of maritime terrorism is a sine qua non to the formulation of effective and holistic countermeasures to address it.

As we see it, the maritime domain is not a threat, per se. Indeed, in the past we relied on the vastness of our oceans as a measure of protection against external security threats. However, this protection has been prejudiced with the advancement of technology and lawless elements that wreak havoc in the maritime domain, thus challenging our states' territorial integrity and sovereignty.

The threats that thrive in the maritime domain start and, thus, end on land. Allow me to explain our proposition, starting with examination of the nature of maritime terrorism. Maritime terrorism is a derivative of the broader concept of terrorism. It's a phenomenon in the current security milieu.

Maritime terrorism has no absolute definition, because it varies according to geographical and cultural variables and has in the past remained the business of the affected state. Indeed, there is no objective, universally accepted definition of maritime terrorism, just as there is no objective, universally accepted definition of terrorism itself. One definition espoused by the Council for Security Cooperation in the Asia Pacific, or the CSCAP, working group on maritime cooperation in February 2002 was this: "Maritime terrorism refers to the undertaking of terrorist acts and activities in the maritime environment, using or against vessels or fixed platforms at sea or in port, or against anyone and their passengers or personnel, against coastal facilities or settlements, including tourist resorts, port areas and port towns or cities."

Please note that the CSCAP makes no distinction as to the purpose of the act. What constitutes it as maritime terrorism is the fact that the violence was done in the maritime domain or against maritime infrastructure, including ports, vessels, and fixed platforms at sea. In the Philippines Human Security Act in 2002, however, to be considered maritime terrorism, the violence done in the maritime domain or against a maritime infrastructure must be pursued in furtherance of an unlawful demand directed against the government and people. Nevertheless, what is important in this aspect is the convergence of the opinion of the international community and our domestic laws on acts that comprise maritime terrorism.

A significant incident that first brought the phenomenon of maritime terrorism to the world's attention was the hijacking of the cruise liner *Achille Lauro* by Palestinian terrorists in 1985. Crew members and passengers of the cruise ship were held hostage while demands were made for exchange for the freedom of a group of Palestinian prisoners detained in Israel. Other high-profile terrorist attacks include the suicide attack on the USS *Cole* in February 2000 and the bombing of the Philippine *SuperFerry 14* in February 2004, killing more than one hundred people. The 9/11 terrorist attack on the Twin Towers in New York set new precedents, not only in maritime terrorism, but terrorism itself. The sheer scale of that attack, its ambitious scope, and coordination, combined with the determination and dedication of the hijackers, surpassed anything previously seen. The attack demonstrated that ordinary means of transportation, like aircraft and vessels, can be turned into lethal weapons of terror in the hands of determined terrorists. The vulnerability of the maritime domain and the potential impact of the attack on the maritime sector highlighted the seriousness of the threat to maritime terrorism.

The spate of maritime terrorist attacks in the Philippines is generally perpetrated by two local terrorist groups, namely, the Abu Sayyaf Group (ASG), or the Bearer of the Sword, and the renegade element of the Moro Islamic Liberation Front. These groups are known to use the maritime environment for movement and logistical purposes and have developed maritime capability for marine operations.

The Abu Sayyaf Group is a self-styled group of extremist Muslim fighters blamed for the Philippines' worst attacks. The ASG gained notoriety in 1991 when it bombed the floating library ship M/V *Doulos*. In 2000, using high-powered speed boats, the Abu Sayyaf kidnapped twenty foreigners and a Filipino from a dive resort in Sipadan, Malaysia. In 2001 the ASG kidnapped three U.S. citizens and seventeen Filipinos from a tourist resort in Palawan. The bombing in 2004 of the M/V *SuperFerry 14*, a passenger cruise liner in Manila Bay, that killed 118 passengers and crew, and wounded 300 others, is the ASG's most prominent attack. Likewise, the ASG demonstrated its capability to launch maritime attacks with the bombing of M/V *Dona Ramona* in Lamitan, Basilan, in the southern Philippines in 2005. In the years after, the ASG sporadically engaged in seaborne hijacking, ambuscades, hostage taking, and kidnapping mainly as resource-generating retaliation activities.

On the other hand, elements of the Moro Islamic Liberation Front, MILF, an Islamist militant breakaway group from the Moro National Liberation Front, or MNLF, mounted a bomb attack in the busy seaport of Davao City, resulting in the deaths of sixteen people and injuring of thirty-five others in April 2003. The said activity was alleged to have been committed by the rogue elements of the MILF, despite statements by the mainstream leadership that they are not involved in such incidents.

The ASG and insurgent forces of the MILF are known to have historic ties with the Jemaah Islamiyah, JI, a regional terrorist group fighting for the establishment of an Islamic Republic unifying Malaysia, Indonesia, Brunei, Southern Thailand, and Mindanao in the Philippines. This group has established cells throughout the Southeast Asian region to carry out its objective. The ASG has been able to carry out bomb attacks partly because of training and support given by JI.

Philippine Response

Response is multidimensional —military, social, economic, cultural, political

Given our experiences, we realize the problem with maritime terrorism starts and could end on land. Hence, to address this, a combination of land-based and sea-based solutions is required.

Addressing maritime terrorism requires comprehensive understanding of the character of its causes, the events, issues, factors, and such dynamics that instigated the formation of terrorist groups and sustain their existence. This entails an in-depth analysis and assessment of their history, objectives, and the persons behind them.

Maritime terrorist attacks in the Philippines are predominantly held in tourist areas near the sea, against passenger ships and port infrastructures, which are vulnerable and cause great damage and loss of lives and limbs. The magnitude of that kind of attack is highlighted with the number of casualties it has caused, and the more casualties, the more attention is drawn by the event. On the other hand, hostage taking and kidnapping committed by the ASG are generally staged using maritime areas due to the nature of our archipelagic domain. The use of the maritime domain, because of its vastness, has aided the terrorists to accomplish their acts with unpredictability in the context of location and time. These acts, however, when done in maritime areas, are only results of causes and activities done previously on land. The root causes in initial steps can be traced to problems originating in the terrestrial domain.

The problem of maritime terrorism in the Philippines has political, socioeconomic, and other underpinnings that simply cannot be addressed by military operations in the maritime domain. As such, the problem of and solution to maritime terrorism necessarily start and end on land. On this premise, the Philippines launched a multidimensional program designed to address the social, economic, cultural, and political issues breeding maritime terrorism. The multifaceted nature of maritime terrorism demands a solution that extends beyond combating the terrorists at sea, but also to address its existence and proliferation on land.

Having said that, the Armed Forces of the Philippines (AFP) formulated the Internal Peace and Security Plan, or IPSP, to institutionalize a people-centered, whole-of-government approach to address maritime terrorism. In essence, the plan brings all stakeholders in a network of cooperation that pursues the long-term well-being of the people, and presents a creative and an effective solution to peace and security in the maritime domain. The IPSP proffers that pursuing military solutions to a fundamentally social problem will not end maritime terrorism. The military aspect is just one facet of the multidimensional nature of the problem of maritime terrorism Hence, initiatives under the IPSP range from combat operations to socioeconomic, cultural, and community-based programs for peace and development, consisting of construction of social infrastructure, literacy campaigns, interfaith dialogues, delivery of basic social services, and involvement of stakeholders in AFP initiatives as the means to solve the issues breeding maritime terrorism.

On the part of the Philippine Navy, we complemented land-based solutions with sea-based operations to preempt, prevent, and defeat maritime terrorism. Preemption requires foresight, and a good estimate of the threat based on effective intelligence and detection. Preemption addresses the issues even before they become a threat. This is our proactive approach to fight maritime terrorism. On the other hand, prevention connotes deterrence or imposition of a counter-measure to avoid the occurrence of an attack. Prevention addresses existing threats or problems.

On preemption, the Philippine Navy is expanding its maritime domain awareness capability through the National Coast Watch System. Essentially, the National Coast Watch System is a network of maritime, human, and technical architecture for domain awareness. The backbone of the system is the strategically located coast watch stations with coastal detection equipment and an assortment of intelligence, surveillance, and reconnaissance (ISR) equipment as well. Detection is complemented by a layer of ISR activities and border crossing and border patrol exercises with our neighboring countries. Through the National Coast Watch System, the Philippine Navy endeavors to keep an eye on our vast maritime domain 24/7. Patrolling our seas for surveillance and maritime purposes is, indeed, a tremendous task given the length of our coastline.

On the other hand, the assistance, detection, control, and interdiction activities demand more than the application of military capabilities. More often than not, this entails enforcement of customs, immigration, and quarantine laws, and other domestic laws against terrorism and transnational crimes. Maritime security efforts in the country, thus, involve participation by a host of other concerned government agencies. To harness the synergy of efforts of these government agencies, our government issued Executive Order No. 57. This establishes the National Coast Watch Council as the central interagency mechanism for a coordinated and coherent approach on maritime security operations and maritime security issues, such as maritime terrorism.

Also, to deter probable maritime terrorist attacks, the Philippine Navy assigns sea marshals aboard domestic shipping lines. Sea marshals are Philippine Navy and Philippine Coast Guard operatives tasked to assist in ensuring the security of domestic passenger shipping plying in Philippine waters. The Philippine Navy experience has also proven that the use of the military conveys a powerful deterrent while satisfying public demands for tough action against maritime terrorist groups. The constant visibility and strong presence of AFP units in terrorist breeding areas restricted their movement and provided an atmosphere of peace and security in the community where they come from.

To deter terrorist acts at sea, the Naval Task Force Stingray was organized by the Philippine Navy in 2001 in response to the Sipadan incident. This is composed of highly mobile seaborne units deployed in potential target areas to restrict terrorist movements and thwart their possible attacks. The unpredictable presence of the Task Force Stingray made it difficult for the ASG to stage attacks in the maritime domain. Furthermore, the Philippine Navy has utilized border-crossing stations and joint border patrol operations to deter terrorist activities in the Sulu-Sulawesi border areas. Border-crossing stations are Philippine posts established at the border areas of our neighboring countries to monitor the passage and entry of undesirable people and goods in border-crossing areas. Joint patrol operations, on the other hand, show the strong cooperation between and among neighboring navies, thus conveying their serious effort to combat maritime security threats, including maritime terrorism.

Recognizing that securing the maritime domain alone will not end maritime terrorism, the Philippine Navy engaged in land-based operations as part of its holistic approach in fighting maritime terrorism. Hence, in 2007 the Navy was part of the Armed Forces of the Philippines' OPLAN ULTIMATUM, which was a combat clearing operation resulting in the neutralization of key terrorist leaders and takeover by the armed forces of their camps in certain areas in Mindanao. OPLAN ULTIMATUM was followed by projects to rehabilitate and develop terrorist-infested areas.

Addressing maritime terrorism has also been the focus of some bilateral and multilateral engagements by the Philippines. The agreement on information exchange and establishment of communication procedures in 2002 among the Philippines, Indonesia, and Malaysia strengthens intelligence exchange and information sharing.

The whole-of-government approach in people-centered programs proves to be the best solution to preempt, prevent, and defeat maritime terrorism. The whole-of-government approach brings synergy and efforts of all stakeholders in government agencies, while the people-centered approach addresses the multidimensional issues that breed and sustain maritime terrorism. The country's efforts against maritime terrorism places the welfare of the people at the center of our operations through programs that will uplift their way of life and isolate them from the tentacles of maritime terrorism. With all modesty, may I say the Philippine Navy's experience proves the efficacy of our strategy against maritime terrorism. Indeed, since the 2004 *SuperFerry 14* bombing, no subsequent high-profile maritime terrorist attack has been recorded in the Philippines. The diminished threat of maritime terrorism is also manifested in the decreasing frequency of maritime violence in Philippine waters, attesting to the success of the country's fight against the maritime terrorism.

However, more remains to be done, and none of us can do it alone—thus, the need for more collaborative engagements. With that, I end my presentation. Thank you very much.

Admiral Tan Sri Abdul Aziz Jaafar, Malaysia:

Thank you, Admiral Pama. Admiral Pama talked about the Philippines' experiences on maritime terrorism. He said that maritime terrorism is a multifaceted phenomenon and is constant, as compared to other maritime acts.

He believes that the problems of and solutions to maritime terrorism start and end on the land. Hence, he believes that the key to combating maritime terrorism lies in understanding the nature and addressing the root causes of the problems.

He later concluded that the Philippines' strategy of placing the welfare of the people at the center of their operations has produced good results and has somewhat diminished the threats of maritime terrorism. Once again, thank you, Admiral Pama.

For the next speaker we will have Staff Brigadier Ibrahim S. M. Almusharrakh, the UAE Naval Forces Commander. Staff Brigadier Almusharrakh will share with us the UAE's experiences in managing and protecting critical infrastructure.

Just a brief introduction of him: Staff Brigadier Almusharrakh took over the post as commander of UAE Naval Forces from Rear Admiral Ahmed Sabab al-Tanaiji on 1 February 2011. He joined the Navy in 1980. He underwent the cadet training at the Britannia Royal Naval College (BRNC) in the UK, graduating in 1984. He is a graduate of the Naval Staff College in 1994 and a graduate of the Naval Comand College in 2004. Staff Brigadier Ibrahim S. M. Almusharrakh, you have the floor now. Thank you.

Staff Brigadier General Ibrahim S. M. Almusharrakh:

In the name of God, the Compassionate, the Merciful. First, it gives me pleasure to thank retired admiral Roughead, the former Chief of Naval Operations, and Admiral Greenert for their invitation to me in order to speak at this symposium. Also, I would like to thank Admiral Christenson for hosting this outstanding event at the Naval War College.

Chief naval officers and chiefs of coast guards, ladies and gentlemen, I am not here to speak exclusively about the United Arab Emirates, but to highlight key points to demonstrate how the sea is essential for the United Arab Emirates and how it fits into the maritime domain and may affect the nation's welfare and economic stability and economic growth of United Arab Emirates. Initiatives and decisions taken by the United Arab Emirates to defend, protect, and secure our littoral territorial waters and exclusive economic zones contribute to the continued security and stability of the the Arabian Gulf and the Strait of Hormuz. The key characteristics and factors have to be pointed out also when it comes to critical infrastructure protection in the context of marine security. In the course of the last forty years the United Arab Emirates has transformed from an embryonic federation of seven small, underdeveloped emirates into a major financial and economic power in the Gulf region.

The United Arab Emirates is a littoral state on the Arabian Gulf with about eight hundred kilometers of coastline extending from the southern coast of the Arabian Gulf to the Gulf of Oman. Along the Arabian Gulf coast are hundreds of offshore islands. Qatar lies to the northwest, Saudi Arabia to the west and the south, and the Sultanate of Oman to the northeast and southeast of the Emirates. For sure, I have to cite the Strait of Hormuz, which is adjacent to the coast of United Arab Emirates. This is considered as a strategic choke point that 90 percent of the crude oil exported from the Gulf region is carried through, and dozens of cargo ships transit through this separation scheme every day.

Now let me outline here some other key features of the importance of the sea to the United Arab Emirates. Economic interest in and economic well-being of the Emirates depend primarily on the oil industry. Petroleum has dominated the economy, accounting for most of the national revenues and significant opportunities for investment. The United Arab Emirates has huge proven oil reserves, estimated as 97.8 billion barrels. Now with gas reserves estimated at 214.2 trillion cubic feet, most recent estimates indicate that this would last over 150 years. The oil and gas sector provides a third of the gross national product, thanks to the successful economic programs implemented by the government in recent years. Diversification of the economy has resulted, but still gas and oil remain the dominant contributor to government revenues. Eighty five percent of the oil reserves are located in the sea in the southwestern part of the Gulf area. Offshore oil fields comprising a great number of rigs spread out from the UAE coast. Billions of crude oil barrels are exported through major sea terminals located offshore. Gas is increasingly important both for export and for meeting local demand for water desalination, for domestic and industrial consumers, and for power generation.

The United Arab Emirates government is pursuing economic diversification through investment in infrastructure, transport, trade, and tourism. Sea trade and commerce are important components of the economy of the Emirates today. Most goods and supplies are imported and reexported by sea.

With regard to the growing demand for electric power, the Emirates has proceeded with plans to start up its own ambitious nuclear power program with significant capacity being online by 2020. Construction of nuclear plants is on its way, about two hundred kilometers west of Abu Dhabi City, along the coast. This is being actively pursued by government officials.

Most of the freshwater is produced by desalination plants located on the seashore as well. Most of our plants are also associated with desalination units. This is just a glimpse at a small number of the Emirates' existing economic assets and currently planned infrastructures that are essential to sustain growth and the well-being of the Emirates economy.

To focus now on the security and stability of these infrastructures, these are referred to as critical national infrastructures. In the Emirates, most of these facilities are close to the seashore or at sea. Such infrastructures include onshore and offshore oil fields gathering rigs and terminals, port infrastructure and facilities, refineries, power plants, desalination plants, seaports, airports, natural gas transport network areas and all service networks, select structures such as key bridges, future nuclear power plants, and industrial complexes, etc.

What do we mean by "critical infrastructure?" These are asset systems, physical or virtual networks. These are so vital to the nation that incapacitating or destroying such asset systems or networks would have a debilitating impact on national security, economic security, and national public health and safety, or any combination of those. What is the Emirates' specific approach to critical infrastructure protection? The protection system is, first and foremost, a kind of infrastructure protection authority in the region. This protection authority for infrastructure works with other government security forces to ensure that critical facilities are secured from potential threats, possible disruption, and imminent destruction. The goal here is to build a safer, more secure and resilient environment by taking all necessary precautions to obstruct and prevent any destructive actions by hostile forces and to strengthen national preparation, timely response, and rapid recovery in the event of a terrorist attack, or natural disaster, or any other emergency. This is done by enhancing protection efforts through an unprecedented partnership, to meet the requirements of critical infrastructure identification, prioritization, and protection, and by providing an overarching approach for integrating the nation's many initiatives for asset protection into a single national effort.

- Infrastructure security, strategic planning, and program management are accomplished with government and private sectors in order to develop long-term infrastructure protection strategies and plans [with the CNIA] serving as the central program management authority for critical infrastructure protection issues.
- Risk management is done in concert with private-sector industries through identification of critical infrastructure vulnerabilities and establishment of appropriate mitigation and preparedness plans and strategies.
- Force provision and deployment involve selection and training of elements necessary to produce qualified security personnel while ensuring a high degree of professionalism in the security and protection fields. We need people

able to work in a sensitive and complex environment through cooperation with national and international institutions.
- Oversight and regulatory authority are done through developing, promoting, and auditing standards and best practices for infrastructure protection, leveraging regulatory solutions only when necessary and in accordance with executive counsel and guidance.
- Stakeholders coordination and liaison are done through coordination of government and industrial stakeholders at multiple levels, executive management and service delivery through the principles of partnership, shared best practices, and the exchange of liaison officers.
- An information fusion center and clearinghouse serves as a fusion point for Center for International Policy intelligence and open-source information to produce threat assessments, maintain domain awareness, and provide relevant information requirements for decision making.
- Research and development assessment and deployment are done through study and assessment in cooperation with other governmental and private agencies inside and outside the country.

CNIA'S CORE BUSINESS AREAS

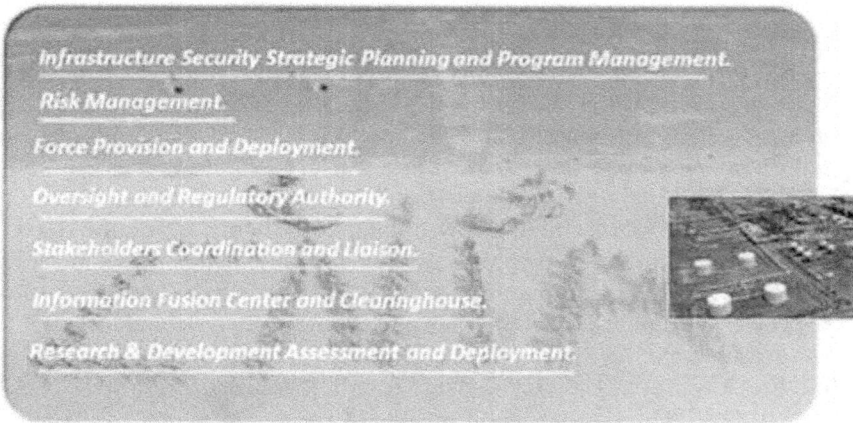

Infrastructure Security Strategic Planning and Program Management.
Risk Management.
Force Provision and Deployment.
Oversight and Regulatory Authority.
Stakeholders Coordination and Liaison.
Information Fusion Center and Clearinghouse.
Research & Development Assessment and Deployment.

In closing, one of the essential elements needed to achieve the nation's critical infrastructure protection goals is to ensure the availability and flow of accurate, timely, and relevant information and intelligence about threats and other hazards in information analysis and incident reporting. Global and regional maritime domain awareness initiatives linked with local initiatives should lead to better preparedness and response to address threats from or at sea and thus provide the necessary protection for the critical infrastructure and sensitive facilities. I thank you for your attention, and peace be upon all of you.

Admiral Tan Sri Abdul Aziz Jaafar, Malaysia:

Thank you, Staff Brigadier Almusharrakh. In his ten-minute presentation, Staff Brigadier Almusharrakh talked about critical national infrastructures in his country, UAE, a very rich and resourceful country. He shared with us the history of and rationale for the establishment of his country's Critical National Infastructure Authority, or, in short, CNIA.

He later explained and also enlightened us on CNIA's seven core business areas, namely, infrastructure security, strategic planning, and program management; risk management; force provision and deployment; oversight and regulatory authority; stakeholder coordination and liaison; information fusion center; and finally, the research and development assessment and deployment.

In his conclusion, he mentioned the requirement for accurate and timely information. Thank you once again, Staff Brigadier Almusharrakh.

Ladies and gentlemen, next I'll invite our final speaker for today's panel discussion. He is none other than Vice Admiral Ibrahim, Chief of Naval Staff for Nigeria. Admiral Ola Sa'ad Ibrahim will deliver his address on his Navy's perspective on resource protection and challenges to maritime security.

A brief introduction of him: Vice Admiral Ola Sa'ad Ibrahim was born on 15 June 1955. A graduate of the Nigerian Defence Academy, Kaduna, and the Armed Forces Command and Staff College, Jaji, he trained with the Royal and Indian Navies. Vice Admiral Ibrahim is a navigation and direction specialist. He holds a bachelor of law degree from Ahmadu Bello University. He was at the Royal College of Defence Studies in the UK as a member in 2002, where he, in addition, obtained a master's degree from the Department of War Studies and Public Policy at King's College, University of London.

Admiral Ibrahim had tours of duty on Nigerian naval ships in various capacities and he is decorated with the Command at Sea Badge for successful command at sea on various Nigerian naval ships. He was Directing Staff and Chief Instructor, respectively, at the Department of Maritime Warfare, Armed Forces Command and Staff College, Jaji.

He was secretary to the Chief of Naval Staff before being appointed to command the naval operations base, Nigerian Naval Ship (NNS) *Beecroft* in 2001. In 2003 Admiral Ibrahim served as Commander, Naval Task Group Operation HARMONY in the Eastern Naval Command, Calabar, before he went to the National Defence College in Nigeria as a Directing Staff in the same year.

He left the National Defence College for the Naval Headquarters as Navy Secretary in August 2005. He returned to the college as Director of Curriculum and Programs Development in May 2006. It was from this point that he headed back to Naval Headquarters as Chief of Administration and subsequently as Chief of Training and Operations.

In February 2009 he was appointed Flag Officer Commanding Western Naval Command, the appointment he held until his elevation to the present appointment as Chief of Naval Staff on 8 September 2010. Vice Admiral Ibrahim is decorated with a Distinguished Service Star and Golden Jubilee Medal. I would like to invite Vice Admiral Ibrahim to deliver his speech. Thank you.

Vice Admiral Ola Sa'ad Ibrahim, Nigeria:

Chief of Naval Operations, United States Navy, Admiral Jonathan Greenert; the President of the Naval War College, Admiral John Christenson; distinguished heads of navies and coast guards here present; distinguished delegates; guest speakers; ladies and gentlemen, I am highly delighted to be here and honored to address this panel, "Global Perspectives to Maritime Security." I'm also delighted to share my thoughts with you on protection of maritime infrastructure and resources against piracy, terrorism, and other forms of insecurity.

Within the past decade, the evolving era of globalization has ushered in significant changes in the maritime environment, in terms of geostrategic and economic values. Apart from increase in maritime trade and shipping, more people live around the coast than ever before, while demand for hydrocarbon and fish resources remains on the rise with the increasing global population. Likewise, the availability of improved technology has made it possible to conduct deep-sea exploitation activities.

Regrettably, on the flip side of the positive values of the maritime environment are emergent threats and various forms of insecurity. Apart from illegal trafficking in goods, humans, and drugs, the maritime environment is faced with the challenges of poaching of fishery resources and crude oil theft and illegal bunkering. Maritime terrorism and militant activities, such as hostage taking and vandalism of pipelines, constitute other threats to maritime security, particularly around African waters.

As we are all probably aware, both the positive and the undesirable attributes of the maritime environment are at play in the Gulf of Guinea and, indeed, in the exclusive economic zone of Nigeria. Against this background, therefore, this short presentation narrows down to the dynamics of protection as they relate to events in Nigeria's maritime environment and the Gulf of Guinea.

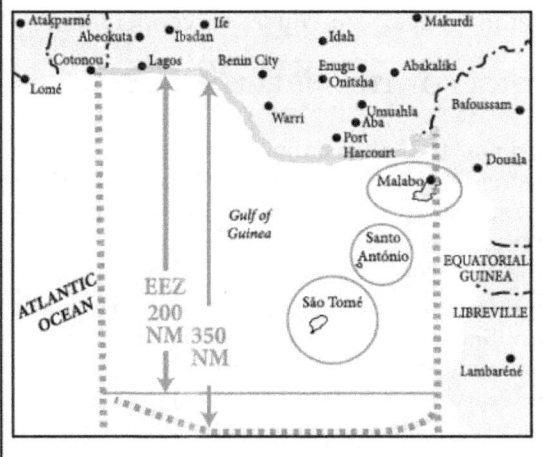

SECURITY ISSUES IN NIGERIA'S MARITIME ENVIRONMENT

Currently, hydrocarbon exploitation in the exclusive economic zone accounts for over 80 percent of national revenue, while over 90 percent of imports and exports are conducted through the numerous coastal ports. Within the past decade, deepwater oil exploitation has extended up to sixty nautical miles from the coast. It is also to be noted that the southeastern flank of Nigeria, of the 84,000 square nautical miles of Nigeria's EEZ, is shared with neighboring states, such as São Tomé and Príncipe, Equatorial Guinea, and Cameroon. Among other things, therefore, these facts demonstrate both the huge dependence of Nigeria on the maritime environment for survival and prosperity, and the imperative of peaceful coexistence with our neighbors.

In line with national foreign policy, Nigeria has consistently adopted a peaceful approach to the resolution of maritime boundary issues and resource sharing with our neighbors. Internally, the amnesty program initiated for ex-militants in the Niger Delta has gone a long way towards abating the threat of kidnapping, hostage taking, and crude oil theft.

Beyond these positive efforts, however, are the persistent attacks on shipping, poaching, illegal bunkering, drug trafficking, smuggling, and environmental pollution. The 13 February 2010 storm which beached over twenty merchant ships on Lagos's coast also revealed disturbing effects of climate change and limited national capacity on salvage operations. Another area of maritime security is the prevalence of transborder crimes on both the western and eastern flanks of Nigeria's national exclusive economic zone. These crimes include attacks on shipping, hostage taking, and poaching, often perpetrated by local and foreign criminal groups who are knowledgeable about the limited interstate security coordination and maritime domain awareness in the Gulf of Guinea. Although maritime terrorism is yet to feature as a prominent consideration, the contending threat scenarios, if unchecked, could provide an attractive atmosphere. The bottom line of the foregoing exposition is the reality that maritime security in the Gulf of Guinea is less about naval wars, but more about resource and shipping protection.

In other words, capacity building in the Nigerian Navy and other local navies must necessarily reflect focus on effective exclusive economic zone presence and maritime domain awareness, as well as interagency and internavy cooperation.

EFFORTS AND CHALLENGES OF THE NIGERIAN NAVY

Nigerian Navy Roles. Under constitutional and other statutory provisions, the Nigerian Navy is charged with the naval defense of the nation as well as with assisting in the coordination and enforcement of customs and immigration and illegal bunkering, antipollution, and fishery protection laws. Apart from hydrographic survey duties, the Nigerian Navy is also tasked to assist in the enforcement of all national and international maritime laws ascribed or acceded to by the government. These roles evidently cover the full spectrum of military, policing, and diplomatic functions of any modern navy. When this is weighed against the background of prevalent threats, it becomes apparent that the Nigerian Navy is under obligation to play a lead role in resource protection within the nation's maritime environment.

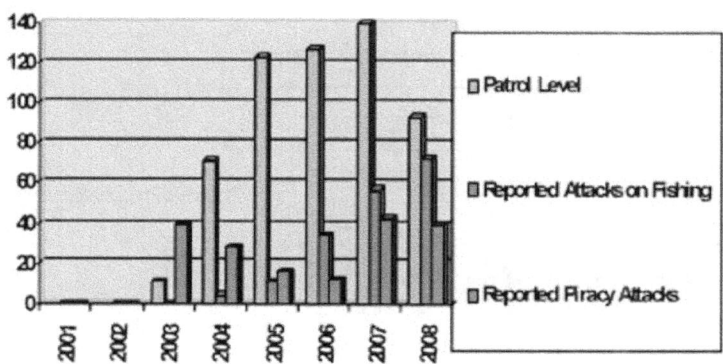

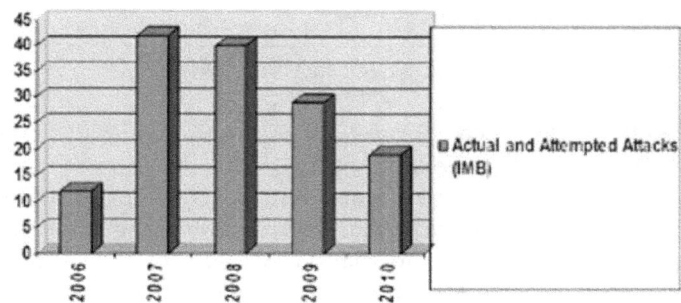

Efforts and Challenges. Towards gaining better comprehension of the challenges of resource protection from the Nigerian Navy perspective, it is necessary to provide illustrations with statistical trends. Following decade-long operations in Liberia and Sierra Leone, the bulk of the Nigerian Navy fleet returned home in 1999 with degraded availability. This period also coincided with the upsurge in crude oil theft, illegal bunkering, and attacks on shipping in Nigeria's coastal waters. Notably, however, the acquisition of four *Balsam*-class vessels from the United States Coast Guard in 2003 significantly increased Nigerian patrol efforts.

As reflected in the statistical profile in figure 1, this led to an appreciable decrease in the number of reported attacks and illegal bunkering. On the other hand, the spike in attacks from around 2007 could be partly attributed to downtime of some of the patrol vessels that were pulled out for maintenance. Likewise, to the acquisition of new patrol crafts, the amnesty program, and increased synergy with the Nigerian Maritime Administration and Safety Agency (NIMASA) could be attributed the

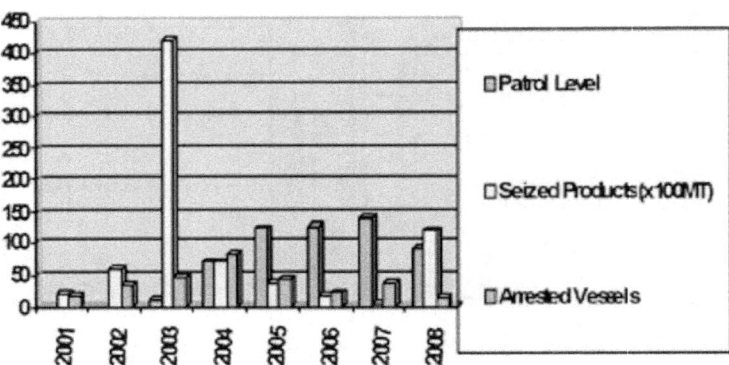

reduction in attacks from 2008 to 2010 as reported by the International Maritime Bureau (IMB).

The overall import of this illustration is to draw attention to the correlation between challenges of inadequate platforms, on the one hand, and the trend of attacks, on the other.

FUTURE PERSPECTIVES

The Transformation Process. Cognizant of the foregoing dynamics, the Nigerian Navy is not in doubt as to the imperatives of effective capacity building in terms of operational assets and strategy. Accordingly, the Nigerian Navy recently developed a comprehensive transformation plan towards addressing its capacity challenges.

The strategic objective of the Nigerian Navy Transformation Plan 2011–2020, therefore, is to achieve and sustain effective capacity to carry out its statutory roles. The key development objectives of the plan are anchored on the pillars of fleet renewal, logistic support and infrastructure, maritime domain awareness, doctrine and training, as well as interagency and subregional cooperation. Primarily, the various capacity-building programs would be based on a new multilevel strategy that guides the improvement of operational effectiveness from the internal waters to the exclusive economic zone.

Platform Acquisition Programs. The future platform acquisition program emphasizes the expansion of the fleet of offshore patrol vessels (OPVs) and coastal patrol boats. In line with this, new patrol crafts are being acquired while arrangements are ongoing for the purchase of long-endurance OPVs.

Permit me to use this opportunity to acknowledge the sustained support of the United States Navy and Coast Guard within the past decade. Apart from the acquisition of the ex–*Balsam* class, the recent transfer of ex–United States Coast Guard cutter *Chase*, now NNS *Thunder*, is expected to significantly improve the presence and the exclusive economic zone protection capacity of the Nigerian Navy. The desire for more vessels of this class remains an open expression of our determination to abate the trend of attacks and other forms of insecurity within the exclusive economic zone.

Maritime Domain Capacity Development. In recognition of the cost-effectiveness and multiplier value of maritime domain awareness in resource protection, a network of integrated sensor systems comprising Automatic Identification System (AIS), radars, and cameras is being developed along the coast of Nigeria. The assistance of the United States Navy and United Kingdom government are highly appreciated in this regard as the installations were made possible under partnership programs with the Nigerian Navy. These efforts notwithstanding, there are outstanding requirements for full maritime domain awareness coverage of a significant portion of the exclusive economic zone. The transformation plan captures this ideal.

Interagency and Subregional Cooperation. Addressing the challenge of operational synergy with relevant national maritime security agencies is also an engaging focus of the Nigerian Navy. Notably, the extant memorandum of understanding (MOU) with the NIMASA is currently undergoing a joint review process towards achieving improved operational synergy. It is worthy of note that the establishment of the joint coast guard unit known as Maritime Guard Command under the MOU has significantly improved maritime security efforts, particularly around Lagos Harbor's entrance. Unfortunately, this modest achievement has translated into recent increased attacks on shipping in the neighboring port of Cotonou. This dimension underlines the critical importance of interstate and internavy cooperation on maritime security. In realization of this, I wish to inform you that both the Nigerian Navy and NIMASA had within the past month engaged the Beninese Navy in joint antipiracy efforts, besides the fact that before now we had a very good relationship with our Ghanaian naval contacts.

Africa Parnership Station Commitment. At this juncture, it is also necessary to acknowledge the valuable contribution of the Africa Partnership Station initiatives towards achieving improved synergy among neighboring maritime security agencies in the Gulf of Guinea. Apart from staff contribution, the participation of Nigerian Navy ships in combined exercises off Ghana and Cameroon within the past two years signals our commitment to the ideals of the Africa Partnership Station. Further, the Nigerian Navy will be hosting the next iteration of Exercise OBANGAME in March 2012. Added to this is a future aspiration for the development of joint centers of excellence for training, including common operating procedure and information-sharing mechanisms.

In conclusion, I wish to make it clear that the challenge of combating threats to maritime infrastructure, shipping, and resource exploitation is far from being won in Nigeria's maritime environment and the Gulf of Guinea.

Nevertheless, the commitment and determination of the Nigerian Navy towards neutralizing this undesirable situation remains unshaken. On a brighter note, the implementation of the ten-year transformation plan constitutes the focal point of the necessary capacity-building efforts in the Nigerian Navy.

Finally, while appreciative of the collaboration efforts with the United States and United Kingdom governments, I wish to place on record the commitment of the Nigerian Navy towards sustaining the various partnership programs on maritime security, as I also look forward to improved synergy at national and subregional levels. Thank you for your attention, and good afternoon.

DISCUSSION

Admiral Tan Sri Abdul Aziz Jaafar, Malaysia:

Thank you, thank you. In essence, he enlightened us on the efforts and challenges in the Gulf of Guinea and further dwelled on the security issues of Nigeria's maritime environment. He reiterated that maritime security in the Gulf of Guinea is not about naval wars but more about resource and shipping protection. Hence, he has recently embarked on the transformation process in the Nigerian Navy—phase one—towards achieving and sustaining effective capacity to carry out its statutory roles. In this regard, he related the six pillars of the Nigerian Navy's transformation plan, focusing primarily on three aspects—platform acquisition programs, maritime domain awareness and capacity development, and the interagency and subregional cooperation. Thank you, Admiral Ibrahim.

Ladies and gentlemen, on behalf of the symposium organizers, I would like to take this opportunity to thank the four panel members for providing us with the insights about the challenges to maritime security, specifically in relation to piracy, maritime domain awareness, maritime terrorism, critical infrastructure protection, and resource protection.

The panel members have also pointed out a few important issues as well as the way forward to effectively deal with those challenges. I believe most of us can readily discuss and comment on the points discussed by the panel members. Before we start, I would like to remind everyone of a few rules. Firstly, please keep your question short, within one minute. Secondly, use the microphone in front of your seat.

You will only speak when I acknowledge you. Introduce yourself first. Be short and be brief. We have only fifteen minutes left. With that, I would like to open the floor for questions and answers. Thank you. Gentleman from Sri Lanka.

Rear Admiral Jayanath Colombage, Sri Lanka:

My question is directed to Admiral Verma. Thank you for an enlightening lecture on piracy. You mentioned these different actions making no difference to the pirates themselves. You also mention having onboard security guards. I believe there is a general reluctance among the merchant marine to have security guards on board.

If my information is right, none of the ships who carried these onboard security teams were ever attacked successfully. Why is it that the shipping companies are very reluctant to carry onboard security teams, which actually can be a deterrent even in the short run?

Admiral Nirmal Verma, India:

You're right on one count, that where we've had security guards, the attempt at piracy has not been successful. There could be two reasons why merchant ships are not keen for this. One, of course, is the commercial interests, which is very unfortunate because I'm talking about Indian shipping companies when I speak with them. They count every penny.

Now Indian shipping has built citadels. There was a time they just wouldn't do it. They talked about cost. In fact, some went on to suggest this may be a passing phenomenon, so why spend a couple of million fortifying yourself?

The other concern is that if you have—I'm talking about the concern from the shipping company side—armed guards, and the armed guards are using a certain category of weapon, it is most likely to lead to the pirates using something more lethal. You can see that happening from the time when they just used small arms and now they're certainly going up in rocket propelled grenades. They try to cause as much damage as they can.

There have been some unfortunate instances where they said, okay, if we can't get the ship, let's destroy it. A couple of ships have been set on fire. In my assessment, these are the reasons why some of them are reluctant. By and large, I would say as the statistics go, at least 35 percent of world shipping which goes through this area is carrying armed guards.

Admiral Tan Sri Abdul Aziz Jaafar, Malaysia:

Thank you. I hope that satisfies your question. Next, please.

Vice Admiral Paul Maddison, Canada:

Good afternoon. Admiral Maddison from Canada. My question will be for Admiral Ibrahim. I'm struck by listening to Admiral Verma describe the piracy on the east coast of Africa and listening to you describe, equally significant, illegal destabilizing activity on the west coast of Africa. It's an interesting contrast.

In terms of the international response, there is a significant growing response in the Indian Ocean and the Somali Basin, bringing many, many navies together, cooperating to deal with that particular threat. We can argue that because of the strategic shipping going through the Gulf of Aden, there is a real compelling reason to be there.

On the west coast of Africa, the activities there, I would think, are very destabilizing for all central West African countries as you work very hard to build maritime security capacity in governments. My question for you, Admiral, is, are you satisfied with the international response to cooperate with you to bring more capacity to deal with the many illegal activities happening and bringing the negative consequences to your nation?

Vice Admiral Ola Sa'ad Ibrahim, Nigeria:

Thank you very much, Admiral. I would like to push perhaps two perspectives here, hoping, in that way, I can answer your question. I would say the challenges in the west coast of Africa, and perhaps to an extent the Gulf of Guinea, are not as huge as that on the east coast. The size and the network of interest relative to the east coast, the Gulf of Guinea, are more manageable.

Beside that, the Nigerian Navy would like to take the leadership position out there along with the Ghanaian Navy. We are visible. We've been everywhere. [As mentioned] in the course of my presentation today, there is support from navies—from U.S., UK. If there is anything the Nigerian Navy can boast of, it is the human capital. We can be on practically any ship with you and be with you to the end of the world. Of that, I'm very, very sure. I am presiding over about twenty thousand human beings, who were likely trained in the combination of what we call political will with resource limitation.

Our ex–*Balsam* class ships were brought many, many years ago, and they are still with us. As a matter of fact, one of them is in the Republic of Benin now on this cooperative venture. They have been extended a few years, a combination of resourcefulness, resilience. You can carry a flag anywhere with those two words. That, I can assure you.

Unlike the eastern flank's failed states, we have a volume of activity. Choke points—that is not like the west coast. You can see how easily it becomes logical for an assembly of navies to bring about order. In the Gulf of Guinea, the Ghanaian Navy is there, the Nigerian Navy is out there.

The training schools are changing, directing staff. Other navies, other coast guards, they're growing. The Beninese Navy is there. Perhaps governments are getting acutely aware of the wisdom of investment in navies. It could take a long while to get to where we expect to get to, but in the Gulf of Guinea, we are not invisible there. We want to be visible, especially the Nigerian Navy, Ghanaian, Ivory Coast, and others. Our problem is not the size of the problem of the eastern African coast. I hope I answered your question. Thank you.

Admiral Tan Sri Abdul Aziz Jaafar, Malaysia:

Thank you, Admiral Ibrahim. I hope he answered your question. Are you happy with that? We have perhaps time for two more questions.

Rear Admiral Shafqat Jawed, Pakistan:

My question is directed to Admiral Verma. Sir, as you have very rightly pointed out, the piracy trend is not now limited to the coast of Somalia; it is extending as far as close to the Indian coast and, of course, the recent incidents which we observed.

We observe the piracy trend coming closer to the Pakistani coast, as well. Of course, the Pakistani Navy has also initiated a lot of antipiracy measures through the years. Sir, one of the antipiracy measures that you highlighted, that you took on, I think, in the Indian Navy very aggressively, was you took action against the mother ships—that data which you have shared with the audience.

My question is what is the impact of these aggressive actions against mother ships, because there could be a possibility of the *quid pro quo* by the pirates elsewhere against Indian shipping. Can you share your analysis on this, including, sir, whether the impact has been positive with regard to the overall trend against the piracy attempts against Indian shipping? Thank you.

Admiral Nirmal Verma, India:

Very valid observations. First thing I would say is that the impact that took place as far as shipping was concerned, which again, was why we took the action that we did when piracy spread eastward—with piracy taking place off the coast of Somalia, the war insurance rates were being applied up to 65 degrees east. As a result, any ships that were entering the ports on the west coast of India, they were not subject to paying these amounts.

Now, when we had a couple of these incidents that took place towards the second half of last year, then the war insurance was applied to 72 degrees, which brought in all the entire coast of India, west coast of India, within the purview of the war insurance. That is one reason that prompted us to take the action that we took.

What happened in our case was that very often you'll find if there is a failed piracy attempt, maybe in some cases the concerned navies breathe a sigh of relief. In our case, actually, the failed piracy attempt was the start of an operation, because we knew that the mother ship would be somewhere in the vicinity. When I say vicinity, it means, you know, a hundred-odd miles maybe, depending on how quickly we could respond.

We do keep an aircraft on rather short notice. That is the reason why we were effective in catching the mother ships. Also helpful was the information exchange that we have with respect to merchant ships in the area, which helped us actually to spot the mother ships, and we took the action that we did.

Now, this bit of your observation about acting in some other area—unfortunately, we are going through this now. You know, these 120 pirates that we have, they've been put through the legal process, as is the case in our country.

We have a case of a ship where the ransom had been paid by the ship owner. While the ship was being released, they actually held back the Indian crew. That is certainly worrisome. We have tried our best to handle this problem. Yes, it is a problem. We will find ways and means to tackle it.

That's why I want to say that Somalia is not tackling piracy at sea. It's a larger issue. Hopefully there are some UN resolutions which come. I mean, there are some enabling resolutions which are there, but [we need] something more active that will ensure that this problem is sorted out where it should be sorted out, ashore.

Like I said, the central gravity of my opinion is the fiscal trail, if you can choke off the money. It almost sounds like investing in the stock market. If you put money on piracy, maybe the returns are so great for whoever finances it and that is a reason why it was going on. Yes, there are repercussions. We are facing it and seeing how best to tackle it.

Admiral Tan Sri Abdul Aziz Jaafar, Malaysia:

Thank you. I hope he has answered your question. I'm very sorry, time has been running out. I have just been warned I have to conclude the session. With that final remark, we have come to the end of our first panel presentation.

I would like to take the opportunity to thank everyone who has made this panel a successful one, particularly the four speakers. Please give them a round of applause. Thank you.

4

An Address

Honorable Ray Mabus
Secretary of the Navy

Admiral Jonathan Greenert, U.S. Navy:

Good morning, everybody. Great time last night. Glad to see you all bright eyed and bushy tailed and ready to go on. That's excellent. It's my pleasure this morning to introduce our Secretary of the Navy, Ray Mabus. This is an individual who has amazing vision. He's been a great mentor for me.

He has distinguished public service as a naval officer. Some of you learned yesterday that he spent time here in Newport on the good ship *Little Rock*, a cruiser, as a junior officer. He understands life at sea. He understands how things get done on the deck plate, and he understands deck-plate leadership. He led during his tenure in the Navy as a naval officer of high standards and integrity, and he has brought those traits to his current job.

He was the auditor for the State of Mississippi, where he was known for innovation and for judiciousness, something we very much need today. He has brought those traits to his current job. As governor of Mississippi, the youngest governor of Mississippi, he ensured that education and training were priorities. So our secretary understands how to plant the seed corn and how to reap benefits later, what the future is about. As the former ambassador to the Kingdom of Saudi Arabia, he understands diversity, and he brought to the forefront the value of diversity and how to get the most out of people.

He has a distinguished educational career. He is a graduate of the University of Mississippi. He has a master's degree from Johns Hopkins University, and his law degree is from Harvard University. He is responsible for both the Navy and the Marine Corps, a unique assignment for a secretary, a service secretary.

He has revitalized our shipbuilding plan. Some of you saw the product of that yesterday in our littoral combat ship (LCS). We are building many more than were previously planned under Secretary Mabus. He has revitalized our acquisitions process, where our negotiations are much more judicious—there is that word again—and producing better ships.

He has a comprehensive—and what I like about it—a tangible energy, vision, and strategy. Please join me in welcoming this morning's speaker, Secretary of the Navy, the seventy-fifth Secretary of the Navy, the Honorable Ray Mabus.

Secretary of the Navy Ray Mabus:

Admiral Greenert, thank you so much for that introduction. I know that just about everybody here has met our new Chief of Naval Operations, Admiral Greenert. I will say what I said at his assumption of command, that I and everybody in the U.S.

Navy will miss CNO Gary Roughead, whom most of you knew, but the one person I thought was capable of building on what Gary Roughead had done and following in his footsteps and equaling his leadership is Jon Greenert. I think we have an outstanding Chief of Naval Operations.

I want to welcome you all here today. I was thinking that one of the first places I went when I was a new Secretary of the Navy two years ago, a little over two years ago—I came here, the International Seapower Symposium, and did the welcome. I looked out over the room and basically knew nobody, saw a lot of strange faces.

In the past two and a half years it's been my great pleasure, honor, to get to meet and work with a lot of the people here today. I see a lot of friendly faces. I see a lot of faces that I've seen both in this country and in your home countries. I see a lot of faces that I hope I get to know better over the months to come, both here and in your home country.

I was glad to see many of you brave the elements last night to come to our reception on the LCS. So I want to welcome you here, the twentieth bienniel International Seapower Symposium. By the way, 40 years ago I was also, as the CNO said, in Newport. I did not get invited to the first symposium—they did not invite lieutenant junior grades to those things—but ISS in those forty years has become increasingly important, because our world has become so increasingly interconnected.

The world is facing some economic issues. They don't touch just one nation or one continent. They've affected every one of us. The boundaries of individual nations today are crisscrossed by global commerce and global telecommunications. But one area that has not changed is the importance of our global maritime commons. This has served as a link between all nations and all peoples throughout human history. Despite some amazing advances in technology and travel, more than 90 percent of all our trade, all the trade for the world, goes by sea. Despite incredible advances in satellite technology, more than 95 percent of all our telecommunications go under the sea. So ISS provides an incredibly valuable opportunity to discuss common concerns, common issues, common visions. Given the nature of the challenges we face, the only way we can manage our shared responsibilities of this century is to have interconnected partnerships. Those have to be strong partnerships.

One of the challenges to every one of our countries has been economic, fiscal. My government, like virtually all governments, is wrestling with matching resources with requirements. But despite those challenges one thing should be very clear: the United States Navy is and will continue to be a global presence, wherever and whenever we are called on.

But the challenges we face today require us not to do things alone, not to do things by ourselves, but to work closely together to deepen partnerships, to share responsibility, to protect and maintain our common interests together.

In his speech last month to the United Nations, President Obama said that when we face global challenges, the U.S. will be part of a global response. He said sometimes the course of history poses challenges; it threatens our common humanity and common security. In responding to natural disasters, for example, or preventing genocide, keeping the peace, ensuring regional security, and maintaining the flow of commerce, in such cases we should not be afraid to act, but the burden of action should not be America's alone.

What he just described—responding to natural disasters, keeping the peace, ensuring regional security, maintaining the flow of commerce—he could have been describing maritime services. As you look across the seas, and in every geographic region in the time since we were last together two years ago, there are numerous examples of where our maritime services are doing just that: on both coasts of Africa, Africa Partnership Station with thirty-four participating nations; in the Caribbean and South America, [we have] Southern Partnership Station, PANAMAX, CONTINUING PROMISE, Amphibious Southern Partnership Stations. These exercises and deployments range from humanitarian assistance, information-sharing, to high-end combat exercises.

In the Pacific, [we are participating in] Pacific Partnership, Exercise ULCHI FREEDOM GUARDIAN, disaster relief across that great ocean and forward deploying littoral combat ships, like the one we were on last night. And [we have] RIMPAC, the world's largest multinational maritime exercise.

In Europe in the Mediterranean, [there is] the Libya operation that so many people, so many countries here, are part of and [we are] forward deploying Aegis guided-missile destroyers. These ongoing exercises around the world serve to strengthen our maritime partnerships, and all are aimed at our common goals, achieving those goals that we all share as members of the maritime commons. I have to say that our individual leadership is also globally deployed. I see representatives from our Navy that live far from the United States sitting here today. Since I took office in May of 2009, I've traveled over 370,000 air miles to more than fifty countries. I've gone on board more than fifty U.S. ships and dozens of foreign naval vessels. In fact, I'm convinced that I'm now suffering some sort of permanent jet lag.

In Admiral Greenert's first three weeks as the new CNO, he spent one-third of [his time] in the air. He went to sea. He met a dozen of his counterparts, ten heads of navy. So, CNO, after you hit the first one hundred thousand miles, come see me; we'll talk.

When I travel internationally, my first priority—as yours is—is to see our sailors and our Marines and visit with them. I also think it's incumbent on all of us as leaders to engage and seek out new ways to work together. Sometimes opportunities that we do not seek are thrust upon us. Piracy is an example of a threat to all our interests that we are responding to with common purpose and with some considerable success. We've all paid the price of piracy, whether off the Horn of Africa, in the Gulf of Aden, or beyond. Lives have been lost. The cost of doing business has gone up. Time and effort have been devoted to this when it could have been spent in other worthwhile endeavors.

We've also worked together in responding to some recent humanitarian crises. Ten nations came together to respond to the devastating earthquake in Haiti. Nations from around the world, thousands of sailors, were involved in the recovery and relief efforts following the earthquake and tsunami in Japan.

As Admiral Greenert talked about, I think there is another area where the risk we face presents us with an opportunity to cooperate. I've had the honor of visiting, as I mentioned, scores of countries, in my role as Navy Secretary, and it's been rare that I went to a place where energy didn't come up as a topic of concern.

Energy security is increasingly affecting how the world looks at its relationships. Governments and militaries across the world recognize that energy can be used offensively and defensively as a weapon, by denying an adversary access to a critical energy source, and that every military can be vulnerable to disruptions in energy supplies or budget impacts due to price shocks.

We're pursuing some advanced fuel alternatives in the United States Navy. We have the opportunity to strengthen a lot of relationships with those—almost all of us—who understand the advantages of energy security. When the U.S. Navy launches the Great Green Fleet, these partnerships will be an integral part of our future force, providing safe refueling ports and economic relationships with countries with whom we share a common vision.

We've also made a whole lot of strides in the last two years since we got together in our ability to operate together. Using same systems or platforms, making sure those systems and platforms can communicate and work together, can be a part of a seamless whole.

Last night I was glad to see so many of you, as I said, come out in a pretty bad rainstorm to come aboard one of our newest ships, littoral combat ship USS *Independence* (LCS 2). That kind of ship is a major part of the future of our Navy and of all navies. You have to be fast. You have to be agile. You have to be flexible. You have to have a smaller crew and modular systems that can be changed quickly and can support missions all the way from high-end combat to disaster relief. You have to be able to operate in shallow littoral waters but also capable of doing blue-water operations as well. You have to be able to defeat things like mine warfare and surface warfare and submarine warfare.

When I became Secretary of the United States Navy two and a half years ago, I looked out at the smallest fleet that America has had since 1916. As CNO mentioned, I've tried to make rebuilding our fleet one of my top priorities. We've gone from building around five ships a year to building more than eleven ships a year, currently. But to do that, you have to get good value. You have to get a fair price for the ships that you purchase. I think that the ship you were on last night, the LCS, serves in this country as a template for how you can do that. Working together with us, industry was able to dramatically reduce the cost of that ship. Because of that, we were able to buy more ships faster, and American taxpayers saved almost $3 billion on the first twenty ships that are under contract now.

These are just some of the things that we have done to work together to cooperate with each other. I think it's incumbent on us as leaders of maritime services to continue to seek out as many ways as we can to work toward a common bond.

Regardless of your country, regardless of your continent, regardless of geography, there is a common bond that exists between sailors. Because, in many ways, we are one culture. We share a tradition more than two millennia in the making. Much of that tradition is largely unchanged, because these traditions are born out of the heritage of the sea. Sailors' lives are still governed, to some large extent, by the structures and roles and rules that guided the lives of our brethren hundreds, if not thousands, of years ago.

Our history of shared experiences, a common seagoing culture, as well as our understanding of the global nature of our roles, our capabilities, go beyond just the boundaries of our individual countries. History has shown that the best response is almost always a response heard from many voices.

More cooperation, more engagement, results in more understanding, which is why I think this meeting, ISS, has been such an important event for the last four decades and will continue to play an incredibly important role in international maritime cooperation. There is no other place that gives the naval leadership of the world the opportunity to see each other, face to face, sailor to sailor, and talk about and address the concerns that we all share, the problems that we all face, the issues that we all have to deal with.

So I'm glad you're here. I encourage you to make the most of our time together. I know that you have. Our shared heritage of the sea provides us a common ground to meet our collective challenges. It is on this ground that we will succeed against those challenges.

So in the common language of sailors from time immemorial, I wish you fair winds and following seas. Thank you very much.

5

Maritime Domain Awareness Operational Game Results

Dean Robert C. "Barney" Rubel
Dean, Center for Naval Warfare Studies, U.S. Naval War College

Professor Thomas Culora:

Thank you. Well, now it's time for me to introduce to you the dean of the Naval War College's Center for Naval Warfare Studies, Professor Robert C. "Barney" Rubel. Dean Rubel is a retired Navy captain with thirty years of service. Commissioned through the Naval Reserve Officers Training Corps at the University of Illinois, he subsequently became a light attack naval aviator flying the A-7 Corsair and later the F-18 Hornet.

As you would expect, he had a number of operational tours, including command of Strike Fighter Squadron 131, and he also served as the inspector general at U.S. Southern Command. While he was on active duty, Dean Rubel's shore assignments were principally involved with professional military education, including as a graduate of the Spanish Naval War College in Madrid, and here, the U.S. Naval War College in Newport.

While here, he has completed three separate faculty tours, first as a Joint Military Operations instructor, then as chairman of the War Gaming Department, and ultimately now as the dean of the Center for Naval Warfare Studies.

In 2006 and 2007 he directed the Naval War College's research and gaming project that led to the current national maritime strategy that you're all familiar with, *A Cooperative Strategy for 21st Century Seapower*. For this, he received the Superior Civilian Service Award. This is an accomplishment—not the award but the accomplishment of writing the actual document. I know he is particularly proud of it and recognized by that award.

Many of you today may know Dean Rubel as a visiting lecturer at a number of international professional military education institutions, including the German Armed Forces Staff College, the Mexican Naval War College, the British Joint Services Staff College, and the Colombian Senior War College.

Professor Rubel has earned a master's degree from Salve Regina University, and at the Naval War College has published a number of articles on a variety of subjects, including security engagement strategy, joint operational art, advanced war gaming, and air warfare.

Dean Rubel is my boss. He is a highly intelligent and handsome man. Did I mention he's my boss? Seriously, it is truly a pleasure to welcome to the podium today Dean Rubel. Please join me in welcoming Dean Robert C. "Barney" Rubel.

Dean Robert Rubel:

Do I hire the right kind of people or what? First, I would like to thank Secretary Mabus for being my warm-up speaker. It was great.

At ISS XIX, recognizing the progress that had been made on Maritime Domain Awareness (MDA), Admiral Gary Roughead called for an MDA game to share ideas and initiatives that had been developed independently around the world.

Subsequently, we got to work to design and execute the game, and we held it here 18–23 July of 2010. The game had thirty-eight participants from twelve countries. The countries were Bahrain, Brazil, Colombia, India, Italy, Japan, Pakistan, Sweden, South Africa, Singapore, the United Kingdom, and, of course, the USA. So we had good representation from around the world. Now I'm here today as the final phase of that game, to report to you all what the results were.

Before I get into the game report proper, I think it's worthwhile to mention why we do international gaming. I know most of your nations do international gaming to one extent or another. This is why we do it: The Naval War College's missions here are to (1) prepare future leaders for our Navy, (2) help the CNO define the future Navy and improve fleet combat readiness, and (3) to strengthen international maritime security cooperation.

How We Conduct Games

- Establish a research question
- Conduct a literature review
- Determine what kind of player decisions will answer the research question
- Develop a Data Collection & Analysis Plan
- Design a game to produce the kind of player interactions needed
- Determine the right players
- Use specialized tools to perform rigorous post-game analysis and provide meaningful insights or information for sponsors

Gaming is a powerful research and education tool, one that I like to think that we're known for here. This covers in a skeleton fashion how we conduct games: We first work to develop a game purpose and objectives with the sponsor of the game, and then we go through this procedure of developing a research question, conducting a literature review to make sure we understand what is known and what is not known about the subject we're studying, etc.

You can see these [points]. I won't belabor them, but I will say that the game report, in full, is available online for all of you. You just go to the Naval War College website and to our War Gaming Department. There is a section on game reports. You will find everything here. Having done gaming for quite a number of years, we've derived some principles of international gaming. These are some of them. The important thing in a game is that it is based on open and honest communication among all the players. Players must be comfortable and committed so that they make the best decisions that they can during the game. That is critical to the success of any game.

Principles of International Gaming

- All navies/coast guards/agencies are equal in terms of legitimacy and stature

- All officers of equivalent rank are regarded as peers – all voices count

- Non-attribution in terms of individual officers

- Each navy plays its own national laws

So let me get to the MDA game proper. Maritime security is both a strategic imperative and a strategic mission for virtually all the navies represented in this room. Effective maritime security is dependent on the development of timely, useful, and relevant information, and on the appropriate sharing of that information.

Therefore, the purpose of this game was to enhance information sharing with international partners for a Maritime Domain Awareness in order to support this ISS. I should say also that the ISS itself is a strategic opportunity to develop and enhance confidence and trust in each other.

These objectives that you see are stated in a way that reflects what a game could be capable of producing. Any war game is always kind of a risk, an investment. Like investing in real estate, you never know quite what you're going to get out of it; but the establishment of clear objectives really goes a long way to upping the odds that the game will produce information that is useful to you. This diagram depicts the game as a whole. The game really consists of five parts. The first part is a social event. You can see on check-in we had a social event, an icebreaker, so that the players could get to meet each other, get to know each other so that we could begin to develop that comfort level and trust and confidence that leads to good decisions during the game.

2010 MDA Game
Purpose and Objectives

- Purpose: Enhance information sharing with international partners for Maritime Domain Awareness in order to support ISS XX

- Objectives:
  - ✓ Examine regional MDA related relationships and networks in order to identify key elements of success, commonalities, and best practices
  - ✓ Expose impediments to effective information sharing
  - ✓ Identify options for broad based international maritime information sharing

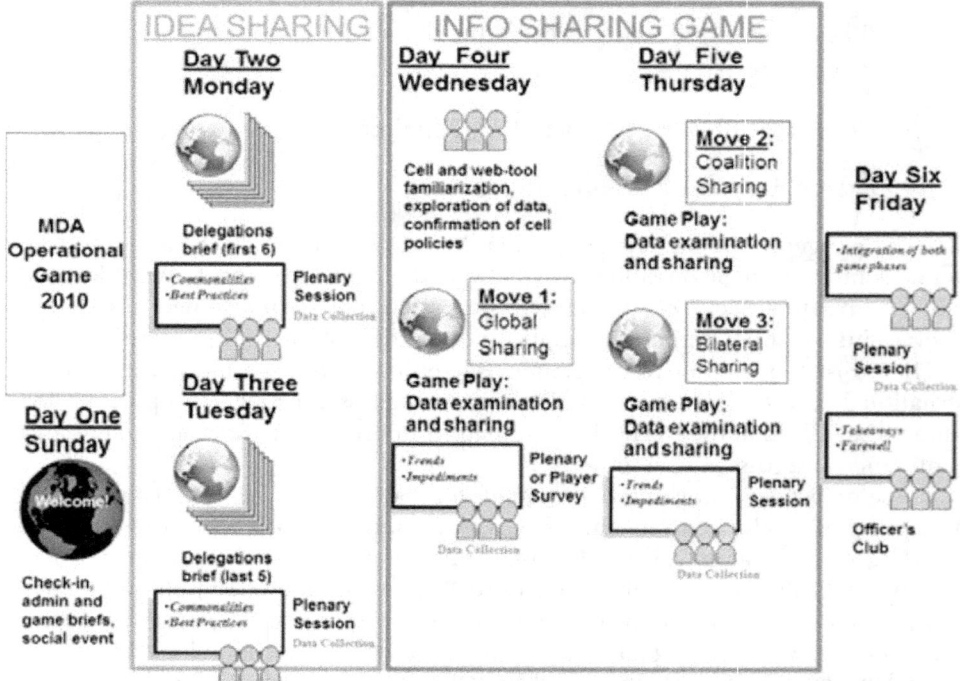

Then we held an idea-sharing workshop. Again, this came out of ISS XIX. It was so impressive to me anyway, the presentations that were made by the various navies up here. A lot of work had been done, a lot of leadership had been exerted throughout the world on this. So we wanted to bring people together to share these ideas.

Then we got into the game proper. Three moves, each featuring a different model of information sharing, which I'll explain a little later. The game was meant to explore the decision terrain of information sharing. Now there is an abstract concept for you, but that's what we deal with here at the Naval War College. I'll try to pull the string on that downstream. Then a plenary session for the players at the end to share their thoughts and experiences on the game proper. Then, finally, a report in two parts, the written report, which is sitting online and available to you, and the report I'm making to you right now. So let's talk about what we learned in the idea-sharing phase. I hasten to add, what you're going to see in the next few slides are the words of the players themselves. These are not my analysts talking, but the players in the game. In terms of the characteristics of successful MDA models out there, there seem to be four major architectures, let's say, that have been established. First, the multiple membership pools, where server and data storage are centralized in a single country. This is exemplified by Italy's V-RMTC [Virtual Regional Maritime Traffic Center] system.

Characteristics of Successful MDA Models

- **Characteristics:**
  - Established by formal Agreements
  - Voluntary in nature
  - Rules for sharing apply equally to all members
  - Limited to unclassified basic ship characteristic and location data
- **Examples:**
  - Multiple membership pools, server and data storage centralized in single country
    - Italy – VRMTC
  - Servers and data storage held in each country with secure internet connections
    - Sweden - SUCBAS
  - Liaison Officer, Interagency, Regional, & Cross Regional Fusion Center
    - Singapore – Changi C2 Centre
  - Linking Regional Nodes: TRMN
    - Italy led cross regional initiative (e.g., Brazil, Singapore, India, Italy & US)

Then you have a different approach where servers and data storage are held in each country, but they're connected with secure connections, like the SUCBAS [Sea Surveillance Cooperation Baltic Sea] system that is up in the Baltic. A third approach is represented by the Changi C2 Centre in Singapore, where you have liaison officers and a fusion center.

The fourth approach is T-RMN [Trans-Regional Maritime Network] that Italy has established. It's a system for jumping across regional systems, and T-RMN specifically links the V-RMTC in the Mediterranean with SISTRAM [Information System for Maritime Traffic], which is Brazil's system in the South Atlantic. These are the four approaches to information-sharing architectures that are out there. They all

Commonalities

- **Commonly understood and accepted term and definition:**
  - Maritime Domain Awareness: The effective understanding of anything associated with the maritime domain (on, below, or above the sea) that could impact security, safety, economy, or environment of a nation

- **Common Reasons for Sharing**
  - Receive information through reciprocal sharing
  - Improve capacity of sharing partners to take actions in their own interests that also support one's own national objectives

- **Technology Integration**
  - Will and desire to synchronize and integrate legacy systems
  - Develop international working group to study technology integration

seem to work in their various ways. A key factor in the success of international and maritime security efforts is that everyone seems to be operating on the basis of a common understanding of what MDA is. The definition is up there.

This is a very important starting point. I think we're very lucky that this seems to be shared by everybody. I believe another reason that navies share information and cooperate is reflected in what I heard two years ago from Admiral Guillermo Barrera from Colombia. He said that every nation that benefits from the seas has a responsibility to contribute to their security. It's another way of saying "think globally, act locally."

While maritime security is about relationships and information, technology is a powerful tool. It can be problematic, as much a hindrance as a help. We need to work together to keep it from becoming an obstacle to cooperation. The technology integration recommendation of the players, although not specific, [is to] develop an international working group to study it. It wasn't specific as to whether this group should be regional or global, but the sense was that a group should be established.

Let's talk about the game itself. I'll summarize the theory and mechanics of the game so that you can better judge for yourselves the validity of the results. Games are not experiments, although this one looks a little bit like one. I must stress that, although this was a competently designed and executed game, it did not have sufficient scientific rigor to be considered an experiment. It proved nothing, but it did illuminate the dynamics of the information sharing enough that we could discern the outlines of a comprehensive potential MDA architecture. I need to explain this diagram a bit. The blue box represents the theoretical set of MDA information a nation would need to secure its waters and contribute to regional and global maritime security. The white box, which is overlaid on the blue box, is a subset of that

Meeting National MDA Requirements through Information Sharing

What sharing structure maximizes the <u>volume</u> and <u>detail</u> of shared information?

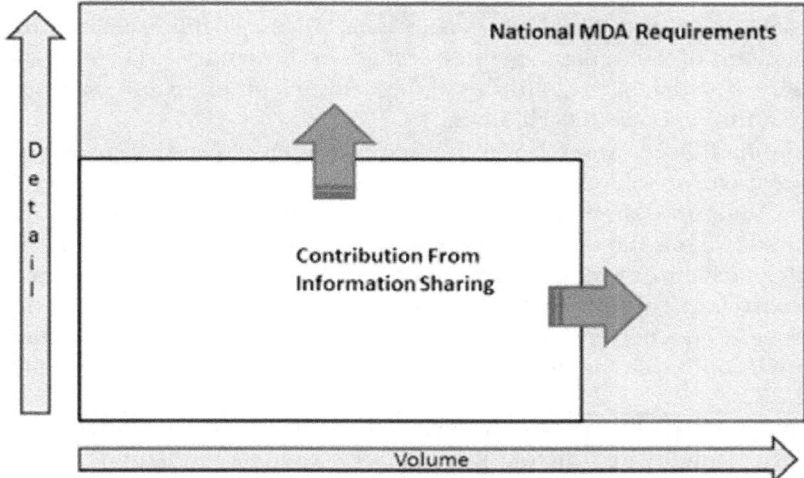

theoretical MDA information set that could be gained by other nations sharing information they have, which is relevant to your MDA information requirements.

What is not depicted here is the gap between the theoretical information requirements and what information is actually available from national sources and

Sharing Models

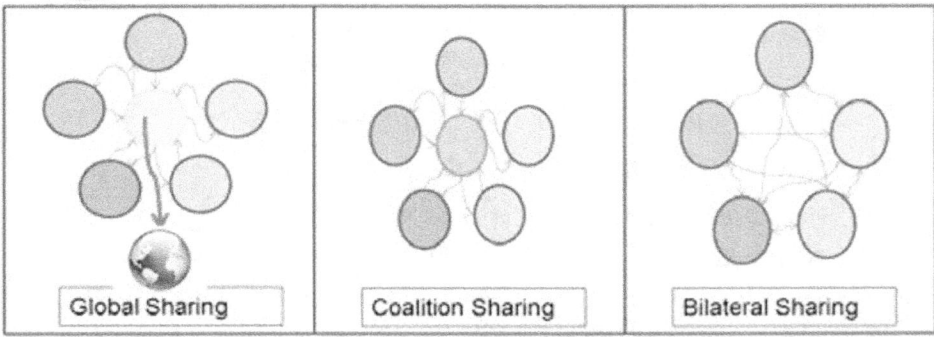

- Open membership
- Low barriers to entry
- Information shared is viewable by all members

- Restricted membership
- Formal agreement
- Legal basis
- Information shared is viewable by all members

- No formal agreements specified (Ad Hoc)
- Sharing occurs directly between two countries

capabilities. The blue arrows indicate that increased international sharing of information might help in filling that gap. Now, these are the three sharing models that we established for the purposes of the game based on what we observed in the real world [see figure, p. 65]. In the global and coalition models that you see, the center circle represents a kind of database. It's very much like V-RMTC in Italy, where there is a centralized database that everybody contributes to.

In the case of global sharing, the world gets to see it, whether they're part of a regional coalition or not. Everybody gets to see it. In the coalition-sharing model, only the members of the coalition get to see what's in the database. Then in bilateral sharing, there is no database. Countries simply call each other up and share specific amounts of information with each other.

The game had three moves. So in the first move the global-sharing model was the only one used. We told players that's the model, use it. Move two, we used coalition sharing, and move three, bilateral sharing. Now, the research question that we established was what is the optimal structure for international information sharing that provides each entity with the most volume and detail of maritime information. This is a research question. The word "optimal" in there does not indicate that we were hoping to find a perfect solution. It was used to provide a basis for evaluation using the philosophy that the more volume and detail of information that you have, the better.

This may not always be the case in the real world, but for game purposes it performs a useful, simplifying function. War games are always distillations of the real

Categorizing the Scenario Information

A research-derived analytical framing device

Tier 1	Tier 2	Tier 3	Tier 4
• Name • Flag • Type • Status • Dimensions • Draft • Last Port of Call • Next Port of Call • Position	• Master Nationality • Owner • Owner Nationality	• Vessel of Interest • Amplifying Information	• Crew Information • Cargo Information • Historical/Miscellaneous Information

world, and good game design dictates that we be both careful and explicit in how we distill down reality so that we can usefully game it. We divided the amount of

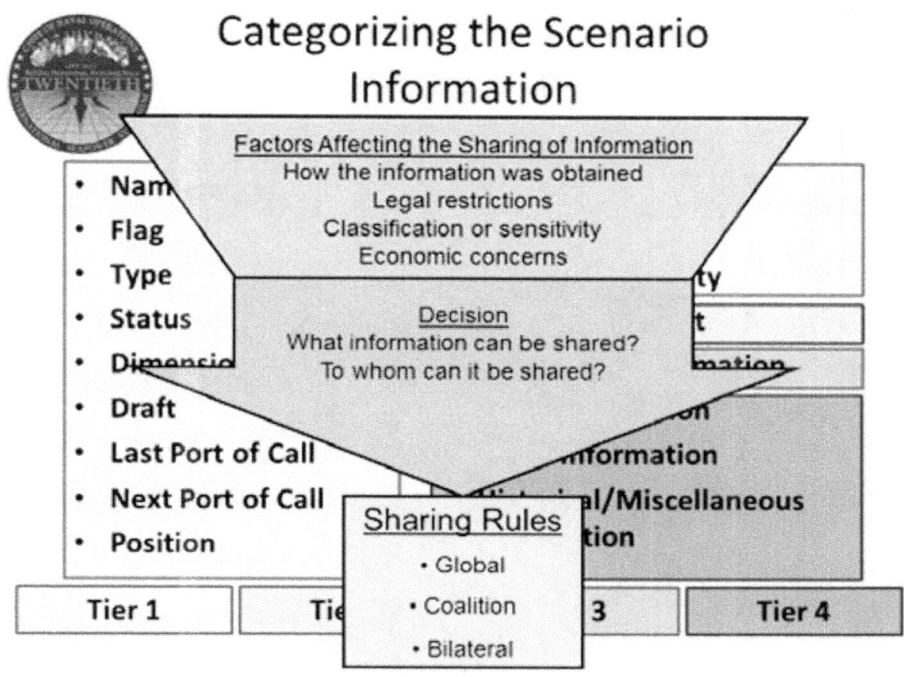

information that would be theoretically available to a particular ship about a particular ship into four tiers of information. These may or may not reflect the real world, but they approximate it. Tier one is the least sensitive and most widely available information. It's normally what is available from AIS or other public sources.

Tier two is more sensitive information that might have been generated by intelligence sources or law enforcement agencies, but it's simply whether a vessel is of interest to somebody or not. There is no detail with it.

Tier three, on the other hand, details why that vessel is of interest. It's clearly more sensitive information. Tier four, finally, consists of proprietary information, law enforcement information, and possibly additional intelligence. This is the most sensitive kind of information by definition for purposes of the game. Each move players had to decide, based on the conditions presented by the move scenario, the sharing model featured in the move, and the actual laws and policies of their countries, what tiers of information they would share with other players. So this sounds kind of experiment-like in nature, but again, it isn't.

McCarty Little Hall, where many of you were yesterday for your seminars, that is our gaming center. We have our own independent gaming network that we reconfigure for every game we do. Each country delegation in this game had one member in a composite trading cell, the blue one. This member communicated with his delegation either by phone or by computer to find out what information he could share in a particular scenario.

For each move we provided all cells with a set of tracks and certain information about those tracks, but the same information was not necessarily given to each cell. Some cells had more information on some tracks than others, etc.

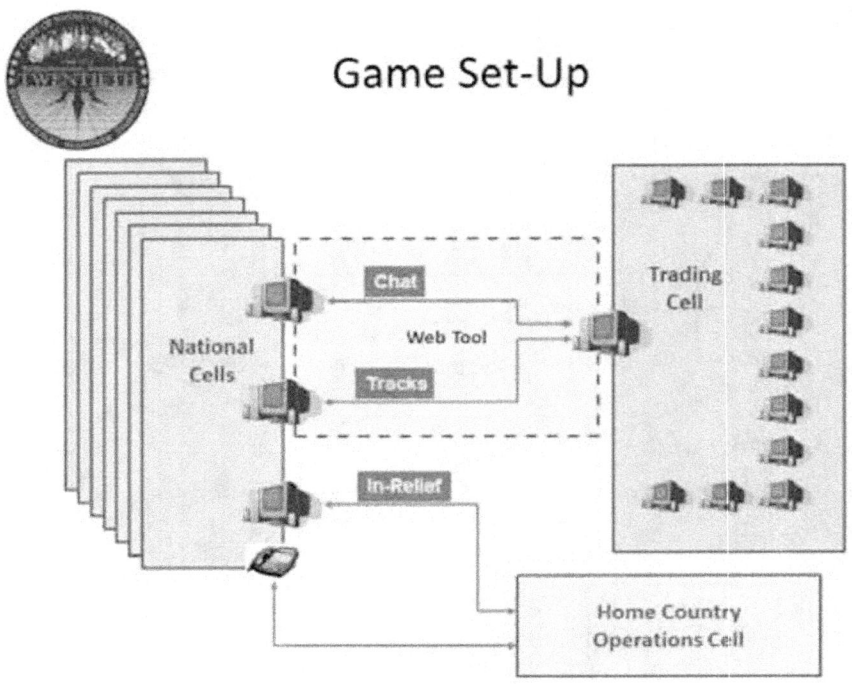

Game Set-Up

There were twelve cells representing twelve countries. Each cell got a somewhat different set of information; then the players had to decide how much of that information they would share.

The delegations, which were in separate rooms, decided on their own what information they would share, what policy of sharing they would impart to their trader, instructions to give them, or they could contact their home country. We used several methods to allow a delegation to call home if it was in doubt, so that we had the most accurate and realistic depiction of the country's policy on information sharing.

There were, in this game, no right or wrong answers. We just wanted to understand the conditions in which countries would either share or withhold information. So let me get right to the results of the game. The assumed legal top cover in the coalition model established a higher level of trust, because players were more confident in their governments' ability to provide the necessary support, but also more confident that they would receive a higher amount of volume and detail and that the information was accurate.

In the coalition model, we said it wasn't meant to represent any specific model out there, but we said, "Just assume you're part of this coalition, your countries have formal agreements on sharing of information and proceed on that basis." On the insights here, you see that trust and confidence are key factors. To a large extent on this basis, the game simply reinforced common sense. The recommendation is, again I want to emphasize, that of the players themselves. Each region has countries with different levels of capabilities. In each case countries that cannot effectively secure their waters and cannot connect into the regional system of Maritime Domain

Awareness represent a seam or a vulnerability in that region and maybe globally. This is why outreach and capacity building are so important.

Trust & Confidence

Observations
- Was commonly understood and accepted during the Coalition Model (maximum info sharing)
- The formal framework of the Coalition Model inspired a high level of trust and confidence

Insights
- Trust and willingness to share are the fundamental factors that enhance awareness and build partnerships.
- Respect and acceptance of individual nations' sovereignty, policies, and culture is vital to a successful information sharing initiative

Player Recommendations
- Regional partnership building initiatives help develop trust and confidence over time

Regional Partnership Building

Observations
- Some nations are unable to participate in MDA partnership due to inadequate technical or legal infrastructure
- Capacity building initiatives should focus on helping increase international civilian, military and law enforcement coordination and awareness

Insights
- Existing regional partnership initiatives focus on technical, manpower, training & economic support but cross-regional coordination not evident
- Regional initiatives enable partner nations to achieve domestic MDA requirements & help break down barriers.

Player Recommendations
- A multinational outreach and coordination group, headed by regional maritime leaders
- Focus on educating nations and integrating regional initiatives through the application of workshops, conferences and games.

Interagency Coordination and its Impact on Information Sharing

Observations
- Domestic interagency challenges must be resolved in order to achieve the full potential of global information sharing

Insights
- No one size fits all answer; every nation's process is different
- Each nation realized that their own interagency issues need revitalizing and improvement
- Navies play key role in MDA, but are only one piece of the puzzle
- Better understanding of interagency process is imperative in achieving the full potential of navies' capabilities

Player Recommendations
- An internal examination of individual interagency processes and procedures is needed in respective nations

The recommendation for a multinational outreach group, in the recommendations there, was not specific as to whether such a group would be global or would be a set of regional groups that would be established.

Within the U.S. military we have been preaching to ourselves the importance of interagency cooperation for years. Despite all this, I would say that our own success has been difficult to achieve. Where we have achieved it, it takes a lot of work. Everyone seems to understand the importance of interagency cooperation in the arena of MDA and maritime security. Achieving it just takes a lot of work and, at times, a willingness to change our ways of operating.

I remember when Admiral McFadden from Canada was up here at the last ISS briefing interagency, and he had up on the slide here a very complex depiction of Canada's interagency process. Everybody—we were all sitting in the audience just going, "Oh, my God."

He stops, and he says, "Listen, just because it briefs ugly doesn't mean it won't work." I think that tells you something about the difficulties and the flexibility of mind we have to have as we try to establish effective working relationships with other agencies, including law enforcement and nongovernmental organizations. It was clear from the game that a common set of international norms as simulated during the coalition-sharing model in the game would greatly facilitate information sharing. There seems to be enough in the way of existing agreements, laws, and policies to provide a good start at creating a uniform and rational set of norms. So the work of a policy group would be to determine how all of these existing provisions could be stitched together and into a framework that we could all use.

Fusion and analysis of information is the ability to make sense of information. Spotting patterns, anomalies, and connections is the payoff to this process. Such output generates cuing and tippers, which then allows individual navies and coast

International Legal Framework

Observations
- Legal and policy were the major impediments to info sharing
- Endorsement of international norms was strongly desired by the players across all three models
- Assumed legal framework in Coalition Model supported this desire

Insights
- Leverage existing navy-navy agreements (TRMN/VRMTC, SUCBAS etc) and/or establish new agreements
- Establishment of an international legal framework and/or body which establishes and governs international data standards and protocols. (i.e. ICAO)
- Leverage existing international law (e.g. UNCLOS, SUA, etc.) in order to create agreements and Memoranda of Understanding
- The Regional Co-Operation Agreement on Combating Piracy and Armed Robbery against Ships in Asia (Singapore led initiative) was discussed as an ideal model

Player Recommendations
- An international Legal and Policy Working Group dedicated to examining these issues would be valuable.

guards to respond effectively. This is both technology and manpower intensive, so efforts to make national technologies compatible and to conduct more intensive training, each would have big payoffs. It was not made clear who should conduct the technology feasibility study, perhaps the International Maritime Organization

Fusion & Analysis

Observations
- A critical element to sharing information cross-regionally
- "Information is only valuable if you can make sense of it"

Insights
- Existing domestic technology is in early development stages and many may not be compatible if regional systems were integrated
- Many ongoing research and demonstration programs address these limitations

Player Recommendations
- Technology Feasibility Study
- Leverage existing commercial off-the-shelf fusion and analysis tools and software
- Further coordination and integration among trans-regional partners is needed

Unity of Purpose
The Power of Commitment

- Statement of principles in support of maritime information sharing

- Create a favorable environment for sharing
  - Increased trust and confidence
  - Increased development of legal support (i.e. domestic legislation, international agreements)

- Provide framework helping working groups to solve legal, policy, technical and capacity issues

(IMO), but this will require further discussion. I know in my seminar yesterday afternoon it was not—there was some doubt whether IMO was the appropriate place.

So what does this all add up to? While we designed the game to examine the relative merits of three distinct information-sharing models, actual game play revealed the outlines of a potential comprehensive structure for information sharing among countries within regions and across regions. I need to say that this section, although based on game results and player inputs, is the opinion of my analysts. In other words, we're shifting now from a direct report of what the players in the game did and said, to our interpretation of what it means; so, take it on that basis. The consensus among players was that if an international statement of MDA and/or maritime security principles could be crafted that most or all nations could agree to, it would significantly assist the advancement of mutual trust and confidence and facilitate

Global Sharing
The Power of Numbers

- Information sharing following the global model
  - Tier 1 level information
  - Widest possible membership (governmental, agency, commercial, NGO etc) with low barriers to entry

- Provides a limited legal basis with additional opportunity to endorse sharing
  - Could be an expansion of existing navy-navy agreements (TRMN/VRMTC, SUCBAS etc)

Formal Sharing
The Power of Law

- Follows the game's coalition model
- Information sharing at all tiers with high volume within a group
- Formal codified sharing arrangements provide legal basis to support wide spread sharing
  - Can take the form of treaty, MOU, MOA, etc
  - Could be nation-nation, navy-navy, or agency-agency
- Can consist of functional or regional agreements
  - May have duplicate formal agreements with identical membership to support different agencies (i.e. customs, immigration, military etc.)

the solving of a range of challenges. Global sharing may be based on a federation of existing networks, or it may be an entirely new one. Effectiveness will be a function of having the largest possible membership, based on the premise that the massive volume of information received and disseminated globally has more value than the small amount of information that finds its way to bad actors. Again, in the game this was with the global system, and it would be nonsensitive information, stuff that everybody felt comfortable with everybody knowing.

The game demonstrated that formal agreements between countries produce institutionalized trust and confidence and, therefore, generate high volume and detail of information sharing at all tiers of sensitivity. Because players recognized the benefits of sharing came not only from the receipt of information provided by a partner but also from the improved readiness of all partners, which is achieved through the widespread dissemination of information, it was determined that the size of the coalition group must be as large as possible in order to keep the volume sharing high, or high enough, to be effective.

This benefit can only be realized through the higher volumes achieved when partners that share bilaterally come together as a group to ensure that the available information spreads completely to all partners. For various reasons, there will always be gaps in the ability of nations to share with others via multilateral agreements. These gaps occur where no sharing exists, or the sensitivity of information exceeds the limits of the existing agreements.

Ad hoc sharing is a structural element that could be, at least, partially used to overcome these gaps. I would say that this kind of sharing would be more effective if there were an existing comfort level between the two nations before the need for sharing arose. This comfort level is generated by meetings like this, by international exercises, workshops, etc. This is where the brief gets ugly. The picture that emerges

Ad Hoc Sharing
The Power of a Phone Call

- Follows the game's Bilateral Model

- Sharing arrangements established based on perceived needs and interests (push or pull)

- Used where:
  - No formal agreement exists
  - Sensitivity exceeds that permitted for a given formal agreement

is of a composite architecture which is founded on a baseline global picture of basic tier-one information. However, the key and the pivot point for the whole architecture are really the regional agreements enhanced, where possible, by cross regional interactions. This structure is then supplemented by ad hoc sharing on a bilateral basis when and where necessary.

Comprehensive Information Sharing Structure

What sharing structure maximizes the <u>volume</u> and <u>detail</u> of shared information?

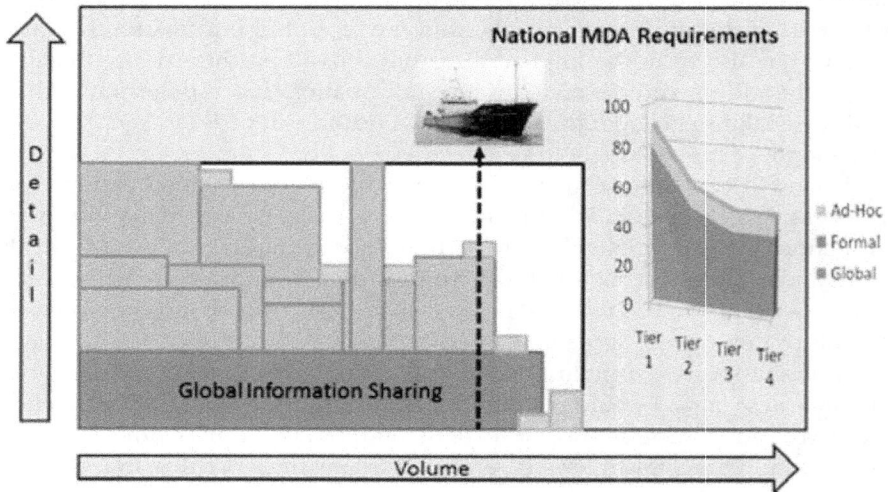

In this slide the blue is the global database, and the red is the information that is shared via formal agreements, and then the green are the individual phone calls, the bilateral information sharing, and the white here indicates that, well, maybe there will be some gaps.

This graph is based directly on the numbers that came from the game. There were thousands of decisions within the game on whether to share or not share. This graph depicts that.

In this area on the right, the percentage, up this side, versus the tier or the sensitivity of information—you can see that there was a lot of information shared. The tier-one information was shared essentially globally, supplemented by the formal sharing agreements and bilateral phone calls.

It's important to note that both tier-two through tier-four information was substantially shared via the coalition, information-sharing, formal agreements, and then bilateral interactions supplemented everything else. I should point out that the provisions on this slide are ideas, not recommendations. However, they do reflect the outlook of the players from the twelve countries participating in the game. We here at the Naval War College have a privileged vantage point in that we can see almost everything naval that is going on around the world, and we keep contact with our alumni and our colleagues not only at the war colleges but out at the operational fleets, too.

In my view, although there is a lot of bad news in the world, there is certainly one massive piece of good news that tends to go unreported. That's the level of international naval cooperation that goes on day after day. If you think about it, there has been nothing like this in history. There has been nothing like this ISS in history. This represents a piece of good news and a basis for hope, really, for the world.

Next Steps

- **Efforts to facilitate greater international information sharing**
  - Develop and endorse a set of international information sharing principles.
  - Establish international working groups (e.g. Legal, Technical, etc)
- **Move forward with a Global information sharing structure for tier 1 information**
  - Expand or federate existing networks
- **Create Formal sharing groups**
  - Coalesce formal bilaterals into groups
- **Continue with Ad-Hoc information sharing**
  - To build relationships
  - To fill gaps between formal arrangements

In closing, I would like to point out that a game such as this is quite feasible to conduct by most countries. We learned a lot from this game, but there is still a lot to learn. I think that the more games like this that we as the global family of navies conduct in more places the better it will be for us all. I thank you very much for your attention. I hope this provided useful information to you and, again, it's online, and if you need help in finding it, we can certainly do that. I'm standing by for any questions you might have.

6

Panel Discussion Two
Beyond MDA:
Building Responsive Partnerships

Moderated by
Vice Admiral Johannes Refiloe Mudimu, South Africa

Panel Members:
Admiral Bruno Branciforte, Italy
Admiral Julio Soares de Moura Neto, Brazil
Vice Admiral Laksdya Marsetio, Indonesia
Vice Admiral Paul Maddison, Canada

Vice Admiral Johannes Refiloe Mudimu, South Africa:

First, members, allow me to extend our appreciation to Rear Admiral John Christenson, President of the Naval War College, and to thank Admiral Jonathan Greenert, U.S. Chief of Naval Operations, for inviting us to participate in this historic twentieth symposium of naval and coast guard chiefs.

It is always, members, very enriching and fulfilling to meet so many leaders who share the same vision in addressing the common challenges we all face. Our duty, of course, is always to grapple with finding appropriate answers to these myriad problems and we provide the security of our people and ensure respect of our territorial integrity and sovereignty, in each of our countries.

This morning's members on the panel will navigate with you the topic "Beyond Maritime Domain Awareness: Building Responsive Partnerships." To help unravel this subject, I have Admiral Bruno Branciforte, Chief of Italian Navy; Chief Admiral Julio de Moura Neto, Commander of the Brazilian Navy; Vice Admiral Marsetio, Vice Chief of Staff, Indonesian Navy; and Vice Admiral Paul Maddison, Chief of Staff of the Canadian Navy.

Allow me, distinguished chiefs of navies and coast guards, to briefly touch on the matter of "Maritime Domain Awareness: Building Responsive Partnerships." To us, maritime domain awareness (MDA) means the ability of a nation to be aware of the situation on the sea, at the sea, and around the sea, where the issues of maritime crime are orchestrated, and on the land and around the sea, where the criminals and perpetrators of these crimes go back to land to enjoy the proceeds of their crimes.

In the few minutes allotted to me, allow me to say today an interdependent global economy depends on secure and unimpeded flow of maritime traffic through the most economic sea lanes, straits, ports, and transit corridors at competitive cost levels. At the same time, through the implementing of provisions of the Convention on Law of the Sea, the security and welfare of all nations are linked to a regime of law and order at sea that suppresses illicit activities, such as drug and weapon smuggling and human trafficking, and combats the threat of piracy and maritime crime.

To achieve economic free flow of maritime trade, maritime nations need to organize, operate, and seek to develop relationships with other governments in pursuit of this noble goal of harmonious seas for all of us to better the economic development of our countries.

To achieve the aim of maritime security, regional economic communities of the world need to be involved in high-level cooperation in order to achieve effective awareness of their respective maritime domains, coupled with the long-term funding of the regional development and sustainment of maritime and air enforcement capabilities.

The unifying concept of maritime security partnerships is information sharing to achieve maritime domain awareness. Comprehensive MDA on a regional basis will permit identification of threatening and illegal maritime activities. Achieving regional MDA must be viewed as a critical step in building regional partnerships.

Examples of effective information sharing for MDA using the IMO-sanctioned Automatic Identification System—a long-range identification and tracking/reporting system for commercial ships—are the Malacca Straits Security Initiative, partnering in Singapore, Indonesia, and Malaysia, and the Gulf of Guinea Network.

It will take a major effort to coordinate all of the existing capabilities, extend them, and to disseminate information on a timely basis to those maritime law enforcement authorities that can take necessary and appropriate action. This requires the need to ensure that the demands of maritime security form part of a respective government's economic growth priorities to secure long-term adequate funding for the development of maritime air and sensor capabilities.

The linkage between economic growth, maritime trade, and maritime security must be pursued with utmost vigor through the following activities:

- Expand regional bilateral relations and agreements. In many cases the base on which to build will be military-to-military, navy-to-navy relationships that can be expanded to include those departments of government that are important to the security task.
- This tradition of common maritime training of regional partners' personnel to maritime security to build a relationship and trust that eventually results in the establishment of maritime security partnerships within each regional economic community. Developing the capabilities of regional maritime security forces will allow them to move their countries towards participation in regional maritime exercises, deployments, and operations.
- The establishment of local, regional shipbuilding. Spare parts and maintenance industries and technical training centers are critical to this activity. Secure, continued long-term funding for maritime capabilities is another key ingredient for the sustaining of maritime security partnerships. The law enforcement authorities and legal skill that will be needed to carry out anti-piracy and anti–maritime crime enforcement must be established onboard naval vessels.
- The establishment of regional maritime contingent commanders with the robust, legal component will facilitate the enhancement of regional legal maritime capacity.

- Utilize cost-effective solutions for improved ocean surveillance, by exploiting data from a growing inventory of commercial, remote imaging sensors and satellites, maritime-directed over-the-horizon radars, and coastal radar surveillance on the territorial waters of regional partners.

This strengthening of the organization of the respective regional economic community maritime secretariats is needed to implement the responsibilities of the region's maritime security policy and to better implement maritime security partnerships at both national and regional levels.

Effective maritime enforcement must take into account that both legal and illegal waterborne traffic crosses national, regional, and continental boundaries. As a result, coastal partners within the region must take coordinated action against maritime crime and pirate activities, while respecting the sovereignty of the nation under which we operate. That will build, that will fortify, that will strengthen nations' relations.

In arranging a system of partnerships for surveillance, information sharing, and law enforcement are essentially regional enablers to solve, to ensure, coordinated action and prosecution within the respective maritime domains. These are

- Location of threats. Maritime threats are everywhere. They may come from the local ports and country waters or from anywhere around the world. This consideration takes into account that the greater part of the world's maritime trade moves all over the world. Even fishing vessels may operate well beyond a country's territorial waters.
- Extent of regulation. International law was developed to govern the maritime domain, but the means of enforcement are often limited. The maritime space is vast, and the surveillance is poor, except in close approaches to major ports. One way to reduce the space in which travel occurs is to fill the gaps in regulations through international efforts, especially through the International Maritime Organization.
- Capabilities of individual countries. This enabler varies from highly capable governments with excellent maritime capabilities to those governments with poor or nonexistent maritime capabilities. While civilians and information-sharing capabilities can be made available worldwide, it is the countries themselves that are responsible for moving about on the surface of the sea to carry out enforcement. One objective of maritime security is to increase the capability and coordination of these enforcers through ocean patrol vessels in sufficient numbers and to achieve greater coverage in the maritime high seas.
- Depth of information. This ranges from the maximum MDA, which would entail knowing the location of every vessel in the regional waters, down to the specific cases of stopping ships and boarding them for inspections as the circumstances admit. There is a substantial element of deterrence to be realized from having a total system in place, as seen in the Strait of Malacca and the Strait of Singapore. Where patrols have increased, there has been a reduction in incidents of piracy.
- Severity of maritime threats. A maritime threat that is carried out could have regional and/or national consequences as well as international consequences. Warlords may seize a merchant ship and load a chemical weapon, or they might poach the local fisheries, depriving the people of their livelihoods.

Hence, our definition of "maritime domain awareness" is the ability to know what is happening on the sea, under the sea, and surrounding the sea. Maritime enforcement establishes facilities for surveillance and information to serve both regional and national purposes, including the recognition that maritime threats can move from one part of maritime domain to the other.

Members, I thank you. Those are my opening remarks on this topic.

Now kindly allow me to call on my erudite speakers who deal with this topic. First among these will be Admiral Bruno Branciforte, Chief of Staff of the Italian Navy.

Just a few notes about this admiral. Admiral Bruno Branciforte was born in Naples on the sixth of November, 1947. From 1965 to 1969 he attended the Naval Academy of Livorno, graduating in Maritime and Naval Sciences.

From 1969 to 1976 he was assigned to different ITN ships—the corvettes *Grosso* and *Todaro*, the destroyer *Impavido*, and the cruiser *Caio Duilio*—as navigator and assistant operations/communications officer, as well as being the flag assistant to the commanding admiral of the Second Naval Division. During these years he specialized in advanced communications and attended Naval Command School. From 1976 to 1977 he was appointed commanding officer of the corvette *Aquila*. From 1977 to 1978 he served as a flag assistant to the commander in chief of the Italian fleet, also attending the Naval War College.

In 1979 he was assigned to the Intelligence Department of the Italian Navy General Staff as a director of the Intelligence Operational Center until 1985 and subsequently as chief of the Information Collection Branch. In 1985, with a rank of commander, he served as an executive officer of the cruiser *Vittorio Veneto* and then as commanding officer of the frigate *Aliseo*.

In 1987 he joined the Navy General Staff as chief of information collection in the Intelligence Department. From 1989 to 1992 he served in Washington, D.C., as the naval attaché to the Italian Embassy. Upon his return to Italy, he commanded the aircraft carrier *Giuseppe Garibaldi* from September 1992 to September 1993.

He then attended the Center for Advanced Defense Studies. Upon graduation, he returned to command of the carrier *Giuseppe Garibaldi*, deployed to the United States to take on board the first AV-8B II Plus aircraft of the Italian naval aviation. Promoted to rear admiral (lower half) in 1995, he was then appointed to the Italian Navy General Staff as chief of the Intelligence Department, from 1995 to 1998, double-hatted as chief of the Plans, Policy, and Operations Department, from '96 to '98. After the General Staff restructuring, from '98 to 2000, he became head of the new General Planning Department. In this role he took control of initial planning of naval procurement, masterminded naval participation in several international operations, and promoted the fleet's operational restructuring and modernization of the landing force.

In 2000 he returned to sea and took his command of the Italian Navy surface fleet until 2001. From December 2001 to February 2002, during Operation ENDURING FREEDOM, he was Italian senior naval representative at Central Command in Tampa. From 2001 to 2004 he served as chief of staff to the commander in chief of the Italian fleet. Promoted vice admiral in 2004, he held the position of commander in chief of Italian fleet from October 2004 to 12 December 2006. On 16 December 2006 he was appointed as director of external security for the National Intelligence Agency for leading its most recent restructuring.

Since 23 February 2010 Admiral Branciforte is Chief of the Italian Navy. Give him a round of applause.

Admiral Bruno Branciforte, Italy:

Admiral Greenert, Admiral Christenson, dear colleagues, ladies and gentlemen, it's my first time at the International Seapower Symposium in Newport as Chief of the Italian Navy, but as a naval attaché in Washington I was here in 1991 when Admiral Trost was CNO of the U.S. Navy and said that the main target of the symposium was the reciprocal knowledge of participants. The same spirit was in the words of Admiral Greenert, during yesterday's session and during the Naval War College reception. I fully agree on this, because if you have to cooperate with somebody, it helps to know who is on the other end of the telephone line.

Now, first of all, let me tell you that I am very delighted to have the opportunity to elaborate on the MDA initiatives and more specifically on the number of efforts under way, and their achievements, as well as their challenges. Indeed, it is my firm belief that maritime surveillance is a key enabler of maritime security and one of the Navy's fundamental challenges in the years to come. Poor knowledge of the maritime domain renders mostly ineffective the possibility to disrupt our local acts at sea. Italy has always been deeply aware of that. Indeed, it is Italy's geographic position that accounts for this belief. Italy sticks out into the Mediterranean Basin, whose sustainable exploitation is essential both for the country's and the entire region's prosperity. This is the reason why in 2004 the Italian Navy launched a pilot project designed to enhance information sharing among regional navies. The initiative has been dubbed the Virtual Regional Maritime Traffic Center, and so far has been adopted by as many as thirteen navies in various positions of the world. I will focus on this initiative and its latest developments later in my speech. As regards maritime surveillance, the good news is that an increasing number of stakeholders in critical maritime regions have recently become aware that it is a matter of utmost importance. As a consequence, especially in Europe, a large number of maritime security initiatives have been designed. Some of them are already under way, while others need to be properly tested. Against this background the European Union has played a key role by emphasizing the need for a robust and reliable MDA—however you say it, and whatever it is called in Europe—as a prerequisite for an enduring maritime security. It follows that a large number of EU maritime communities are potentially involved, as well as various EU member states, and have consented to make progress toward a higher degree of information sharing.

Along with many others developed at the supra regional level, worth mentioning are the most renowned networks being developed all around the world, the Maritime Safety and Security Information System (MSSIS), the European Commission's projects [inaudible], such as BLUEMASSMED and MARSUNO [Maritime Surveillance North], the European Defence Agency Maritime Surveillance Networking (MARSUR) Project, the European Maritime Safety Agency's [EMSA] Safe Net and CleanSeaNetSea, the Singapore Regional Maritime Information Exchange, the V-RMTC Americas, the Sea Surveillance Cooperation Baltic Sea (SUCBAS), as well as the rewarding outcomes of the the recent USJFCOM [U.S. Joint Forces Command]–sponsored multinational experiments and the NATO-led ACT [Allied Command Transformation] MSA concept development and phase.

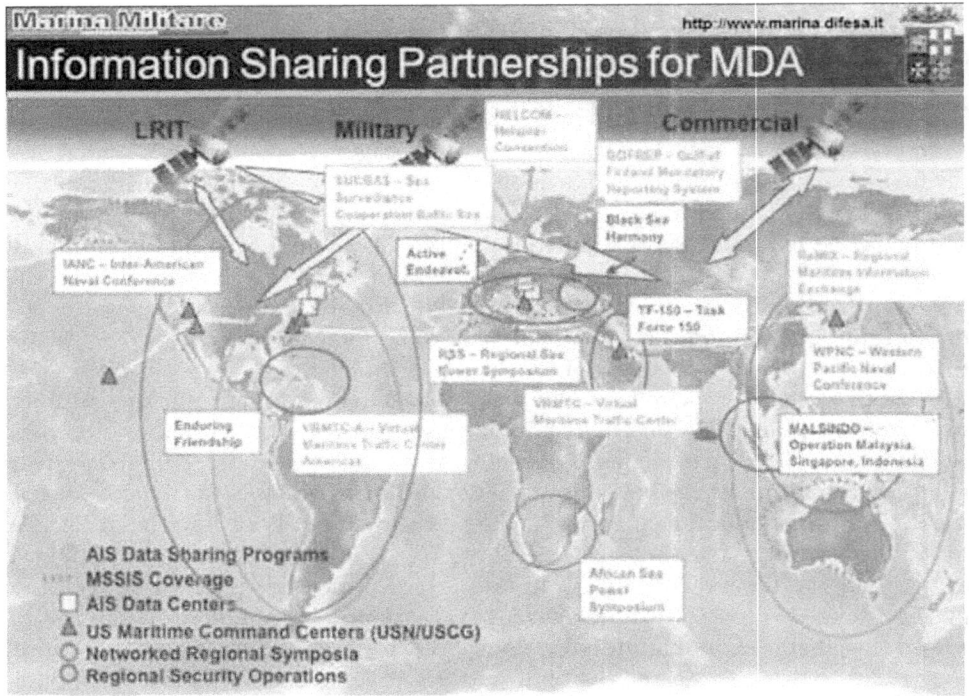

Additionally, mention is also to be made of the larger numbers of interagency initiatives at the national level. Incidentally, sometimes their implementation seems more challenging than those at international level. Needless to say, none of the foregoing networks and initiatives is a definite answer to both regional and global information-sharing challenges. Nevertheless, some of them have turned out to be successful in addressing them. In specific, some of them have succeeded in overcoming national barriers by laying the foundation of interagency cooperation. Others have fostered dialogue and collaboration among similar bodies operating in a given region. Despite the successful results, further efforts have to be made to involve a larger number of stakeholders in maritime domain awareness. Several surveys have been carried out to identify major challenges to a more comprehensive MDA. It is not my intention to argue for or against the points raised by very knowledgeable experts. Anyway, I cannot avoid making reference to the most sensitive. In order of importance, I think they are

- political issues, namely political willingness and mutual trust. They are the most frequently mentioned obstacles.
- legal issues resulting from contrasting privacy and data protection related to legislation and regulation.
- exchange of classified data, as it precludes above all interaction between civilian and military domains.
- different views about MSA, its importance, and its consequent implementation reflect peculiarities of each world region in the domain of maritime security.

Luckily, efforts have been made to progressively remove these barriers.

European Union institutions are making commendable efforts in achieving common information sharing. In my own view, such a common environment will pursue a twofold objective—first, to meet user communities' requirements, second, to allow the agreement of specific info-exchange standards.

The common information-sharing environment's advantages include the contribution provided to smoothing both legislative, as well as confidential matters, and simultaneously the promotion, whenever necessary, of specific information-sharing policies. Let me share with you some facts on how we have progressed in the Mediterranean. As most of you are well aware, in the last seven years the Italian Navy has gained remarkable experience in the MSA domain through the development of V-RMTC, a network initially launched to share information of regional maritime traffic by connecting navies' operational centers through an Internet portal. The system, as it turned out, was susceptible to further developments with the passing of time. With V-RMTC, the Italian Navy developed a system and scientists reported interaction at the task regional level. In its initial stage, the project saw the participation of sixteen navies, totaling an average of two thousand contacts on a quarterly basis. Seven years later the figures increased considerably. As many as thirty navies shared data, totaling more than a million contacts.

The latest V-RMTC development plan is the Trans-Regional Maritime Network (T-RMN), the idea for which was launched here in Newport in the course of the 2007 ISS. On that occasion, why did we acknowledge the need to adopt a new approach in the field of global maritime information sharing? In ISS 2007, the Italian Navy offered V-RMTC as a starting point to experiment on this approach. The extremely positive outcomes from the testing phase led to the development of T-RMN.

Through this newly designed network, the V-RMTC server was linked to similar and compatible systems in other countries—Brazil's system, Singapore's OASIS [inaudible], and probably, we hope, in the future, others. These sound and concrete results have been possible because of the effort of each participating navy; but [success] comes also from the philosophy of the system it serves. That may inspire a possible solution to create a global MDA. The key factors of the model's success come mainly from its peculiar features and the adopted tools approach. Regardless of the current technology I would like to highlight the following: confidence, clarity, and mutual trust among all member navies; simple infrastructure with no extra cost and extremely user-friendly interface; a flexible architecture facilitating compatibility among extraregional systems; the possibility to join the community through a trial period in order to evaluate pros and cons; a shared governance based on steering and operational working groups where all navies have the same dignity, regardless of the amount of data provided to the community.

The advantage is for all participants to share instead of exchanging information. [It is] non-mandatory policy, leaving it to the navies the decision whether it is pertinent to share, or not, specific data. Therefore, it is not binding or not superseding the single nation's prerogatives. In my opinion, these features were essential to overcome constraints and concerns. Moreover, in line with the outcomes of the global maritime partnership game, I am convinced that the federative approach followed has proved to be the most fruitful, since it allows us to benefit from the unique regional peculiar knowledge.

Of course, V-RMTC success is strongly linked with the navies' attitudes to cooperate. While the broader MSA requires a larger number of partners beyond the navies, the V-RMTC experience brings some lessons learned that may provide useful ends for any future development of MDA at regional or at global levels. Let me share with you just this, the most relevant point.

- MDA must be endorsed first at the regional level by getting [inaudible] with an open-door policy shaped by the principles of mutual trust and transparency.
- The quantity of shared data is irrelevant, as even a single entry may turn out to be extremely valuable.
- Games and exercises involving partners may be vital to prove schemes' effectiveness and, thereby, overcome national sensitivities.
- Governance must be equally shared by empowering partners.
- And yes, an effective integration of regional MDA-related initiatives may be achieved by taking into account the different experiences gained and the points of view expressed in various world regions.

Thank you very much for your attention.

Vice Admiral Johannes Refiloe Mudimu, South Africa:

I wish to thank Admiral Bruno Branciforte for the brilliant presentation that he has made. We will now, members, proceed directly to our second speaker, Fleet Admiral Julio Soares de Moura Neto, Commander of the Brazilian Navy.

Admiral Moura Neto was born 20 March 1943, in Rio de Janeiro. He joined the Brazilian Navy in 1959, attending the Naval High School in Angra dos Reis, Rio de Janeiro State, graduated from the Brazilian Naval Academy in Rio de Janeiro in 1964.

His sea tours include commanding officer of monitor *Parnaíba* in 1981, and commanding officer of the destroyer *Mariz E. Barros* in 1987, and commander of Destroyer Squadron 1 in 1992. As flag rank, Admiral Moura Neto was assigned to command the First Fleet Division in 1998.

Admiral Maura Neto got his fourth star on 31 March 2003. As fleet admiral he was assigned to General Director, General Bureau in 2003, Chief of Naval Operations and General Director, General Bureau of Navigation in 2005, Chief of Navy General Staff in 2007, and as of 1 March 2007 he took the billet of Commander of the Brazilian Navy.

During his career he attended all the usual courses of a surface and naval officer; in particular, a one-year BS degree in communication at Admiral Wandenkolk Instruction Center and the command and staff officer course in maritime politics strategy at the Naval War College in Rio de Janeiro and the Superior Naval War Course in Portugal are to be mentioned.

Admiral Moura Neto is married to Sheila Royo Soares de Moura. They have three sons and three grandchildren.

Admiral Moura Neto has received several Brazilian and foreign awards and medals throughout his career; among these we can count the Defense Order of Merit, Naval Order of Merit, Military Order of Merit, [and the] Air Force Order of Merit as well as many others. He received Argentinian Navy Medal, Spanish Naval Order of Merit, Paraguayan National Naval Medal, Uruguayan Naval Merit Honor Medal, Italian Medalha "Decorazione d'Onore Interforze Dello Stato Magiore Della

Difesa," as well as many other decorations. He is a highly decorated officer, ladies and gentlemen.

Thanks very much. The floor is yours. Thanks, Admiral.

Admiral Julio Soares de Moura Neto, Brazil:

Thank you, Admiral Mudimu, for the floor, and thank you for the words. Admiral Greenert, Chief of Naval Operations, in name of whom I greet all my colleagues, chiefs of the navies and coast guards present today.

Admiral Greenert, thank you for the welcome, warm welcome to all of us at this symposium. Admiral Christenson, President of Naval College, congratulations for the outstanding organization of this important event. Dear delegates and officers of U.S. Navy and other navies, ladies and gentlemen. Well, good morning. It is a great pleasure to be here and to have the opportunity to say some words about regional maritime awareness and Brazilian responsiveness. I will follow this summary:

- Brazilian challenges,
- Regional maritime domain awareness, with the following topics:
  - Brazilian Maritime Traffic Information System,
  - Regional Maritime Traffic Center of the South Atlantic Maritime Area,
  - Data exchange between SISTRAM and U.S. Maritime Safety and Security Information System (MSSIS),
  - Regional data center of Long Range Identification and Tracking System (LRIT), and
  - Trans-Regional Maritime Network,
- Brazilian responsiveness,
- "Blue Amazon" Management System, and
- Final considerations.

BRAZILIAN CHALLENGES

Enforcing the law, norms, and regulations related to navigation safety and security of operations on open sea and inland waterways requires a great deal of work by the Brazilian Navy.

The Brazilian jurisdictional waters include about 3,600,000 square kilometers and 900,000 square kilometers related to our continental shelf beyond the EEZ, which encompass a total area of 4,500,000 square kilometers, roughly half of the dimension of Brazil's territory.

Due to dimensions of those waters and their rich and complex environments, an analogy with the universally known Amazon rain forest was created, calling this huge maritime area the "Blue Amazon" as a way to alert the Brazilian society on the importance and richness of the sea.

Brazil has 8,500 kilometers of coastline with more than forty ports, and 40,000 kilometers of waterways, including approximately 22,000 kilometers in the Amazon region alone. The Brazilian search and rescue (SAR) area is a maritime area of about 13,000,000 square kilometers. I guess these geographic facts speak for themselves, showing how important the sea and the waterways are for my country.

Related to regional maritime domain awareness, I'd like to mention its status from a Brazilian perspective.

As we can see, the Brazilian Maritime Traffic Information System, that we call SISTRAM, gathers available data from Brazilian and foreign military and civilian ships and aircrafts, AIS stations, LRIT, and various contributing systems related to maritime traffic. The system was developed and is maintained by the Brazilian Navy.

The development by the Brazilian Navy of the Regional Maritime Traffic Center of the South Atlantic Maritime Area, that we call CRT-AMAS, represents an important step in establishing a network for maritime traffic information exchange and encompasses some countries of the South Atlantic maritime area (in Portuguese we call it AMAS)—Argentina, Brazil, Paraguay, and Uruguay.

The system allows signatory countries to visualize in real time through the web an updated surface picture of the South Atlantic maritime area, allowing them to rapidly access events that may compromise safety at sea.

The AMAS coordinator, called CAMAS, is a two-year function shared by Argentina, Brazil, and Uruguay. The Regional Maritime Traffic Center System is installed on the AMAS coordinator network as well as the Local Command and Operational Coordinators (COLCO) of Argentina, Brazil, Paraguay, and Uruguay.

Now let's talk about the data exchange between Brazilian Navy's SISTRAM and the United States Maritime Safety and Security Information System. Highlighted, in the picture, is the exchange of AIS information between the two systems.

In the Brazilian case, the AIS information is collected from our naval ships, as well as land, island, and offshore stations run by the Brazilian Navy, and exchanged with the U.S. Navy through an AIS server connected to the MSSIS. It is believed that by the end of this year the data exchange between SISTRAM and MSSIS will be completed.

Another initiative that I would like to present to you is the Regional Data Center of the Long Range Identification and Tracking System, called RDC LRIT Brazil-Uruguay. The RDC LRIT is a joint initiative between Brazil and Uruguay to increase the regional MDA using LRIT system capabilities.

This year we are finishing the last phase of installation for the LRIT data user in the Peruvian Navy, contributing to foment the MDA of that country. Currently the RDC LRIT is fully operational and is ready to provide service to other countries. We hope that soon other navies will join our RDC LRIT.

Now I want to talk about the Trans-Regional Maritime Network initiative that Admiral Bruno Branciforte mentioned. In addition to regional agreements on maritime traffic control, the Brazilian Navy joined SISTRAM with the Virtual Regional Maritime Traffic Center, V-RMTC, operated by Italian Navy, contributing to provide a broader maritime information network known as Trans-Regional Maritime Network, T-RMN. The T-RMN also includes two other systems, the OASIS from Singapore and the MSIS from India. As is shown in the picture, recently, Brazil is experiencing the growth and spreading of its sea lines of communication across the areas covered by the Trans-Regional Maritime Network.

In terms of responsiveness, I'll discuss some thoughts that all together summarize the Brazilian approach. Under Brazilian law, that supports our legal basis, the constabulary responsibilities are shared among the Brazilian Navy and other Brazilian federal agencies. In parallel with our current capabilities—[which] include naval patrol and inspection, environment protection, as well as search and rescue operations—the Brazilian Navy, in its vision of the future, is seeking to improve the "Blue

Amazon" Management System (SisGAAz), that is, the framework to monitor, detect, and improve intelligence and law enforcement in Brazilian jurisdictional waters and in search and rescue areas in a multiagency environment.

As I told you, to apply the concept of regional maritime domain awareness and efficiently meet all the needs of maritime safety and security in this area of responsibility in the South Atlantic, the Brazilian Navy is developing the "Blue Amazon" Management System, a complex system integrating SISTRAM and all the previous systems presented, adding, among others, monitoring capabilities by radar satellite and long-range radars to coordinate the responsiveness in our jurisdictional waters and SAR area. The "Blue Amazon" Management System encompasses monitoring and command and control of the Brazilian jurisdictional waters and the Brazilian search and rescue area.

The reliability of information and the prompt reaction are direct results connected with the capability to collect, process, analyze, and disseminate data as well as to coordinate, control, and provide interoperability with the response forces, both on the national and international levels, if needed.

As we are coming to the end, I have some final considerations to share with you.

In recent years, especially due to increase of the maritime traffic and international commerce, a greater understanding of the importance of the ocean and its environmental and security issues was paved in the international community. On the other hand, we're also presented with so-called new threats: smuggling, drugs and weapons trafficking, piracy, terrorism, and illegal immigration.

It is a challenge for all nations to cope with these new threats—according to the legal system, both national and international to provide support, preventive and repressive actions, and when necessary, to face the unlawful acts at sea, and to enhance awareness of all that is associated with the maritime environment which can impact on the protection, security and economy of our countries.

MDA needs more than technical applications. It needs regional and transregional agreements which are able to level the differences in technologies and capacities of the nations. Now, to provide interoperability among states, there needs to be a building of common confidence and trust, in order to cope with the threats and challenges that know no boundaries and are posed to the global maritime traffic.

Finally, I reiterate that Brazil is willing to support the actions and decisions of regional and multilateral forums to increase regional maritime security and global cooperation. The international field is the best way of confronting and solving the major issues present on the oceans. Under the Brazilian perspective, the agreements tend to become stronger, fostering mutual trust and cooperation, but a greater effort should be made in order to bring more states to participate in sharing of maritime traffic information and to build responsive partnerships.

Thank you so much.

Vice Admiral Johannes Refiloe Mudimu, South Africa:

Thanks, Admiral Neto, for speaking on regional awareness and national responsiveness.

Now, members, our third presentation will come from Indonesia, Vice Admiral Marsetio, Vice Chief of Staff, Indonesian Navy.

Vice Admiral Marsetio is currently the Vice Chief of Naval Staff of the Indonesian Navy. He graduated from the Indonesian Naval Academy in 1981. He was recognized with the Akademik Medali as a top graduate in his class.

From 1981 to 2001 he served in a variety of flotillas, including Indonesian warships. He had command of patrol ships [inaudible]. From 1992 to 1995 he served ashore as staff officer. From 2001 to 2006 he served in many strategic appointments which led to many high-level postings.

He was promoted to commodore in 2006 and appointed as vice assistant to the chief of Naval Staff for planning and budgeting. In 2009 he was promoted to rear admiral and appointed the commander of the Military Sea Lift Command, followed by a posting as commander of Western Fleet Command.

In 2010 he was promoted to vice admiral and appointed the Vice Chief of Naval Staff. During his career Vice Admiral Marsetio completed many of his military courses and education required to reach the highest level of leadership in the Indonesian Armed Forces and has always been honored as the best graduate, for which he was awarded the first star medal.

He was also an inaugural student of the National Resilience Institute and was recognized as the top graduate for 2004 with an award of the Seroja Wibawa Nugraha Award. He has also attended many overseas courses, such as the Royal Dutch Navy NBCD School and Command Team Training course in Netherlands in 1986; Royal Navy College in UK, 1991, Naval Operations School in Italy, 2002, and Senior Executive course APCSS [Asia-Pacific Center for Security Studies], USA, in 2007. Vice Admiral Marsetio is always willing to share his knowledge and experiences with others as he is going to do today. Despite his many responsibilities, he finds time to teach in many institutions within the Navy, the Indonesian Armed Forces, and the civilian universities, such as the University of Indonesia, the Surabaya Institute of Technology, and Indonesian National Defense University.

He is also very keen in maintaining and updating his international network—hence MDA, Admiral, you are well suited for this topic—by attending many overseas courses and workshops, such as mine countermeasures [conferences] in Denmark, 1994; a weapons symposium in Phillipines in 1997; ACL Malaysia, 1998, in Korea; Maritime and Technology Seminar in the UK, 1999; mine counter-exercises in Singapore in 2000; and last ASTRAL UK in 2001; a strategic defense review meeting in 2002; a class ammunition seminar in Norway in 2008; and UN peacekeeping meeting in New York in 2009; a defense technology Asia seminar in Singapore in 2009, Langkawi Maritime Seminar in Malaysia in 2009; Naval Maritime Seminar in Sri Lanka in 2010; Defense Technology Conference in Singapore in 2011; and the fifth Navy Chiefs Meeting in Vietnam, 2011.

Currently Vice Admiral Marsetio is a doctoral candidate at the Gadja Mada University and is looking forward to completing his research in the very near future. Vice Admiral Marsetio is married to Penny Iliana, and blessed with two sons. His youngest son, who happens to follow his father's footsteps, recently graduated from the Indonesian Naval Academy, July 2011, and was also honored with an Akademik Medali as top graduate in his class. Vice Admiral Marsetio, the audience is yours. Thanks very much.

Vice Admiral Laksdya Marsetio, Indonesia:

Thank you, Admiral, for your introduction, I think it is complete and encyclopedic. Thank you very much.

Admiral Greenert, Admiral Christenson, chiefs of navy, ladies and gentlemen, I would like to first thank the United States Navy for the hospitality and for bringing together the chiefs of navies from all over the world for this meeting. I would also like to convey our congratulations to Admiral Greenert for his new assignment as United States Chief of Naval Operations. Admiral, we wish you all the best in the future. On this occasion I would like to present the Indonesian Navy perspective on regional interoperability in managing maritime issues.

I will start my presentation with a brief introduction describing how the Indonesian Navy views its maritime domain, followed by some maritime issues in the region, existing naval cooperation's operation in regard to regional interoperability, future efforts, and then conclude the presentation with hope that there will be an exchange of ideas, views, and opinion and that may enrich our viewpoints as we discuss the way ahead. Chiefs of navies and delegates, in a researched look at the ASEAN [Association of Southeast Asian Nations] region, geographically waters cover most of the region with many sea lines of communication and sea lanes of trade passing through the waters carrying more than half of the world's export commodities.

Such conditions make the region a point of interest for many countries. The international community's views of the Asian waters is one of the Asian nations' strategic interests, since Asian nations are getting more dependent on the seas which have been a fan to the economy in the ASEAN region. Such condition means Indonesia has to control and manage many entry points and sea routes. They not only bring benefit but can be utilized to increase the economy of the littoral states in the region.

They also bring challenges to the region and become issues related to maritime security. Some of these continue to be concern for the regional states, such as maritime environmental issues, as damage to tropical reefs, major oil spills, or exploitation of fisheries, and also transnational maritime crime.

This latter issue, which includes economically motivated activity such as at-sea robbery, illegal fishing, illegal logging, smuggling, trafficking in persons, and illegal immigration, has a synergistic effect which exacerbates interstate conflict and nonstate political violence. For instance, the smuggling of people, weapons, and other contraband may provide terrorists or other insurgents the means to move weapons and personnel, raise funds, and recruit new members.

Aside from that issue, our state is well aware that there remain some territorial disputes between states as well as the imminent threat of terrorism and insurgency. Despite some differences of understanding on the definition of terrorism, it has been suggested what may appear as another act of piracy may, in fact, be a training ground for a future terrorist mission.

Since it is globally agreed that our trusted neighbors could independently manage or overcome their maritime issue with all available resources, Indonesia is in need for a system to increase and enhance the capability in order to manage or overcome the challenges that we have to face. Such situations have developed the idea to conduct operations with respective neighboring states. With a vast area of

Major Challenges

- Political issues
- Legal issues
- Classification of exchanged data
- Different views about MSA

water, the Indonesian Navy is committed to strengthening this effort in order to tackle the various maritime issues that we face today. A number of naval cooperations conducted are focusing on maritime security and since territorial stability has long become the region's core of interest. More so in the present, we fight around maritime border issues. This is a principle that implies countries conduct a battle within their respective territorial waters while utilizing information sharing with neighboring countries for coordination.

As one might expect in the region, the Indonesian Navy has been conducting several activities, such as coordination patrol or naval exercises with our neighboring navies, namely, INDINDO COORDINATED PATROL with India, INDOTHAI with Thailand, MALINDO with Malaysia, INDOSIN with Singapore, PHILINDO with the Philippines, and exercises HELANG LAUT with Brunei, and AUSINDO and CASSDEX with Australia.

In the future we are also planning to conduct activites with China and Vietnam. Furthermore, we also deploy our antipiracy group in the Gulf of Aden and also work closely with several navies in that area of operation.

The thing is, navy leaders and delegates, as we look deeper into naval cooperation in the region, we can find that there are also several bilateral naval exercise programs conducted between states such as Malaysia and Cambodia, Vietnam and Thailand, and Malaysia and Phillipines, and naval programs within the multilateral framework, such as the Western Pacific Naval Symposium or the Indian Ocean Naval Symposium. Aside from interregional cooperation, extraregional powers often participate in offering support, including the United States, Japan, China, Russia, India, and South Korea. This form of support and assistance principally offers an interoperability and [inaudible] of coastal states in manufacturing maritime security in the region.

This will in turn reciprocally guarantee the smooth flow of traffic, economy, and financial maritime trade. However, numerous observers have a good assistance operation and Southeast Asia has barely touched the surface of these issues, and most cooperation has never addressed the core and source of the problem, seeing the focus more on confidence building and preferring diplomacy rather than conflict resolution. Nevertheless, taken together, these developments constitute significant progress. Their allowance for information sharing has been enhanced. States seem firmly committed to these activities. This could be seen during the International Maritime Security Conference 2011 held last May in Singapore as part of IMDEX Asia [International Maritime Defense Exhibition & Conference]. In this forum the Indonesian Navy highlighted the importance of engaging civilian institutions in maritime security cooperation.

Also worth noticing is the establishment of the ASEAN Navy Chiefs' Meeting, also known as ANCM, in Vietnam in July 2011. The meeting saw the heads of ASEAN navies agreeing to formulate an agenda of activities to be jointly conducted in order to improve the people's prosperity through maritime security cooperation. It is, indeed, too early to say that the above movements and effort are sure signs of positive improvement, but it is clear that it is a significant growth in the scope of regional cooperation.

In the form of cooperation, they focus mainly on [how] better bilateral confidence-building measures have now developed to include personnel and expert exchanges and, when fully expanded, will include information sharing and coordinated maritime patrol. This is a sign that regional states have started to soften their sensitivity toward sovereignty issues, although it remains a priority in all occasions.

This newfound attitude toward sovereignty has drawn a lot of extraregional power interest within the context of capability improvement and involvement of extraregional forces, thus increasing the programs of cooperation known and increasing the prioritization of maritime security.

Admiral and honored guests, now let me discuss the Indonesian Navy's perspective on interoperability among the navies in the Southeast Asia region. Interoperability can be defined as the ability of diverse systems and/or organizations to work together. In this context, regional interoperability is the ability of regional navies to work and conduct operations together, using their own equipment. Based on that system of regional-level cooperation, naval cooperation described previously, it is a fact that navies are capable to operate bilaterally with each other. As we shift our focus to multilateral cooperation, we can find that a number of regional navies have been involved in Exercise KAKADU, headed by the Royal Australian Navy. Another display of regional interoperability is the Cooperation Afloat Readiness and Training (CARAT) Exercise. In offering several bilateral activities between Indonesia, the United Sates, and regional navies simultaneously, we see how regional navies are able to cooperate with an extraregional power.

In view of this example, it can be surmised that navies in Southeast Asia have yet to be fully interoperable with one another due to the fact that the region has yet to witness a combined operation that involves all states in the region. Cooperation initiatives, including the ANCM, which will soon operate the ASEAN

Information-Sharing Portal, also known as AIP, among participating countries and develop combined exercises are a good indication this regional-level interoperability can be realistically achieved. For security, granted, and a way ahead, especially to enhance stability and maritime security in the Southeast Asia region, in the perspective of the Indonesian Navy, there are three efforts that need to be made.

- First, establishing strategic partnerships with interregional states and extraregional powers. This partnership has emerged as a simple option for managing in a complex and globalizing world. Such relationships generally contain several common elements forging links between countries that are neither allies nor adversaries, but they serve a range [of interests] both common and divergent. The balance of capability among regional navies is a major factor in creating interoperability.
- Second, enhancing regional interoperability. This field very much depends on the stand and perspective of the country in responding to the cooperative framework being established. This is caused in part by a sense of a combined operation informing the exclusivity of all navies in the region. Many areas lack the means and support in coding software and it must be fully discussed to ensure a real interoperability between regional navies.
- Third, encouraging participation and involving related civilian agencies in maritime security. It is also important to give attention to the fact that such involvement may increase the effectiveness and efficiency of such a force.

Distinguished delegates, in conclusion, maritime security is closely intertwined with economic stability at regional and international levels. It is our common hope that through this forum we can exchange ideas, perspectives, and opinions that would contribute to the management of maritime security in order to [make a] positive contribution and impact on regional and global economic development.

The Indonesian Navy deliberately shares this perspective to this forum where we may all agree to consider that the time has come for us to fully enhance our partnership to find the most beneficial solution and realize interoperability among us to maintain maritime security.

Before I conclude my presentation, I would like to, once again, thank the United States Navy, for hosting this highly successful symposium. We should continue to sustain this good momentum [in] the future. Thank you very much for your kind attention. Fair winds and following seas.

Vice Admiral Johannes Refiloe Mudimu, South Africa:

That was very interesting. Thank you.

Members, I think our fourth intervention [sic] and the last in this panel will be "Closing the Seams: Interagency Cooperation," which will be presented by Vice Admiral Paul Maddison, Chief of Maritime Staff.

Vice Admiral Maddison was commissioned in 1980, and earned his Bridge Watchkeeping and Above-Water Warfare qualifications in HMC ships *Terra Nova* and *Qu'appelle.*

Vice Admiral Maddison's seatime has been equally divided between Canada's Atlantic and Pacific Fleets, including [time as] combat officer of HMCS *Skeena* (1988), executive officer of HMCS *Winnipeg* (1994), and command of HMC ships *Calgary* (1997) and *Iroquois* (2002). Other seagoing appointments have included staff anti-submarine warfare officer to NATO's Commander, Standing Naval Force Atlantic (1989); staff weapons officer to the Commander, Canadian Task Group deployed to the Persian Gulf (1991); Combat Officer, Sea Training Atlantic (1992); Executive Officer, Sea Training Pacific (1996); and commander of the experimental Standing Contingency Force (2006).

Vice Admiral Maddison's shore appointments have included aide-de-camp to the Governor General (1985), command of a joint Space Control Center crew in Colorado Springs (2000), Director General, Maritime Force Development (2005), and Assistant Chief of Military Personnel (2007). In 2008 Vice Admiral Maddison was appointed Commander, Maritime Forces Atlantic and Joint Task Force Atlantic in Halifax, Nova Scotia. He returned to Ottawa in 2010 to serve as Deputy Commander, Maritime Command and Assistant Chief of the Maritime Staff.

An avid hockey enthusiast who still straps on the blades when he can, Vice Admiral Maddison also enjoys watching Aussie Rules football, keeping fit, studying naval history, fishing with his son, discussing the meaning of life with his daughter, and actively seeking that ever-elusive work-life balance that would enrich all of the above. He met his love, Fay, on a blind date during a port visit to Hong Kong, and humbly admits that only through Fay's personal sacrifice and unselfish commitment as a military spouse has he been able to stay young at heart and serve Canada in uniform for so long.

Vice Admiral Maddison was promoted to his present rank and assumed command of the Royal Canadian Navy in July 2011.

Vice Admiral Paul Maddison, Canada:

Well, good morning. *Bonjour.* Thank you for that introduction. Admiral Greenert, Admiral Christenson, distinguished colleagues and friends, let me begin by stating how much I—like I'm sure all of you—have been energized by our efforts here to address the shared challenges we face on the world's oceans, in what the great naval strategist Alfred Thayer Mahan, writing from a desk a few hundred meters from here, described as "a wide common, over which men may pass in all directions."

I wish to acknowledge Admiral Greenert's leadership in bringing us together to build on a strategic trust between us all and for affording me the great privilege of speaking to you all today, not as commander of Maritime Command, but as commander of the Royal Canadian Navy.

I have been asked to address the issue of interagency cooperation and maritime security and defense. Ultimately, what I propose to lay out for you is a strategic imperative for cooperation at sea. First let me review some observations regarding Canada's evolving efforts to "close the seams."

The world's oceans, in my view, defy simple organization charts of federal agency responsibilities. Oceans are inherently multi-jurisdictional for coastal states, requiring integrated action across a whole range of activities, from defense and security, on the one hand, to resource stewardship and the protection of oceans' ecosystems, on the other.

The sheer size of Canada's home waters had already been driving federal agencies towards strategic cooperation in our ocean approaches well before 9/11 lent to those efforts an urgent defense and security imperative. Canada's 2004 National Security Policy sought to enhance this framework of federal cooperation through "unity of maritime effort" rather than through unity of command, and focused on breaking down barriers to effective information sharing and collaborative planning, rather than on driving large-scale organizational change across government. This approach respected each federal agency's mandates while also preserving the essential legal protections of a free and open society.

There is no elegant way to make any of the processes we have evolved in Canada look pretty on a PowerPoint slide, so I don't have any. In the real world we have made it work in Canada because of leadership, personal relationships, and the high degree of confidence and trust that are built by bringing different organizations together to work in common purpose. For example, our progress in advancing an integrated approach to continental maritime security has been due, in no small way, to the strong relationships that have always existed between the U.S. and Canadian defense establishments and especially between the Royal Canadian Navy, the United States Navy, and the United States Coast Guard.

Since 2006, Canada's three marine security operations centers, or MSOCs, have been instrumental in improving our "unity of maritime effort." These centers, located on our east and west coasts and on the Great Lakes, bring together National Defence, Canadian Border Services, the Royal Canadian Mounted Police, Transport Canada, Department of Fisheries and Oceans, and the Canadian Coast Guard. Canada MSOCs are all about horizontal information and intelligence sharing to enable effective, collaborative planning and the formulation of "whole of government" responses to maritime security events, based on the concept of rallying around and enabling the lead agency that has maritime jurisdiction over the event.

The key for the MSOC partners is to identify the anomaly from among all of the legitimate activities occurring at sea as early as possible and to do that through policies and technologies that enable actionable multiple-sensor and multiple-database information to be both exposed and discovered through shared user entitlements.

I don't wish to understate some of the challenges that we have encountered. More often than not, we have found the key difficulties to be associated with differences among federal and provincial partners in terms of their service cultures and the ways in which they approach risk, rather than in, as many people assume, legal or technical impediments. This is why I believe it is strategic trust between partners that is essential to closing the seams at the national level.

Canada's evolving approach to interagency maritime security is a reflection of our geography, history, and national governance, but the issue of strategic trust and strategic cooperation is relevant to all of us here today, because our solutions at the national level shape the manner in which we drive towards achieving consensus regionally and, ultimately, internationally.

So permit me, then, to lay out the strategic imperative for cooperation, an imperative that is tagged by a sense of urgency due, I believe, to the fact that we may very well be on the cusp of historic and momentous change in the global maritime domain.

As I am sure all of you fully appreciate, today's rules-based maritime order sits upon a delicate balance between two central and essentially competing ideas that have existed in a state of constructive tension for some five hundred years, since they were first disputed by the English and the Dutch in the seventeenth century: The first, *mare liberum*—the idea that the seas cannot be made sovereign, and hence, are free for all to use. The second, *mare clausum*—the idea that the seas can be made sovereign to the limits of effective state control.

This delicate balance was achieved not in bloodshed, but rather through an unprecedented degree of international consultation and collaboration in the closing decades of the twentieth century. The result was a unique global convergence of maritime interest that was codified within the 1982 United Nations Convention on the Law of the Sea.

The convention was forged out of a compelling need to reconcile the economic and national interests of the world's coastal states with the traditional defense and security interests of the great maritime powers. That makes the 1982 conference among the crowning achievements of international law. But what made it possible was the fact that both the maritime powers and the coastal states risked suffering equally from the perpetuation of an unregulated, disputed, and unstable maritime order. Whether or not that international consensus will continue to hold in the face of building pressures on coastal states, both large and small, is one of the abiding strategic issues of the twenty-first century.

To understand why, we need to only look to the Arctic, where we are likely to see more change in the coming three decades than has occurred since Europeans first arrived in Greenland. That change is being driven by three main factors:

- First, the steadily increasing global demands for strategic resources, including food, minerals, and energy, and rapid improvement in the technologies needed to bring previously inaccessible seabed resources to market.
- Second, the desire—indeed, the need—for the developed economies to secure assured access to those resources. And
- Third, the role of climate change, which is serving as a catalyst for accelerating change, especially in the world's littorals, whether as a consequence of its physical environmental effects or because, for instance, of the profound social implications of migrating fish stocks on the coastal populations dependent on fish protein to sustain their families.

The high north will be open as a commercially viable sea route for the first time in recorded history, much sooner than many thought possible even a few years ago In all likelihood, that route will emerge across the Arctic Basin well before the fabled Northwest Passage, becoming potentially the preferred option for transoceanic passage between Europe and Asia. Shipping patterns worldwide are likely to be altered significantly as a result.

This is why the five Arctic coastal states—Canada, Denmark, Norway, Russia, and the United States—are working to establish their claims to the vast energy and mineral reserves that have already been discovered, or are believed to lie in the Arctic Basin and its periphery. These resources are likely to become commercially exploitable in the near future, bringing with them a host of economic opportunities, but also vastly increased levels of human activity that will have to be effectively regulated.

In short, a range of factors have emerged to deepen the economic, political, and legal stakes at issue in the Arctic, creating the potential for increased strategic competition in the coming decades. However, as the maritime boundary delineation agreement reached in 2010 between Russia and Norway attests, the intensification of ocean politics in the Arctic has been moderated thus far by strategic cooperation.

It is reasonable, then, to contend that the region's existing disputes will continue to be reconciled through law and diplomacy. Although the Arctic states, including Canada, hold two different interpretations regarding the various provisions of UNCLOS, none appear to be incompatible with the logic that underpins the convention itself.

From the geopolitical perspective, strategic cooperation should be a core, long-term national interest for each of the Arctic states, as it reinforces the 1982 convention from which we each stand to gain so much. It is in this spirit of strategic cooperation that the Canadian Forces have invited the Danish and American navies, as well as the United States Coast Guard, to participate in the annual NANOOK series of exercises in the Canadian Arctic Archipelago, as we build on our abilities to operate at very high latitudes for sustained periods during the navigable season and provide, with our other federal partners, the same ability to regulate our Arctic waters as we currently achieve in our Atlantic and Pacific approaches.

Elsewhere in the world, intensifying ocean politics have been met by significant increases in interstate tension and confrontation. Nowhere is this more apparent than in the Asia-Pacific. The South China Sea, in particular, much like the Arctic Basin, is a region rich in seabed resources. Unlike the Arctic, its importance to global commerce is real today, rather than emergent tomorrow.

From a legal perspective, the region is overlaid with multiple overlapping territorial claims, a factor that has for the most part defied diplomatic efforts at resolution. Still, China has identified its maritime claims in the South China Sea as a core national interest at a time when ocean policy has been increasingly central to the Sino-American relationship in two crucial respects—first, in relation to the United States as an Asia-Pacific power that is vested deeply in regional stability and security, and second, in relation to the role played by the United States as the world's preeminent maritime power. In both instances, how China and the United States approach their differences will be crucial to the trajectory of the twenty-first century. A fundamental significance to this trajectory is the expansive interpretation of its rights as a coastal state that China advocates, an interpretation that would provide aspects of sovereign authority well beyond what the 1982 convention permits. China is not alone in making such claims. That it does so may simply indicate the need for a new legal balance between coastal states' needs for regulation and stewardship of their ocean approaches and the international community's rights of free movement and access.

That alone would be a development of cardinal importance to the global system. However, it might also foreshadow something even more profound. It could lead to an unraveling of the international consensus through which the 1982 convention was derived and to an erosion of a stability in ocean politics that the convention achieved. Shifts in the balance of global power have led before to fundamental changes in the legal framework that underpins the global system, and they may very well do so again.

The consequences of such an unraveling would be enormous and would potentially lead to a far darker world than the one we now inhabit. This is not a future to which I believe any of us would want to aspire, but rather one which we—energized by the strategic trust built through gatherings such as this—should be prepared to stand against for the common vital interests of our nations and for the greater good of all.

We have been speaking, over the past couple of days, of matters of common interest. This is where strategic trust begins, through frank discussions of our challenges but with a firm commitment to seeing past those issues that may divide us as the instruments of national policy our navies will always be, to work towards what I firmly believe is among the greatest public goods of this globalized era, a regulated ocean commons.

There are areas where our navies are already working towards that greater good. Obviously, we've heard many examples already. In the Caribbean Basin and Pacific approaches to Central and South America, a range of nations from the Americas and Europe are cooperating effectively to stem the flow of narcotics at sea. Off the Horn of Africa we have witnessed since 2008 a largely spontaneous but nonetheless a remarkable assembly of naval power to suppress piracy, while the international community continues to seek more enduring solutions ashore.

In other words, navies are not only a means of military action employed in pursuit of national interest as states interpret them. They are also the principal guarantor of good order in that wide common upon which men may pass in all directions, as Mahan described it.

Every sailor here is, first and foremost, a professional mariner and understands that our oceans remain crucial to sustaining life on this planet. Each one of us understands that the ocean's riches are crucial to the future of all coastal states, many of which are struggling to secure a better life for their citizens. Each one of us understands how a regulated ocean commons underpins the global economy on which our prosperity and, indeed, our very way of life depends.

So in conclusion, what I speak of here today is not starry-eyed idealism, but rather that point at which national self-interest and common global interest converge fully. I am speaking of strategic choices that are ours to make, that will require strategic trust to be established and sustained among pragmatic, determined men and women of action, such as are gathered here in this great hall of higher learning. I believe it is within our collective grasp to realize its great purpose. Indeed, there may be no higher purpose, and all we need to do is resolve ourselves to achieve it.

Thank you. *Merci.*

Vice Admiral Johannes Refiloe Mudimu, South Africa:

Thanks, Admiral Maddison. Admirals, chiefs of navies and coast guards, I think we can agree that we have navigated you through this very important issue, "Beyond MDA: Building Responsive Partnerships."

Now is an opportunity for all of us to [provide] input of some kind, either in the form of a question or a comment. I'm very inspired by the team as led by Vice Admiral Branciforte on linking regional MDA initiatives; regional awareness, national responsiveness by Admiral Moura Neto; Vice Admiral Marsetio on regional interoperability; and "Closing the Seams: Interagency Cooperation" with Vice Admiral Maddison.

I think in the spirit that permeated through this presentation, I was very inspired also by Admiral Marsetio. He says, "Together we can." Indeed. Members, in the last two days the spirit is "yes, we can." I think this is clearly typified by the recommendations and suggestions that have been made by the panel here.

I think we have fifteen or twenty minutes. I invite comments or questions. In so doing, members, if you could identify yourself and refer the question to a specific speaker or make a general comment. The floor is all yours. Thanks very much. Participants, questions? The presentations were very clear, I agree, very, very clear. I will not provoke questions myself! Yes?

Admiral Jonathan Greenert, United States:

My question is for you, Paul. Could you elaborate a little bit on the Arctic? As you look at the Arctic kind of in a temporal sense, how do you see the evolution, the opening? You gave examples of what could happen. Could you speak to the timing of such, and what may concern us all by, if not priority, by how you see these things occurring—be it travel first, be it resource issues first, be it whatever—as you guys have studied it there in the Canadian Navy?

Vice Admiral Paul Maddison, Canada:

Thank you very much, sir, for the question. A couple of years ago I was told that major shipping companies, such as Maersk and Daewoo and others, design the ships that they're going to build twenty years in advance. I was told that companies were building ice-capable transoceanic shipping, had designed them to be built [by] the 2020s, because the predictions about the opening of the circumpolar route were coming forward so fast. It was expected that we would reach a point where we would begin to see shipping leaving Singapore, Shanghai, Tokyo, Seoul and going not west through the Singapore Strait and towards Suez but northeast, over a shorter, quicker route, and to Rotterdam and other European ports. That could come within the next fifteen years or so.

The rate at which climate change is occurring is not linear. It seems to come in disruptive moments, and we all wake up and go, "Hmmm, the world has changed." I think that the merchant fleets of the world are preparing for that change. That brings a number of sort of security and safety—perhaps more importantly safety—aspects with it from an Arctic search and rescue perspective, from an Arctic environmental and pollution response perspective. There are a number of demand signals that are building because of this for more activity and infrastructure to be developed in the Arctic, in order to support what we will see as much more activity. We are already seeing significant increases in exploration [and] resource extraction activities from all of the circumpolar nations. I just learned recently that Canada has become the world's number-two diamond producer because of mines that are rapidly developing north. The natural gas, the oil reserves, all of this will bring activity which will have to be regulated in terms of ensuring that the environment is protected, that the northern people are protected, and that we have amongst our nations built the strategic trust and cooperation necessary to work together to support the trade and the activities that will occur in the Arctic.

The northern route that the Russians use will open earlier and last longer. So you have the northern route, and you have the circumpolar route. The Northwest Passage, which many people often talk about, in my view, is no longer a critical sort of strategic part of this discussion. The Northwest Passage, compared to the circumpolar route, is like comparing I-95 to a dirt country road—you know, going out towards the cottages—in terms of supporting large volumes of containerized trade.

There is much that Canada has to learn from our Arctic partners, from Norway, from Denmark, from the United States, and from Russia. My chief of the defense staff recently visited Moscow, talked about the Arctic. I spoke with Admiral [Vladimir] Vysotsky [Commander in Chief of the Russian Navy] yesterday about the Arctic. My chief of defense staff will be hosting an Arctic CHODS [Chiefs of Defense] conference in Yellowknife [Northwest Territories, Canada] in 2012 to enable the dialogue that has already begun. Does that answer your question, sir?

Admiral Jonathan Greenert, United States:

Yes. Thank you, sir.

Vice Admiral Johannes Refiloe Mudimu, South Africa:

Any other input or questions from members? Yes, Admiral.

Commodore Mark Mellett, Republic of Ireland:

I'm Commodore Mark Mellett from the Irish Naval Service. I was very taken with your comments, Paul, in context of that remarkable agreement, the Convention of the Law of the Sea in 1982. I think it was achieved on the backs of diplomats who actually went there with strategic trust in mind in terms of codifying what is a remarkable agreement.

Would we go a step further and say, as we look to the future, that as long as the agreement is not ratified by all maritime states, that we have strategic risk facing us down the road?

Vice Admiral Paul Maddison, Canada:

I would say because of the numbers of signatories, the legitimacy of UNCLOS III is unquestioned. The respect that it has and the way it is applied by not only signatories but by non-signatories, I think, will continue to give it the legitimacy that it has sustained since 1982.

I think it is critical—listening to Dr. Carmel, I think it was yesterday, when he spoke about the new age of globalization and the complexity and the speed at which change is happening in this increasingly active, energized globalized world—to have a system that normalizes relations, that allows everyone to sort of align with it as we deal with one another. I think [that] is vital.

My message this morning with respect to UNCLOS was that we need to be very careful and not to allow the complexity, the disruptive events in the world, to challenge the freedom of the sea and the rules based on international maritime order to a degree that precedents of interpretation are set and not challenged and then allowed to become, for all intents and purposes, a new agreement.

To go back to your original question, I don't see UNCLOS at this particular time as being at all at risk. Thanks.

Vice Admiral Johannes Refiloe Mudimu, South Africa:

Any other questions?

Rear Admiral Jayanath Colombage, Sri Lanka:

I am admiral from the Sri Lanka Navy. It's great to see the guardians of the ocean across the world talking in unison about importance of MDA and beyond. Basically MDA, to me, means what is that ship doing, where is she going, where is she coming from?

Two years ago when the Sri Lankan government was fighting with the [Liberation Tigers of Tamil Eelam (LTTE)], we came across a situation where this political organization ran more than fifteen merchant vessels carrying large quantities of weapons, explosives, ordinance, and war-fighting materials, traveling in international sea routes, calling on many international ports. So despite all the initiatives that we saw today, things can be exploited.

Therefore, I mean, I would request the expert panel's opinion on this. Are the laws governing these nonstate actors sufficient? We know the LTTE heavily abused the flag of convenience, heavily abused the end-war certificate. This is not just one gun or two, but hundred thousands of guns. So I request your opinion on how effective are these initiatives across the world. Thank you.

Admiral Bruno Branciforte, Italy:

I think everybody at this table and probably in the room can answer this question, because as we said many times today, MDA is an interagency problem. What you said is right. Who has to operate against these types of threats? I mean, the illegal traffic of weapons [affect] a lot of agencies in each country. So we have to work all together.

I can tell you how we, for example, operate in Italy. The government decided to have one fusion center in the Navy Operational Center, in which we fuse all the information coming from all the agencies involved in this type of activity, also the trafficking of weapons, illegal trafficking.

It means that all the operations that are carried out at sea and ashore must be followed, monitored, and communicated to these centers. Only in this way we can analyze which are the tracks of the ships, and see the ports that each ship visits, and what is the cargo that ship is carrying.

Of course, the constitution of this national database can be exchanged with many other nations, and we are not sure that the same type of center will be operating in other nations in the same way. Each nation must have, of course, its organization, its initial national organization. Only in this way can we exchange real information.

What navies can do is, as you said, track the movements of these ships, but people at sea must know what are the tracks [of the vessels], their movements, what is the cargo they are transporting, and if necessary, be able to stop them or to signal the same information to the ports where this ship is arriving. This is the final goal.

Of course, to operate at sea, what we need is all this information fused in one center nationally. All this information must be exchanged with the other nations if you're able to do it.

Vice Admiral Johannes Refiloe Mudimu, South Africa:

Any other member want to add to the answer? Anybody in the house want to add to the answer, add some light on this topic? I think your question has been answered. Any there other members with a question or comment on the topic?

Rear Admiral Matthew Quashie, Ghana:

Rear Admiral Quashie, Chief of Staff of the Ghana Navy. I would like to use this opportunity to thank the CNO of the U.S. Navy, the President of the War College, and all of my colleagues that are here, that you offered this opportunity to talk about issues that are common and global to us.

When you look around the world, my part of the world, we have issues. The issues are more economic, and I believe that world navies work together for a common good.

I think that there's a big de-link in the area that I come from.

We have tried in our own way, led by countries like South Africa, to get together and also protect our commons, but you need equipment to do that. That is what we lack the most. I believe the U.S. and other countries, they have done a lot. Ghana, for example, has benefited from the largesse of the United States in terms of platforms, training, and other collaboration, but I still believe there is a lot more that has to be done. In my country, for example, we have oil companies exploiting in our region, but they have serious security challenges. Sometimes we talk and request assistance, but it is difficult for countries to give it to us. They kept telling us that, by their laws, you cannot support the military directly. I think that is very unfortunate, because without security, they cannot perform. I think that's the place, security—well, not as important as the shooting, until there is a problem and then they come. When they come, we don't have what it takes to do that the job. I'm also aware of what proportion of the GDP the U.S. wants countries to spend on their military. Where I'm coming from we cannot do that. It's far more than we can afford. I think it's about time, if you want the circle to be properly completed, it's about time nations who can go out of their way in a very big way to support poor nations like us.

If you go along the west coast of Africa from Equatorial Guinea, all the way to Senegal, through the other Portuguese country, Guinea-Bissau, these countries—it's very difficult to get platforms. I think that it's about time, this should be an extension of that issue.

We need to look at the countries who are able and capable to support us in a very big way, so that we can bridge that gap. Otherwise, when it comes to our part of the world—you can do a lot elsewhere, but when it comes to our part of the world, the game will be lost. This is a great opportunity for all of you.

I think very soon the African countries will be meeting. When we meet, we're going to come up with something. We are going to throw it out to you. When it comes to you, please don't hesitate. We need your support; otherwise, what we are doing here will not be completed globally. That is all. I thank you very much.

Vice Admiral Johannes Refiloe Mudimu, South Africa:

Thanks, members, for listening and the questions that have been posed and the eloquent speakers. You can give them a round of applause. Thanks very much.

7

The Hattendorf Prize

Awarded to
Dr. N. A. M. Rodger

All Souls College, Oxford University

Rear Admiral John Christenson, United States:

Good afternoon, and welcome to this very special event. I would like to thank the Chief of Naval Operations, Admiral Jonathan Greenert; the First Sea Lord, Admiral Sir Mark Stanhope; Professor John Hattendorf; and Dr. Nicholas Rodger for joining me on the stage. Please, have a seat.

Today the Naval War College makes the first award of the newly established Hattendorf Prize for Distinguished Original Research in Maritime History. It is particularly appropriate for the Naval War College to make this announcement here at this international symposium.

Professor John Hattendorf presents the Hattendorf Prize Medal to Dr. N. A. M. Rodger (center) of All Souls College, Oxford University, while Admiral Jonathan N. Greenert, U.S. Navy; Admiral Sir Mark Stanhope, Royal Navy; and Rear Admiral John N. Christenson, U.S. Navy, applaud.

This new prize is made for world-class achievement in original research that contributes to a deeper understanding of the broad context and inner relationships involved in the roles, contributions, limitations, and uses of the sea services in history.

This prize reflects the essence of Professor John B. Hattendorf's professional values and goals for his field during his continuing service here since 1984, as the Naval War College's Ernest J. King Professor of Maritime History, to serve the Navy by improving the quality and range of scholarship in maritime history, striving to engage globally with an appreciation for scholarship in different languages and from different national, cultural, and regional perspectives, and to see maritime history as a broad field in global history that builds on insights that cut across traditional academic and national boundaries.

Before we present this award to this first, most deserving recipient, let me take a few moments to talk about the distinguished scholar for whom the award is named. Professor John Hattendorf is truly a legend here at the Naval War College and within the international circle of naval historians. The professional journal U.S. Naval Institute *Proceedings* has described him as, "one of the most widely known, respected naval historians in the world." I could not agree more. He earned his bachelor's degree from Kenyon College, his master's degree in history from Brown, and, in 1979, his doctorate at Pembroke College, Oxford.

The foundation of his knowledge of naval affairs comes from his wartime service as a naval officer during the Vietnam era. He served aboard the destroyer USS *O'Brien*, earning a commendation from the commander of the United States Seventh Fleet for outstanding performance of duty during combat operations in April 1967. He later served at sea in destroyers *Purdy* and *Fiske*.

He was a key staff member and confidant of War College President Admiral Stansfield Turner during his historic presidency. They called it the Turner Revolution, and it reinvigorated the College and set it on the course we follow to this day. Admiral Turner knew just how good Professor Hattendorf was, so he sent the young lieutenant to Oxford to earn his PhD.

He is the author, coauthor, editor, or coeditor on more than forty books on British and American maritime history and naval warfare. He has called maritime history "a subject that touches on both the greatest moments of the human spirit as well as on the worst, including war." He has won numerous awards for his contributions to the field of maritime history and literary achievement, including the Navy League of the United States Alfred Thayer Mahan Award for Literary Achievement. We are truly blessed to have him here at the Naval War College all these years and on the stage with us here today.

The purpose of the Hattendorf Prize is to honor and to express appreciation for distinguished academic research and writing in the field of maritime history. With the intention that this is to be the most prestigious award that any scholar can receive in this field, we hope that it will serve as a permanent beacon to encourage and to promote the new scholarship in this very important and newly reemerging and reinvigorated field of study.

By having this award associated with the Naval War College and awarded on an international basis to the world's leading scholars who have distinguished themselves in this field, it will serve to reinforce this College's role as the U.S. Navy's most important link between sea services and the broader academic community.

Equally important, it adds for the College a new and complementary component that highlights and extends the College's interest in regional studies and international cooperation. In this, it can form a focal point in the future life of the College that provides broad intellectual stimulation through new historical research and historical insight, while at the same time serving the College's educational mission in helping to promote its role as "a place of original research on all questions relating to war and to statesmanship connected with war, or the prevention of war." It is an award that promotes and continues the inspiration that Luce and Mahan laid here more than a century ago when they turned to historical understanding as a fundamental element in the College's educational and research approach.

In permanently endowing the Hattendorf Prize, I would like to thank the Naval War College Foundation. Retired captain John Odegaard, the foundation's executive director, is here with us this afternoon. Thank you, John.

We want to recognize the great generosity of the donor, Pam Ribbey, whose late grandfather, Captain Charles Maddox, was a 1935 and 1939 Naval War College graduate, and faculty member from 1939 to 1941. Her permanent endowment of the prize allows us to present a $10,000 cash prize and a bronze medal designed by Professor Hattendorf's youngest daughter, Anna Hattendorf.

What a great day. Thank you all for being here. I would like to ask our most distinguished group here to assemble there center stage as we present the award.

Professor Thomas Culora:

The President of the U.S. Naval War College takes great pleasure in awarding the Hattendorf Prize for Distinguished Original Research in Maritime History to Dr. N. A. M. Rodger, research fellow of All Souls College, Oxford. The Naval War College is pleased to recognize you as the first Hattendorf Prize laureate.

This award is predicated on your distinguished achievement as an assiduous historical researcher as well as the author of beautifully written and intellectually impressive studies of Britain's naval history. Your scope, embracing more than a thousand years of naval history, is informed and given depth by an equally broad understanding of your subject.

Your impressive command of sources ranging from medieval documents in Latin to modern archives and scholarly works in a broad range of European languages has established a new and more comprehensive approach to writing a national naval history. You have written that "the naval historian has to be aware of what other historians are writing to do justice to his own subject, and explain its importance to others. To do so he has to integrate a wide range of knowledge." "It goes without saying that this demands a great deal of reading and not inconsiderable literary skills, so it is not surprising that successful naval histories which take this approach are rare." Your works exemplify that description and have themselves become prizes for us to read.

This award honors you and your work, expressing appreciation for your distinguished academic research, insight, and writing that contribute to a deeper historical understanding of the broad context and interrelationships involved in the roles, achievements, and uses of navies within the context of both maritime and general history.

Presented this twentieth day of October, 2011, at the U.S. Naval War College, signed John N. Christenson, Rear Admiral, United States Navy, President, Naval War College.

Admiral John Christenson, United States:

Dr. Rodger, the auditorium is yours.

Dr. N. A. M. Rodger, United Kingdom:

Well, Admiral Greenert, Admiral Christenson, ladies and gentlemen, my first task, very obviously, is to express my profound gratitude to the Naval War College Foundation, to the Naval War College for the honor they have done me in presenting this prize, this medal, an honor which, as far as I'm concerned, is, if possible, increased by the fact that it bears the name of my old friend John Hattendorf.[1] I can tell you that nothing that Admiral Christenson said of his merits and achievements was in the slightest degree exaggerated.

I've often thought that historians, naval historians like myself, are able to do more service to navies than the navies sometimes realize. I like to take what opportunities come my way to tell admirals this, but I must say I never dreamt that I should find myself with an opportunity to say it to all the admirals in the whole world who matter.

I do think that history is of value and importance to navies. Perhaps here, actually, is the one place where it shouldn't be necessary to say it, here in the United States Naval War College, which was the first institution in the world founded to study history as the foundation of naval policy. We are, after all, only a few yards from the rooms in which around 130 years ago the then-captain Alfred Thayer Mahan was writing the first of his great books.

Here, least of anywhere in the world, the influence of history on seapower scarcely needs to be underlined. Yet, I think there are still things to be said which are worth saying, things worth saying in eight minutes. Actually, one of them, you may be surprised if I start by saying, one of them is to offer you a caution—what history won't do for you.

It certainly won't save you from mistakes, nor must you imagine that historians are infallible. A historian is a prophet of the past, not the future. If you look at Mahan, whose influence is absolutely unquestionable and whose works are still read by everybody, you can see that there were some important things which he did not realize, did not understand.

It's very notable that Mahan's naval world is a world dominated by a handful of rival great naval powers, all of them European. For him, there is one successful navy which triumphs in war, in fact, usually in battle, and then dominates the whole world.

Of course, that was the picture in the nineteenth century in his lifetime, but it wasn't, in fact, a picture that was going to go on forever. The world was already changing even as he wrote, and he, himself, had a small share in changing it. The main way in which it was changing was the rise, at the end of the nineteenth century, of significant naval powers outside Europe.

---

1. Dr. Rodger's following remarks were later expanded into an article: N. A. M. Rodger, "The Hattendorf Prize Lecture: The Perils of History," *Naval War College Review* 66, no. 1 (Winter 2013), pp. 7–15.

The British had managed to dominate the seas of the world for a long time, because they had no rivals outside Europe. If you could dominate European waters, then by extension you could dominate the rest of the world as well. This is not a trick you can pull off if there are significant naval powers on the other side of the world. Then you need to have a fleet in two places at once, or two fleets at the same time.

It's the rise of other naval powers which actually changes the world as Mahan described, and, of course, one of the principal other naval powers outside Europe was precisely the United States Navy, whose rise Mahan devoted his career to promoting. In a way, he blew up his own world, or at least he contributed to doing so.

There is another thing, I think, involved in this. The rise of the other naval powers is a function of the tremendous economic success of free trade—as we would say, globalization—in the nineteenth century. In the 1840s, probably Britain was the only advanced economy in the world. By the 1890s, there were at least a dozen. As advanced, prosperous economies with industry and technology developed in other parts of the world, many of them built navies. The more navies they built, the more impossible it became for any one navy to dominate the seas of the world, the faster history advanced towards the situation in which we live today—this situation which is exemplified by your presence here a world in which there are very many important navies all over the place, and nobody can achieve anything very much in the naval world without cooperation, coalitions, alliances, and so on. You know that. That's why you're here.

Mahan, I think, never really envisaged that. The naval world he depicts was one in which this sort of alliance situation has no existence. It's partly because he seems to have been very largely unaware of economics, which, again, I think is something which nobody would say today. All strategy is based on economics. Certainly all naval strategy is based on economics. I think that's obvious, hardly needs elaboration. It must be obvious here. I suppose it's the reason behind that very handsome logo that you've been looking at all week with its apparent message that the Swiss Navy rules the waves.

In all events, we can all agree that economics matter. There, I think, is something that Mahan actually probably wasn't really aware of what was going on. So don't think that historians can do everything. But nevertheless, you can't get away from history. All our human experience, as individuals and as organizations, is experience of the past. The present slips through our fingers every second.

The future, which would be very useful to know about, is regrettably inaccessible. In fact, all we know is the past, recent past, distant past, as the case may be. As a matter of fact, you have only to read or listen to the speeches, the writings of politicians, journalists, and, indeed, of admirals to find that people continually, automatically, without thinking of it, make reference to past analogies. They draw explicit parallels with events in the past, and they use unconscious images and language which betray the parallels which they're adopting without thinking. History is always with us. We can't get away from it.

The problem is that all too frequently the history which people are using is a history which is irrelevant, distorted, or altogether imagined. This is a bad foundation for policy making. If you cannot avoid the past, it's a very good plan to try basing your plans on a past which really happened and has some relevance to the world in which we live, rather than an imagined, mythical, or entirely distorted past which represents, as it might be, things you half remember from school, inherited prejudice, things you heard in the pub, or whatever the other foundations are for the things which people assume and talk about.

History won't solve all your problems, but I can guarantee that policy making on the basis of bad, imagined, or fantastical history certainly will cause you a very great many problems.

In that respect, historians have, I think, an essential role in at least clearing the ground and avoiding the most elementary pitfalls, which is why this college maintains so powerful a history department and continues to keep history in the center of its intellectual activities in support of the United States Navy and of all the other navies whose officers come to study here.

I hope, I think, I believe the same can be said of all navies which take their professions seriously. I wish the same could be said of all other organizations of government. Navies, I think, are well ahead of other people in taking history seriously.

Still, it deserves to be said as often as people will listen that if we don't pay attention to history, we won't escape history; we'll just become the prisoners of historical myths. On that basis, we're extremely unlikely to make the right decisions.

So let me finish by once again giving my profound thanks to the Naval War College Foundation and to the Naval War College for the honor they have done me.

Admiral John Christenson, United States:

I think you'll all agree that we made a fantastic first selection for the first award. Professor Rodger, thank you. First Sea Lord, CNO, Professor Hattendorf, all, thank you for joining us on the stage. I'm going to turn it back over to you, Tom.

8

Regional Breakout Group Reports

Moderated by Professor Thomas Culora
Chairman, Warfare Analysis and Research Department, U.S. Naval War College

Professor Thomas Culora:

Thank you, sir. Now it's time to hear the reports from the regional breakout groups. Many of you participated in those groups yesterday afternoon. The report was there were some lively sessions throughout, within all the regions. I think we're very much looking forward to hearing the reports from those groups.

We have about an hour and forty minutes, which means that each speaker will have about ten minutes to present the group's report. I talked to some of the presenters. They said that that is very doable.

I will take a cue from the admirals who have moderated their panels so expertly and use the red and green cards, if I need to. I will assist the speakers by, about eight minutes into the speech, holding up the red card, so you know you have a couple minutes left. We have a lot of groups to get through. I want to be able to give everybody an opportunity to speak.

The first group today is going to report from the Atlantic Ocean group. If I may invite Commander Beirão from Brazil to the podium on my left to give your report.

ATLANTIC OCEAN

Commander André Panno Beirão, Brazil:

Admiral Greenert, Chief of Naval Operations, in the name of [Brazil], I greet all chiefs of navies and coast guards present here. Rear Admiral Christenson, President of the Naval War College, congratulations for the outstanding organization of this important event.

Dear delegates and officers of friendly navies, ladies and gentlemen, good afternoon. It's a pleasure to be here to represent the breakout group Atlantic Ocean. Well, we hope to show here some thoughts discussed by the group.

First of all, our group represents a big ocean. In spite of its apparent stability, we know for sure the contemporary risks and threats, and only through partnerships towards maritime domain awareness [can we] increase safety and security in Atlantic waters.

The key issue that was proposed for the group was "what are the changes that we have to face in order to cope with piracy, smuggling, trafficking and other illicit activities in our ocean, and how can partners help mitigate risks, costs and, therefore, threats."

The very first challenge to face is the social and political understanding of the necessity of keeping the investments in security. It seems especially hard at this moment when some countries need to solve important economic problems. In other words, how [do we] justify increasing the defense expenditures?

Atlantic Ocean

- Argentina
- Brazil
- Canada
- Guyana
- Iceland
- Ireland
- Portugal
- Suriname
- UK
- Uruguay
- US

The second challenge pointed [out] in our group was the frequency of interagency coordination for the nation to share data. The lack of global standards demands bilateral or regional partnerships, which we consider a fundamental step towards the full knowledge of the maritime domain. International legal issues have to be addressed. While regional agreements already exist, the countries in the Atlantic Ocean need to be aware of what is going on in other parts of the globe.

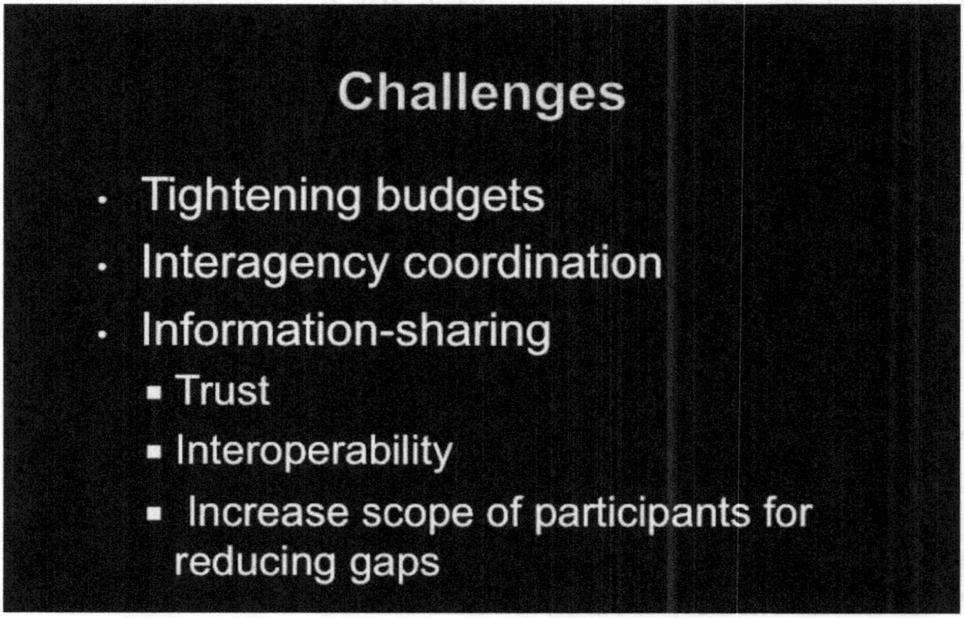

Challenges

- Tightening budgets
- Interagency coordination
- Information-sharing
  - Trust
  - Interoperability
  - Increase scope of participants for reducing gaps

The outcome of this desired cooperation is represented by a term already mentioned during this symposium—that is, sharing information.

To achieve this aim, we have to address key issues like
- fostering relationships based on trust,
- overcoming technological asymmetries among partners, and
- developing comprehensive agreements to fill gaps.

Observations

- **Maritime security cooperation needs to be gradual**
  - Additional countries joining regional arrangements
  - Natural emergencies and attacks can force rapid adjustment and development

- **Each Navy is to some degree dependent on how neighboring navies adapt to changed circumstances**

- **Technical interoperability**
  - Protocols and standards have to emerge

In this discussion there are some aspects that we can accept based on prior experiences. First of all, the progress on maritime security cooperation needs to be gradual. Bilateral or regional arrangements are more effective when other countries join the association, and that is what's happening right now in Atlantic South America. However, natural emergencies and attacks can force rapid adjustments and development.

Of course, each navy is, to some degree, dependent on how neighboring navies adapt to changed circumstances. In other words, a good domestic effort will not be totally effective unless neighbors have a similar concern. Another point is that technical interoperability is needed, but protocols and standards may have to emerge rather than be imposed. After reviewing the challenges, and with due considerations, the group agreed to present some directions to address and mitigate the questions and problems. First, once this threat reappears in the wave of globalization, the private sector must be heard during the selection to start discussions for specific issues.

This whole process [brings us] back to maritime domain awareness. The development of maritime security standards and protocols are best handled regionally, but built over a common ground. Finally, we consider [it] relevant to continue or increase enduring multinational cooperation structure. This concludes our presentation. Thanks for your attention.

PACIFIC OCEAN

Professor Thomas Culora:

Thank you very much, Commander. I would now like to invite the spokesperson for the Pacific Ocean breakout group, Lieutenant Colonel Akhmar from Brunei.

Lieutenant Colonel Saiful Akhmar, Brunei:

Admiral Greenert, Chief of Naval Operations; Rear Admiral Christenson, President of the Naval War College; distinguished leaders of navies and coast guards around the world; distinguished guests; ladies and gentlemen, good afternoon and *salaam alaikum.*

It is my pleasure to apprise you of the results of the discussion in the Pacific Group breakout group yesterday afternoon. My name is Lieutenant Colonel Saiful Akhmar from the Joint Command and Staff College in Brunei Darussalam.

Let me say first and foremost, it was really a challenge for the group initially to select a willing volunteer to present this report. However, after much coaxing the consensus was reached and, partly through my own volition, an officer from the army is standing in front of you this afternoon. You can now rest assured in the belief that I am not in the wrong symposium.

Ladies and gentlemen, our group focused our discussions on three discussion points, which were facilitated by Professor Peter Dutton of the Naval War College. Our thoughts and ideas were captured in summary, or are captured in summary in this one PowerPoint slide, as we were told to do, but it does not actually reflect the richness of our discussions.

Pacific Ocean

- **Follow-on to ISS with a Virtual Exercise**
  - Senior Leaders can share insights and developments regionally and globally on a more regular basis.
  - Maintain momentum developed at ISS

- **Develop HADR SOP**
  - Pre-planned responses
  - Engage all stakeholders in advance, including NGOs
  - POCs updated and current
  - Existing Submarine Rescue Web Page as potential model
  - Think through options for overcoming language barriers between rescuers and victims
  - Leverage social media to facilitate disaster response

However, it was clear that every party in the group was interested in achieving effectiveness in collaborative efforts in responding to crises in the Pacific region. What [is] important [is] that the group identified several gaps in these efforts that require filling, and not without apparent challenges. In essence, the discussion group geared [its] thoughts towards HA/DR (humanitarian assistance and disaster relief) efforts within the region. The three points—or rather two for now—on the slide reflect the main initiatives that can be pursued over the next two years. Allow me to elaborate on the first point, virtual exercise, which perhaps will lead to thematic focus for a future ISS. This, perhaps, is a means to enhance MDA, not only for individual nations but also for the region as a whole. Latching onto this, I must mention his name, [Vice] Admiral [Gerald R.] Beaman [Commander, U.S. Third Fleet] brought out the maxim that is pertinent to HA/DR response, which is "the issue is not if, but when, HA/DR response is required."

The group also later identified that clear coordination would result between neighbors in the region if training initiatives took examples of the multilateral approach, those that have already manifested from existing training exercises, such as RIMPAC, Pacific Partnership, Panamax and so on.

Another quintessential requirement that was discussed pertained to the involvement of the whole-of-government approach, plus NGOs (nongovernmental organizations), to bring the capacities to bear within a virtual environment. On this aspect, it is one thing to have boots on the ground, as we from the army would normally say, conducting HA/DR operations. It is another thing to realize that boots on the ground do not work in isolation.

Today it is a necessity to coordinate efforts with government and NGO elements, and a major step towards enhancing joint interagency and multinational operations in the HA/DR context.

The group also correctly identified that a multilateral approach almost always manifests some sensitivities, but also realized the advantages it will bring when it comes to responding to a crisis in a vast area, such as the Pacific—in essence, a collaborative effort vis-à-vis virtual means to connect the links in order to develop a fuller understanding of what is occurring in the Pacific environment.

As for the second issue, the group identified that preplanned response measures can be captured better in the form of an SOP, or standard operating procedure. Again, this relates to the virtual exercise alluded to earlier.

[Rear] Admiral [Arthur] Johnson, [U.S. Navy]—a good friend of mine from the breakout group who actually nominated me—articulated that we need to think of better ways to make use of new tools and technologies, and consequently roles can be assigned in advance after recognition of incoming disasters in order to respond to such disasters.

Out of this, the matter of design, implementation, operationalizing measures identified from the virtual exercise should be captured in the form of an SOP, which in effect will result in achieving a common operating picture amongst all stakeholders. One contributor in the group mentioned also the existence of a multinational force SOP (MNF SOP), under the remit of U.S. Pacific Command, which perhaps will contribute towards achieving a common operating picture.

Our group also had the privilege of being introduced to the Naval Criminal Investigative Service's manual, which is called the *Guide for Investigating Acts of Maritime Piracy*. This, again, [is] an example of an SOP that offers a uniformity approach to piracy and helps in understanding measures of collecting evidence. Another form of arrangement would be to have a mutual logistic support arrangement, which definitely will outline accountabilities for nations within the Pacific.

I move on now to our next point, I hope, which is in the next slide, which is common command and control suites or processes drawing on the Internet and the social media. The group identified that there may be a need to have a common platform for nations to communicate in real time. The group also identified that sometimes too much focus can be paid to hardware platform or suites and not enough to information sharing and what exactly is necessary to communicate. This is further exacerbated by multiple languages within the region, especially when it boils down to determining the threats, either nonhuman threats or threats to operational security. The sharing of a common language in communications might help improve awareness and identification of emerging threats.

Pacific Ocean

- **Additional Non-Traditional Security (NTS) ideas**
  - Common C2 Suites
    would improve interoperability
  - SOP sharing
    Piracy Investigation and Prosecution Manual developed by NCIS can overcome some of the legal challenges
  - Climate Change is a NTS concern:
    Increasing coverage by Warning Systems for NTS threats based on weather or natural disasters
  - Regional HADR Exercises
    Incorporating whole of government, NGOs, and virtual collaboration for partners throughout a region

Further to these, members of the group also explored the utility of the electronic media—such as Skype, Facebook, Twitter—as another means of enhancing information sharing and a matter of ensuring that the real information needs of all involved parties in crisis response are met.

Our friend from New Zealand in the group [Rear Admiral Tony Jonathan Parr] shared how the New Zealand military struggled in the past to operate in an unclassified Internet environment and social media. Relating to the recent earthquake in New Zealand, it was found that within five to seven days nations contributing aid used Facebook and Internet [sites] in the English language. These became a major means by which the public was informed.

Ladies and gentlemen, it would be incomplete not to mention the principal challenges to crisis response and information sharing in the Pacific region that was shared in the group discussion which eventually led to the three proposed initiatives articulated earlier.

The group identified, amongst many, the following: First, the challenge of climate change affects crisis response for Pacific Island nations. Second, data identification of [human-centered], nontraditional threats and also, third, our friend from Korea raised the challenge of security of navigation, especially when it involves the import or export of hydrocarbon resources.

These challenges also entail legal procedures, or lack of [them], to address piracy and the paucity of forces to handle issues. [Other challenges are] the ability to share information once any perceived threat has been identified and how to respond. A good working example was highlighted pertaining to the Eyes in the Sky air patrols and the intelligence exchange group for the Malacca Straits, which has effectively reduced the number of piracy incidents.

Last but not least, another challenge or perception identified was the lack of determining intersection of mutual interests between the NGOs and the affected states and the military.

Admirals, distinguished guests, ladies and gentlemen, let me close by sharing a maxim often used in my college. I quote, "We often identify lessons from our endeavors, but we rarely learn from them." By building on this thought on behalf of our group, a sense of urgency must be created to enhance a common awareness that will allow the Pacific group of nations to operationalize actions that are deemed required to collaborate and coordinate responses within the region. I thank you.

Professor Culora:

Thank you. After that, I think you're ready for a lateral transfer to the navy. I would next like to invite up Captain Saqib from Pakistan who will give the report for the Indian Ocean regional breakout group.

INDIAN OCEAN

Captain Saqib Khattak, Pakistan:

Bismillah al rahman al rahim: in the name of Allah, the Beneficent, the Merciful. Admiral Greenert, Chief of the Naval Operations, United States Navy; chiefs of the navies and the coast guards; distinguished guests; ladies and gentlemen, good afternoon and *salaam alaikum*. I am Captain Saqib from the Pakistan Navy and a student of the Naval Command College [NCC] at the Naval War College, under the able command of Admiral Christenson, able and kind commander, Admiral Christenson.

Unlike my predecessors who prepared well for this occasion, unfortunately, I did not. The reason is that I was not coming to this place, I was going towards McCarty Little Hall, because I thought I was supposed to say something in front of the same gathering which we had there yesterday. But my naval attaché accompanying me told me, you don't have to go there, you have to speak in front of all the chiefs of the navies of the world.

So you can well imagine how much I am prepared to speak in front of you. Anyway, I'm going to take this on. Yesterday, it happened the same way as my friend from Brunei told you, there was no volunteer. The moderator kept asking us time and again, and kept looking at everybody. Whenever he looked at me, I looked the other way, and during the whole course of our breakout nobody volunteered.

In the end I thought that I was going to speak there, so I said okay, I'm going to go ahead with it. Had I realized that I'm going to speak in front of you, I think I wouldn't have volunteered. Anyway, I'm here just two months more for my Naval Command College course—here to learn more about how to speak in front of the chiefs of the navies.

So I start off with a story [from] Vice Admiral Manson Brown from the U.S. Coast Guard, Pacific Command—I did not know his name until just two minutes ago. I just asked. He told me a very good story yesterday. In such breakouts or something that he was in, a volunteer was being asked to moderate. Nobody was volunteering even there. In the end he said, "'I want to volunteer.' I raised my hand and said I want to be moderator for this occasion." Later on, within a week, I think, he was then rear admiral. He got the good news of his performance then, and he got his third star to his credit. I may get one after this occasion.

Having said so much, I think I will not take much of your time, sir. I would like to say what Admiral Alfred Thayer Mahan said about the Indian Ocean and its significance. He said, and I quote, "Whoever controls the Indian Ocean dominates Asia. This ocean is the key to the seven seas. In the twenty-first century, the destiny of the world will be decided on its waters."

You can well imagine then in the twentieth century what was said about this Indian Ocean and its importance. It is not only important for the Indian Ocean region states only, but it is important for the world as it starts from the Strait of Hormuz, goes down to the Gulf of Aden, around the Cape of Good Hope and towards the east into the Malacca Strait. It is, I would say, the most significant ocean, because the whole world is dependent on the trade passing through this route. Whatever we discussed yesterday, and there was very, I would say, good input given by both the Australian and Indian counterpart, the four points that came up in our discussion are as highlighted here. I will go through them one by one.

Indian Ocean

1. Piracy is a land and a maritime issue; it is a global issue because it affects the global supply chain and because of its extra-regional financial aspects.
   - States should share lessons learned and develop SOPs for counter piracy operations and for information sharing associated with the mission.
   - Countering piracy may require a UN mandate to facilitate cooperative and "from the sea" solutions that address both the land and maritime dimensions.
2. A critical challenge to maritime security is that small boats remain outside the current MDA framework.
   - Develop a multilateral legal framework with associated funding to bring small boats into a improved maritime security framework.
3. Given resource constraints, one challenge is how to maintain a balance between the use of Navy and Coast Guard assets for war-fighting and law enforcement missions and cooperative endeavors such as disaster-relief and counter-piracy.
   - Do states need to address this concern more comprehensively by considering a high-low mix of platforms and capabilities?
   - Can states substitute capacity-building of local partners for the suboptimal use of high-end assets to address low-end threats?
4. Final Initiative: A web-based information and coordination site for disaster-relief assets' locations, capabilities, and availability.
   - Modeled on International Submarine Escape and Rescue Liaison Office (ISMERLO)

We talked about piracy. We said that piracy is not only a maritime issue; it is a land issue as well. It is a global issue, because it affects the global supply chain and because of its extraregional financial aspects. The states should share lessons learned and develop SOPs for counterpiracy operations and for information sharing associated with the mission. Countering piracy may require a United Nations mandate to facilitate cooperative and from-the-sea solutions that address both the land and maritime dimensions.

One point that came to light was why are we going for the cure. Why are we not looking at the prevention part? As we say, prevention is better than cure. Being reactive to what is all happening regarding the piracy issue and handling that, we may look into the aspect of seeing what the pirates want. They want money. They are not educated. So why not hold the bull by the horns and address the issues of the pirates, so that the pirate operations are minimized, and then we can go for the cure.

The second point that came up, [which is] a critical challenge to maritime security, is that small boats remain outside the current MDA framework. Since the small boats, which are, I would say, innumerable and can't be counted, they're without any geographical areas—maybe they don't have GPS on board, or maybe they are not registered. So many unregistered boats that ply around are not in any database, and they are involved in such activities. We don't have anything about them.

We need to focus on this issue country-wide and get them registered, so that we can have control on this issue. We can develop a multilateral legal framework with associated funding to bring small boats into an improved maritime security framework.

The third point—given resource constraints, one challenge is how to maintain a balance between the use of navy and coast guard assets for war fighting and law enforcement missions and cooperative endeavors, such as disaster relief and counterpiracy. This point came up because the issue was that the navies are basically meant to prepare for the war. This is our secondary mission, to look after the HA/DR issues. Why use higher-value assets to handle this low-key note? This is one of the points that came to our discussion. We said, do states need to address this concern more comprehensively by considering a high/low mix of platforms and capabilities? Should we go for that? Can states substitute capacity building of local partners for the suboptimal use of high-end assets to address low-end threats?

The last point that came to our discussion and was concluded was regarding a final initiative of web-based information and coordination site for disaster relief, assets, locations, capabilities, and availabilities. In light of ISMERLO, that is, the International Submarine Escape and Rescue Liaison Office, that we get together regionally and we discuss how if a submarine accident happens and how should we handle the situation, how to move the assets from around the globe and focus, concentrate on that point, and this came truly after the incident of *Kursk*.

We had discussed a lot on that, and I am happy to inform you here that I am the only submariner of the NCC. I am happy to be part of Admiral Greenert's family, too. Piracy issues and regional issues that we have in the Indian Ocean can be addressed, in my opinion, if we sit together, we talk openly, and we talk frequently. Then we can discuss this issue and handle the situation as nations, as global players, and I think this will come down to the minimum.

This is what I had to say. I don't have any concluding remarks, but I would just like to say that, in my opinion, prevention is better than cure. We should get into the mind-set of the pirates and get them what they want, negotiate with them and minimize this so that we make the Indian Ocean a peaceful and a better place for the entire world. I thank you, sir.

MEDITERRANEAN, BLACK SEA, AND CASPIAN SEA

Professor Thomas Culora:

Thank you, Captain. I would now like to invite Captain Yayci from Turkey. He will address—he will speak to the regional breakout group that dealt with the Mediterranean, the Black Sea, and Caspian Sea.

Captain Cihat Yayci, Turkey:

Admiral Greenert, Admiral Christenson, admirals and delegates and distinguished guests, first of all, let me thank the U.S. Navy and War College for organizing this very important and very beneficial symposium. I am representing the Mediterranean, Black Sea, and Caspian Sea region, and our working group results are as follows.

Mediterranean, Black & Caspian Seas

1. Value in separate regional Cooperation and Operational initiatives like BLACKSEAFOR and Black Sea Harmony
2. Multi and bilateral exercises are excellent training opportunities for all participants
3. Naval cooperation helps reduce, but does not eliminate bilateral information sharing challenges
4. To get information, have to give information
   1. Move from "Need to know" to "Need to share"
   2. Balance against need to protect information
5. "One size fits all" does not work in this region

Separate regional cooperation and operational initiatives, like Black Sea Naval Cooperation Task Group (BLACKSEAFOR) and BLACK SEA HARMONY, confidence-building measures, and Black Sea Coast Guard Forum, as well as Five Plus Five [5+5], V-RMTC, and ADRION Initiative in the Mediterranean, are very believable initiatives. So in a way there are no gaps in the Black Sea. As far as ensuring almost complete maritime picture, we have maritime domain awareness.

Still, there are risks, although they are not threats. Those risks [need] to be checked, not to turn into threats due to intentions or capabilities. This is also right for the Mediterranean. Indeed, there are initiatives and operations for the cooperation of navies, NATO, and United Nations, like the Italian Navy–led V-RMTC, the Turkish Navy's MEDITERRANEAN SHIELD, NATO's ACTIVE ENDEAVOR, and United Nations UNIFIL (United Nations Interim Force in Lebanon). To sum up, the gaps can be filled only with the cooperative and multilateral efforts of all littoral states. Simultaneously, littoral states must work towards establishing an effective MDA. Also, multi- and bilateral exercises are excellent training opportunities for all participants.

Black Sea Naval Cooperation Task Group, BLACKSEAFOR, is a very excellent, unique example for this. After the Cold War, six littorals came together under the umbrella of Turkish-led initiative, BLACKSEAFOR, Black Sea Naval Cooperation Task Group, in 2001. At that time it was very hard to operate together, but now the navies have achieved successful interoperability. Partnership and cooperation have paved the way for an improved regional interoperability.

In the context of MDA and MSO, BLACK SEA HARMONY is another success story. However, cooperation has reduced but not eliminated bilateral or multilateral sharing challenge. In this context interagency cooperation is highly needed to efficiently maintain maritime situation awareness and effectively conduct maritime security operations.

For this purpose, firstly, it is a prerequisite to integrate the systems by relevant nation maritime commands and agencies to establish a joint maritime domain awareness for national, regional, and global aspects. Also very important [is] bringing a shared understanding to today's maritime challenges and creating opportunity for the relevant parties to better understand each other.

On the other hand, it is a fact that regional awareness will come through regional ownership, which should be complementary to the global ownership. In this manner, first of all, we should all recognize some practical hindrances. For example, although it is not a threat, a nation's reluctance to share information is an important hindrance and leads to a perception of that nation as willing to receive but reluctant to give. This is just not conducive to bringing out effective partnerships and cooperation. For this, moving from "need to know" to "need to share" for balancing against the need to protect information should be considered.

To sum up, in terms of the fight against illicit activities, no country can be expected to overcome problems alone by its own measures. Coordination and cooperation should be strictly maintained. That's why Operation BLACK SEA HARMONY and Operation MEDITERRANEAN SHIELD—although these are initiated by the Turkish Navy and created with NATO's Operation ACTIVE ENDEAVOR in the area—[and] all MDA activities are almost linked to NATO's system and V-RMTC.

In that regard, to be committed to working with partners, allies, and neighbors to limit the operational space of potential threats by posing greater regional and international cooperation, information sharing, exercise, and operation deployments should be considered. However, we are mindful of the fact that political apathy and technical difficulties are the main hindrances in this effort, but those hindrances can be overcome by the common willingness.

Without forgetting or neglecting that each country has its own unique characteristics and therefore approaches like "one size fits all" don't work in this situation, we should work together to extend our support to the countries in need of technical assistance.

The main thing is a matter of will, and these gatherings are exceptional opportunities, like ISS, for us to reach a common understanding that global peace, security, and stability can be successful through nations' efforts and regional cooperation and coordination. In this sense some progress is made.

Also, thanks to gatherings like the Venice Regional Seapower Symposium and Black Sea navies' commander meeting gatherings, similar to this one, although smaller, but in any case, these are the platforms where we can discuss maritime issues together.

Lastly, with the advancements achieved over the last decade [inaudible], the Black Sea, Mediterranean Sea, and Caspian region clearly can be used as an example of how to get different players in order to produce adequate MDA. Thank you very much.

CARIBBEAN

Professor Thomas Culora:

Thank you, Captain. I would now like to invite Lieutenant Commander Dindial from Trinidad to speak about the Caribbean Sea regional breakout group.

Lieutenant Commander Norman Dindial, Trinidad and Tobago:

Admiral Greenert, Admiral Christenson, chiefs of navies and coast guards, other senior officers, good day.

First of all, I would like to thank my regional counterparts for keeping with the tradition and volunteering me to present on behalf of my group. Thanks very much, and I appreciate the opportunity to speak before this illustrious grouping.

Good day. I am Lieutenant Commander Norman Dindial from Trinidad [and] Tobago, Defence Force Coast Guard. I have the simple task this afternoon of providing an overview and brief summary of the dialogue and key points produced by the Caribbean cell breakout group.

This group—the majority of member states comprising small island developing states and, to a lesser extent, islands belonging to provinces of larger kingdoms and sovereignties—has a diverse cultural, economic, and ethnic background.

The eastern Caribbean has one major commonality. The great majority of the islands all have had or still retain strong colonial ties and heritages. This genesis has led to the formulation of great compatibility within the region's domestic laws, as reflected by coastal states in enactment of their domestic legislation. I refer particularly to the Westminster style of government which we've seen in the region.

The majority of small island developing states within the region have all signed on in part to various United Nations conventions, including the most recognized and agreed-on today, United Nations Conventions on the Laws of Sea, UNCLOS 1982. This has allowed the coastal states to claim their respective territorial seas and exercise their legislative and criminal control within the different maritime zones and boundaries.

The coastal states themselves, although having various degrees of jurisdiction within the maritime boundaries, seem to fall short. The problem exists with

Caribbean

1. Greatest Concern: Cooperation between countries is essential. Criminals see the Caribbean without borders. This has a potential magnifying effect of a problem in one country within the region impacting the stability and security of the broader region
2. Identification of the weak link is exploited by the trafficker
3. Primary Threats: Illegal Immigration, Drug Trafficking, Humans Trafficking and Small Arms Trafficking
4. Challenges: Effective regional response to catastrophic incidents and potential long-term economic impacts. Possibility of post-catastrophic event terrorist activity and relationships

enforcement of the jurisdiction within the coastal state's control. The reasons may vary from the lack of resources to interdict and prosecute [or] inadequate funding to maintain assets to perform these tasks to ministerial challenges within the state's local framework.

Whatever may be the reason, this has led to the criminal elements viewing the region as having a noneffective border control. These elements have capitalized on these gaps that have existed. States within the region with stronger water protection are therefore looked on as hard targets, refocusing and diverting criminal activity to coastal states that are perceived to be weak links. One such example that comes to mind is a recent state of emergency that was declared by Trinidad and Tobago in order to strengthen our maritime borders. This has resulted in other states within the region, such as Grenada, seeing more illicit activity being focused and pushed towards the northern islands.

The major types of activities identified by the group, however, are trafficking in illegal arms and psychotropic substances, illegal immigration and human trafficking to a lesser extent. All the region has various challenges specific to individual coastal states. The group focused on one element that attracts international attention and support and that transcends throughout the maritime boundaries. This one specifically relates to humanitarian aid and response to catastrophic events.

There are many items and frameworks that have been developed throughout the region through the hosting of the Cricket World Cup, the Summit of the Americas, and the Caribbean Heads of Government meetings that all have been recently concluded. There is a consensus throughout the group, however, that the region should strengthen the mechanisms that exist, such as the Caribbean Disaster and

Emergency Management Agency (CDEMA), to better support the states when the need arises, to access both regional and foreign assistance.

The group crystalized these in the four points that we can see on the board today. That's a summary for the group's participation. Thank you very much, sir.

NORWEGIAN, NORTH, AND BALTIC SEAS

Professor Thomas Culora:

Thank you, Commander.

I would now like to invite up to the podium Commodore Amundsen from Norway who will speak about the Norwegian, North, and Baltic Seas regional breakout group.

Commodore Henning Amundsen, Norway:

Admiral Christenson, Admiral Greenert, distinguished leaders of the navies, ladies and gentlemen, I'm honored to stand here, privileged. The word "Norwegian" was probably the reason why I was chosen in the group. The high-intensity maritime cooperation in the northern area is gathered around the Baltic and has been so for a long time. Most Baltic countries are involved, except Russia. The model is expanding from its beginnings in Swedish and Finnish cooperation. There is an annual rotating chair. Now Denmark holds the chair.

I. High Intensity Maritime Cooperation

1. **Examples**
   1. Baltic Sea Surveillance Centers
   2. Ordnance disposal (de-mining)
   3. BALTOPS
   4. North Coast Exercises
2. **Methods**
   1. Bottom-up approach, practice driven
   2. Multiple organizational memberships
   3. Interwoven, voluntary information sharing
   4. Focus on common standards, not common hardware
   5. Growing and flexible membership

All navies deliver information to the national fusion centers. Each country shares the information that [it] wish[es] to. There is no single fusion center in the system.

It's essential that the officers manning the Sea Surveillance Centers know each other at staff levels and are completely comfortable picking up the phone, knowing who will answer. This has increased information sharing and building confidence.

I have to say, by the examples here, it's really trained and exercised regularly. Related to the ordnance disposal and de-mining, there is a Baltic Ordnance Safety Board taking care of that. We all know the training in the Baltic, which is the U.S.-led BALTOPS exercise. Then, as NATO has decreased its exercises in the area, there are North Coast Exercises, so the nations in the area take responsibility, especially Germany, Denmark, Norway. The method used has been a bottom-up approach. It's been practice driven. There was multiple organization of membership. However, it's different in each nation. Nations decide on a voluntary basis what information they would like to share.

It's the focus on common standards, not common hardware. The reason for that is that nations have different interests. If you go for one system, some nations lose.

There is a growing and flexible membership. Russia is invited. I have to say that Russia was actually participating, but stopped in 2006. The UK has applied for membership. My own nation, we are not a member, but observers in the Baltic. I think the simple reason for that is the fact that once you go outside of the Baltic Sea, you come to the North Sea and the Norweigian Sea, and we built a joint operational picture on maritime domain awareness with the NATO nations in the area, and different systems apply.

However, we have asked the Baltic nations, as we have the same sharing of information between customs, the police, and the navies. Whenever someone needs something, they pick up the phone and there is one number to dial, and we can sort it out. It's also exercised.

I also would like to say in the growing and flexible numbers here, EU development is a key issue as well. The EU has an active agenda regarding MDA at the moment. A common approach is being developed for not only the Baltic, but also the Atlantic and Mediterranean areas. Seven European countries are actively involved in this effort.

As I understand within the breakout group, the aim is to build a Europe-wide picture, so there are not so many separate systems. How that will evolve? I don't know. We had a chat about challenges to further cooperation and identified those three main focuses or challenges. The limit of state capacity shouldn't limit the work or progress. Because we all believe there's extremely good work going on, we should continue to improve relations in the region and within the group. That—everybody concedes that point.

[In] going for automated systems, which I am sure they have seen in the Mediterranean as well, there's a lot of false alarms. So there is still work to be done if you want to have a completely automated system. The idea must be that if you get AIS information and other information built into one system, you have to have some filtering to pick up what you want to look at.

That is a challenge. There is a huge amount of information. It should be possible to use maximum machine automation in order to ease the work. The key enabler in the Baltic has been that there is a common vision, there is a deep well of trust. I was told the model had been exported to an extent and the African Partnership Station was mentioned as one of those.

II. Challenges to Further Cooperation

1. **Patchwork of institutions**
   a) Efficiency costs
   b) Information leaks (to third parties)
2. **Budgetary constraints**
   a) How to maintain momentum?
   b) Limits of state capacity
3. **Too much information**
   a) Too many alarms

III. Export this model?

1. **Key enablers**
   a) Common vision
   b) Deep well of trust
2. **The model is already being exported to an extent**
   a) Africa Partnership Station
3. **Arctic challenge in the near and medium term?**
   a) Baltic as prototype?
   b) Arctic nations will agree …. ☺

Then the challenges came up. If we went to the Barents region further north and maybe there was a possibility to use the Baltic agreement as a model, but as I see it, the Arctic issue is mainly one for the five Arctic nations. As you are all aware, and my Russian friends as well, we have signed an agreement on the border, and there was a number of joint efforts under way. We work closely together with the Russians, both the navy and the coast guard, and we have biannual exercises. POMOR is the national one where it's Norway and Russia.

There is an exercise called NORTHERN EAGLE, which is U.S.-driven, which I'm sure will be up for discussion to open it up for the five nations in the Arctic. That is my view. The Arctic nations will agree with a little smile. I'm sure that when we sit down around the table with all those five nations, we'll come to a common understanding and solution for the best for the region. That concludes our work. We feel we are comfortable with what is going on in the region. We believe that we are on the right track, and there is a high amount of willingness to share information. Thank you.

GULF OF GUINEA AND GULF OF ADEN

Professor Thomas Culora:

Commodore, thank you very much. I would now like to invite up here Rear Admiral Higgs from South Africa. Admiral Higgs will speak to us about the regional breakout group that dealt with the Gulf of Guinea and the Gulf of Aden.

Rear Admiral Robert Higgs, South Africa:

Admiral Greenert, Admiral Christenson, admirals, delegates, distinguished guests, I'm delighted to stand here today as a first-generation South African talking [about] the issues of my continent. The issues with regard to Africa are becoming more and more pertinent, primarily as a result of piracy. However, as we focus on piracy, it is imperative that we do not neglect the other issues of the continent beyond piracy—the poaching of natural resources from people outside the continent; the inability of coastal nations to actually secure what rightfully belongs to the people of Africa; illicit trafficking; human trafficking; the issue of drugs, etc.; the need to protect free trade. But I think one must see it in that broad context.

Gulf of Guinea and Gulf of Aden

Key Challenges
- Sea-Blindness
- Need for regional maritime strategic frameworks
- Naval capability is limited and unevenly distributed

Information-Sharing Issues
- Impressive progress has been made!
- Language, coordination, and compatibility challenges persist
- More training, exercises, and interaction needed

In that context I would like to kick off with the first thing which we discussed. Chris Jesparrow facilitated a very good session with nearly twenty-four nations who were discussing the issues of the Gulf of Aden and the Horn of Africa. Probably the most visible and the most enduring issue and concern amongst everybody there was the issue of sea blindness.

It's the issue of sea blindness, and in our continent it's possibly also a function of our colonial past where the focus was internal. We have to change that around, and we have to get that thing turned around. I will tell you now what we are doing about that.

The reality is that sea blindness has led to significant capacity problems in the navies and the coast guards of the African continent. Maritime forces do not get the resources and the political support which they need to actually get on top of the situation.

This is a result largely of a land-based cultural mind-set, an absence of a maritime culture, [and] a lack of understanding of the importance of the sea and the wealth which the sea brings to the people. This pervades amongst political people, but also military officers who are non-naval.

There is little understanding, also, of the difficulties it takes in raising a navy, because, right, a navy is not only raised; it's in maintaining a navy and in operating a navy and making sure that it works that way. The broad feeling is that political leaders and citizens need to be sensitized and educated to the importance of the sea and naval and maritime forces.

The issue is for the people, the navies, the maritime people, the coast guard people of the continent to stand together and use seminars, symposiums, educational programs, etc., to instill what needs to be instilled.

Currently the AU, the African Union, is also a victim of sea blindness, but that is changing. [It] needs to view things more holistically. But at the same time what has happened in the last few months is the issues concerning piracy, particularly from the SADC [South African Development Community] side, has created an opportunity for common purpose. That is what I'm going to speak to now.

At the 2003 International Seapower Symposium, four Navy leaders got together. It was [the] naval chiefs of Ghana, Kenya, Nigeria, and South Africa. They said they have to emulate the ISS. That resulted in the first Seapower for Africa Symposium being held.

There were twenty-four nations, twenty-four African nations, who attended that. We invited nobody external to the continent. It was just the continent. It was not meant to be secret, but we had to get our act together first, because this is a new Africa.

I can recall being at the War College in 1994, 1995. People said if you got seven or eight African countries together, you were lucky. We had twenty-four. It was a good start. That was in Cape Town. Then we followed up with our second Seapower for Africa Symposium, which was held in 2006 in Abuja, and the Nigerians did it better than us. We went in there, and together we made sure that it started moving up. It was good.

We reported back on what had been achieved since the first Seapower for Africa Symposium. In fact, it made such an impact that President Obasanjo invited the naval delegates to his farm palace afterwards and hosted us. It was wonderful.

Then the third Seapower for Africa Symposium took place in 2009. In 2009 we had thirty-four African nations present. We invited a number of people, as in Nigeria, from outside the continent, and we had twelve nations from outside the continent, largely at three-star level, who came to Cape Town. It was very successful. We started pulling things tighter and tighter together.

The fourth Seapower Symposium was scheduled for Libya. Of course, other things happened. At the moment Senegal is about to host the fourth Seapower for Africa Symposium at the end of next year. What I'm telling you is Africa is getting its act together.

Simultaneously, when piracy started coming into the waters off Mozambique, to the SADC water—South Africa's a member of SADC—our authorities said we have to do something about this. We can't have the scourge coming into our waters.

The chief of the navy, together with our defense minister, started rallying around, in an interagency, interdepartmental way, to rally the resources and the brains of our country on how to get on top of the issue. That was handled very successfully by our defense minister. After that, the authorities went around to mobilize SADC because South Africa alone cannot fight pirates. We are, at the moment, in the process of formalizing a SADC maritime security strategy—and those are the countries from Tanzania, [Democratic Republic of the Congo], and Angola southwards, to pull things together. Since early this year we had a frigate continuously stationed off Mozambique, ensuring that piracy doesn't come further south. If it is not a South African mission, it's a SADC mission. That is the important thing to note. At the same time as we talk about the Indian Ocean, in the Atlantic Ocean, we also had one of our 12,000-ton combat support ships deployed for eighty-two days off there, in conjunction with a number of Gulf of Guinea states, helping bring common purpose and an African agenda, two things, because de facto we couldn't deliver the consequences of that. That is where we are now.

We've just heard in the next few weeks the issue of a maritime security strategy is going to be tabled at the AU. The reality is that if we want to turn Africa around, we [have] got to get the AU asking the governments how their navies are coming on, and how their coast guards are coming on, and what they are doing with regard to interoperability, and how they are potentially interfacing with SADC and interfacing with each other to come up with other regional ways of getting on top of the issue.

In the nature of the game in our continent, as our chief of the navy plays most magnificently, he is to go around and to get people to buy into things, to consult, and to talk, and to get things going. The reality is our country, or our continent, is probably the wealthiest of our continents, but it's also the poorest. We have to somehow bring back confidence to the continent and get things going there.

As I was saying, this is central to it. There is a common purpose here. In a nutshell, that is what has been happening with regard to activities. There's a lot of training which is going on, which was kicked off in 2005 with the first Seapower for Africa Symposium. There are a lot more people from the continent who are doing staff courses in other African nations' staff colleges.

I bumped into a young sublieutenant a few minutes ago who was in our combat officers'—our SWOS [Surface Warfare Officers School] course a year back. We're starting to get on top of things. At the same time I was delighted to see the international SWOS desk here encouraging people to participate in the four courses.

The reality is we can start getting ships into Africa, and we're going to do that. It's the people, preparing the people, which is going to take a lot longer. That is the way to move.

In our discussions we also said what is, in particular focusing on the U.S. Navy, the preeminent navy, what are they doing to attract? Are we appreciating it?

I think there was a great sense of appreciation, particularly for the IMET [International Military Education and Training] program, for the War College for getting the African naval leadership of today and tomorrow to come to do the NCC, to do the [Naval Staff College], to do SWOS, to do everything like this. This is remarkable, sir.

People remarked on this. When we said what about the U.S., because obviously you [are] hosting this, we need to talk to you. That was perceived to be very good in building capacities of the navies and also helping tackling sea blindness, helping build up expertise and commonality.

Your other tangible programs, which you are involved in at the moment which are highly regarded—and of course, those are largely on a bilateral basis, so I can't go into details on that—they are recognized, and they are very, very good.

The issue which also came up was how the major players in the world can somehow help overcome sea blindness in the political leadership of our continent. The big thing was possibly when people from state or foreign affairs come and visit your country, if you can somehow get there to be a navy point in the agenda.

Navies are very, very well received today. In fact, one of the things which our defense minister is trying to do in rebuilding South Africa from our very difficult past is bringing in a youth service. It's not conscription. It's a youth service, but the leadership of the country wants it based on the navy culture, because the navy culture is what is held in high esteem.

It comes from people living together with care for your fellow shipmate, living together in very difficult circumstances for a long time in a hostile environment, and making it work. That is being used at the moment in our country to build our nation, sir. So in a way the navy message has got to get out. I could appeal not only to the United States, but to other nations. If you have leadership coming in, don't leave the political leadership on [its] own. Those are the targets. We must get them in to overcome sea blindness globally. They must come in, and you must show them what you are doing in your naval academies, show them what you are doing, show them how you can get people to do 24/7 stuff. Politeness, respect for authority, respect for everybody else, particularly in this new era, it is very important.

Coming down further into it, the issue with regard to, in our case, helping Africans to build Africa is very important. The old paternalistic colonial days are yesterday's days. That's short term. We have to turn that around. People are going to see it in a different way.

I really enjoyed what Professor Rubel put on his table when he talked about MDA war gaming. He said to respect each nation in [its] own right. Each navy is a sovereign navy in itself. There may be these capable, or more capable navies, but there is no such thing as a second-class or third-class navy.

I think, sir, what comes through here is most definitely that each navy is treated with great respect. It is the ethos of the War College. It is wonderful. It is very good.

It helps build the self-esteem of everybody, from the tiniest of navies right through to the most powerful of navies.

Sir, in closing, thank you very much, indeed, for the opportunity. We had a great discussion with almost twenty-four African representatives. One of the issues which we had is language. How do we overcome the language thing?

I'm very fortunate; my mother tongue is English. There are not many people who speak English as a first language. You have to be aware of that and be sensitive to bring people together so that they can communicate and feel forgiven when they don't speak perfect English. We have to go along that way, and it will help us get on top of it.

With regard to the hardware, the hardware will come. I know that. The hardware can come very quickly. South Africa has programs in place at the moment, and I'm sure a lot of other nations have also. The big thing is the human capital. We have to get the human capital going as soon as possible, the human capital as it is now. Also, as I mentioned, the target is the political decision makers. We have to get them to understand. We have to unshackle their minds. I think that's it. Sir, thank you very much, indeed, for the opportunity.

ARABIAN GULF AND OMAN SEA

Professor Thomas Culora:

Admiral, thank you very much. I would now like to call up our last speaker for the afternoon of the regional breakout groups, Commander Abdulla from the United Arab Emirates. He will talk to us about the Arabian Gulf and the Oman Sea.

Commander Abdulla Sultan Hassan Al Khozaimy, United Arab Emirates:

Admiral Greenert, Chief of Naval Operations, U.S. Navy; Rear Admiral Christenson; chiefs of the world navies and coast guards; ladies and gentlemen, I represent the Arabian Gulf and Oman Sea group report. I thought at the beginning that we are the only group that had the challenge to nominate the speaker. It doesn't surprise me, and I didn't prepare a lot of words to say, but I'm not going to repeat what we heard from the previous group speakers.

Since yesterday, we've been listening to the guest speakers, and the panel speakers, and most of them, they highlight the importance of information sharing and the military domain awareness.

Also yesterday we listened to the speech of the commander of the United Arab Emirates Navy. He highlighted the importance of the Arabian Gulf, and he mentioned the huge amount of commerce using the Arabian Gulf, from oil production and infrastructures and the area.

So we discussed the challenges and the antipiracy information sharing. We highlighted the interoperability and equipment, so for the GCC [Gulf Cooperation Council] countries and GCC navies, I don't think we have any issues in this, but you all know that in the Arabian Gulf and Oman Sea there are a lot of partners over there sailing.

So the issue of government matching in communication and providing channels for new information, for classified information—right now, in the GCC, we are

Arabian Gulf/Oman Sea

1. **Principle Challenges to Anti-Piracy Information sharing**
   a) Interoperability/Equipment
2. **Principle Challenges to Piracy Response**
   a) International Legal framework
   b) Interoperability
3. **Regional Maritime Security Initiatives**
   a) Continue to support and broaden participation in ongoing series of conferences/workshops/regional forums
   b) Broaden anti-piracy discussion to include networks, financiers etc.

connected through the Naval Operations Centers, and we have a Naval Coordination Center down in Bahrain, established in the area in 2010.

The issue is—the challenge here is the interoperability and equipment with the partners, the players down sailing in the area of Arabian Gulf and Oman Sea.

The second point was the principal challenges to piracy response. We discussed, our group, that international legal framework. As we listen to the guest speakers and some of the guest speakers and panels, most of the countries of international security, they have the political will, but we don't have the road map to address this from the United Nations, or the Security Council, under any mandate or any resolution.

We know most of the piracy comes from Somalia. We in the Arabian Gulf, we don't report anything until now, any piracy incident. Only we report some thuggery and human trafficking in the Arabian Gulf. Most of these, in Oman Sea, the Gulf of Aden, are as my previous speakers or my previous group speakers have highlighted.

We are within national legal framework to address this through the United Nations or the Security Council. Funding, this issue, funding through United Nations—there is a lot of activity going on over there. A lot of navies are sailing around the Gulf of Aden, those from EU, under Fifth Fleet command, or under CTF 30. There were different countries available there, China, India—they are separate. So for coordination and effort, unity of effort, to be vital, we think that if things will come through the United Nations or the Security Council it will be more of a resolution. It will be more of a benefit.

We all know that Somalia is a failing state. We in the United Arab Emirates, in early 2010, we hosted a forum under the Ministry of Foreign States addressing the Somalia issue and the piracy issue. Also, we hosted different bilateral forums addressing this piracy. Because, yes, United Arab Emirates, for example, most of the GCC countries, they are away from Gulf of Aden. As you know, the oil and commerce and the trade which we receive and transfer through the sea are very important. We have ships using that, ships using those roads.

The third point is regional maritime security initiative. We and GCC, we have bilateral [partnerships], and we have the GCC Head of Navies Conferences and meetings annually and seasonally, and at any time. On this issue we do not have any problem. We will continue to support and broaden the participation with an ongoing series of conferences.

For example, we hosted in the middle of 2010 the IONS, Indian Ocean Naval Symposium, down in UAE. This is enhancing maritime security down, not only in the Indian Ocean and the Arabian Gulf. I think this symposium is a great opportunity to all the participants in this symposium to highlight maritime demands that we have.

Also, we host and participate in many workshops hosted by the Fifth Fleet commander, under NAVCENT [Naval Forces Central Command], or bilateral, or GCCs also, and regional forums, as I said, like IONS. We are looking forward to broadening the anti-piracy discussion to include networks and financing and commerce, the shipping companies, to include them in this reform.

In conclusion, we think that we have to address and we have to hold the international will with our partners, and we have to work closely with our partners in order to have better coordination channels for flow of information and better maritime domain awareness. Thank you for listening.

Professor Thomas Culora:

Thank you very much. Well, whether they were volunteered or [were] in some cases, conscripted, pulling these briefings together is really no easy task. I would like to, first of all, thank the moderators from around the War College [who] helped do that, but certainly I want to extend a special thank you to all of the presenters who gave their time and energy to share some very important insights and concerns within your region. Again, a round of applause for everyone who presented. Great job.

9

An Address

Dr. Nicholas Eberstadt
American Enterprise Institute for Public Policy and Research

Professor Thomas Culora:

Good morning, Admiral Greenert, Admiral Christenson, distinguished leaders of navies and coast guards around the world. I trust you all had an enjoyable evening last night. It was truly wonderful to see everyone there, especially with your spouses. It looked to me like everyone was having a nice time.

Now it is my great pleasure to introduce our next speaker, Dr. Nicholas Eberstadt. Dr. Eberstadt is a political economist and demographer by training. He did his undergraduate work at Harvard University and holds two master's degrees, one from the Kennedy School of Government at Harvard and another from the London School of Economics. He received his PhD in political economy and government, also at Harvard University.

He is currently a senior advisor to the National Bureau of Asian Research, member of the Visiting Committee at the Harvard School of Public Health, and a member of the Global Leadership Council at the World Economic Forum. He researches and writes extensively on economic development, foreign aid, global health, demographics, and poverty.

He is the author of numerous monographs and articles on North and South Korea, East Asia, and countries of the former Soviet Union. He has written several books; his most recent title is from 2008, *The Poverty of "the Poverty Rate."* In this book he highlights how income-based measures of poverty cannot offer a faithful portrait of consumption patterns or material well-being.

Dr. Eberstadt has [served] or is currently serving on a number of boards and councils, including as current commissioner of the Key National Indicators Council, member of the Global Agenda Council, and the World Economic Forum. He's a member of the Visiting Committee at the Harvard School of Public Health, and a senior advisor on the National Bureau of Asian Research.

He also serves as a consultant to the World Bank, U.S. State Department, the U.S. Agency for International Development, and the U.S. Bureau of the Census. You can see he's a very busy person. We're very fortunate to have him with us this morning. I hope you're looking forward to Dr. Eberstadt's remarks as much as I am. Please, join me in welcoming to the podium Dr. Nicholas Eberstadt from the American Enterprise Institute for Public Policy and Research.

Dr. Nicholas Eberstadt:

Thank you for that. Professor Culora, thank you for that lovely introduction. Ladies and gentlemen, it's an honor for me to have an opportunity to talk with such a distinguished group. It's also a pleasure for me. I was at the dinner last night, and I saw some of the *bonhomie* and the camaraderie that has developed in your group over these last few days. When you talk about partnerships developing for securing prosperity and peace in the future—what a wonderful example I thought that was.

I'm going to talk in the next few minutes about the role of demographics in international security over the next several decades. We can look ahead twenty years with respect to population trends for the world. We can't project economic trends forward twenty years. We certainly can't project political trends forward twenty years, but we have a secret weapon in looking at demographic profiles twenty years from now.

Quite simply it is this: The overwhelming majority of people who will be in the world twenty years from now are already alive here today. So we know a lot about what the future labor force of the world is going to look like. We know a lot about what the retirement/pensioner population is going to look like.

These changing trends have a direct impact on economic potential, on social stability, and other important factors that bear upon international security. If we look at the trends that are emerging now and we look at the profile of the world twenty years from now as best we can today, we see we are going to be entering into a very challenging era. It's going to be a very different era from the one we've been familiar with over the last generation.

Not Your Father's World Labor Force

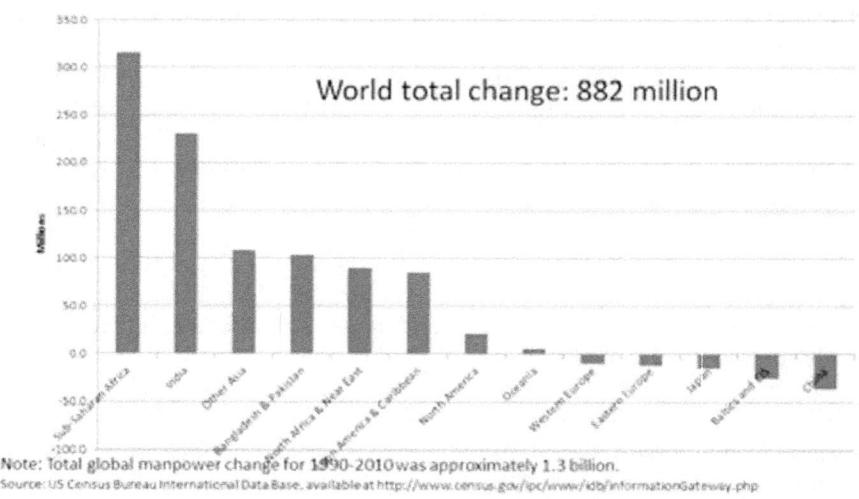

I think you can all read more rapidly than I can talk, so let me say something else while you're looking at this slide. Let me give you a little bit of background, a little bit of perspective. All of us in this room are children of the global population explosion. We were all born in the twentieth century. In the twentieth century the world's population did something it had never done before. It grew by a factor of almost four. It almost quadrupled between 1900 and the year 2000.

The reason the world's population exploded during the last century was not because people suddenly started breeding like rabbits; it's because they finally stopped dying like flies. Between 1900 and the year 2000, the human life expectancy jumped from about thirty years to about sixty-five years. It's a tremendously good thing. The twentieth century really had a health explosion. The population explosion was a health explosion.

That was auspicious in so many different ways. It's one of the reasons that the world's income level almost rose fivefold over that time period. We're entering into a very different era now, driven by a very different trend. The trend that is reshaping the world at the moment is seemingly an inexorable march to subreplacement fertility, which is to say the birth patterns which have continued indefinitely would lead to a peaking and then an indefinite drop in the world's population.

We may not appreciate just how far this march towards lower birthrates has gone already. Almost half of the people in the world live in countries that are subreplacement today. Since we know that the rich countries are only a small share of the world, this means the overwhelming majority of countries with subreplacement fertility are lower-income countries. Almost all of East Asia is subreplacement, and much of Southeast Asia, much of South Asia, the Middle East increasingly, and also Latin America and the Caribbean are increasingly subreplacement.

What does subreplacement fertility do to societies? Three important things that bear on economic potential and social stability. The first is that it leads to a peaking and then an indefinite decline in manpower, unless there is compensating immigration. The second thing it does, it leads to a peaking and then an indefinite decline in total population. The third thing that it does is it leads to profound population aging, the graying of societies. It may sound counterintuitive, but it is small families rather than long lives that make for gray populations. When the base of a population pyramid is squeezed, a larger proportion of older people live in a society.

Let me show you what this means for our world and for some rising powers and for some current powers. Over the past twenty years the world's labor force, its working-age manpower, grew by about 1.3 billion people. Over the next twenty years it's going to grow by less than 900 million people.

In terms of actual tempo of growth, the world's labor force is going to be growing only half as fast over the next twenty years as it grew over the past twenty years. The composition of the world's population labor force growth is going to be very different. Over the past twenty years about half of the world's manpower growth was in India and China, which was a very lucky accident, because these were major global economic growth centers. Over the coming twenty years the lion's share of world labor force growth is going to be in sub-Saharan Africa, which is a region which still hasn't worked out its formula for sustained economic growth.

Not only that, but the working-age manpower in Europe, in Japan, and in many other developed areas is actually going to be shrinking. There is going to be a big drop in working-age manpower in China. This is going to make for a much more challenging environment for increasing prosperity in the years ahead. Some time in the years ahead we're going to get out of this global economic crisis we're in now.

Once we get out of that, it's going to be very difficult to maintain the sorts of growth rates for societies and economies around the world that we enjoyed over the past generation, on the coming generation's demographic inputs.

The narrative that I hear in Washington in international security concerns the rise of China. Over the last generation the Chinese economy has undergone the most remarkable transformation of any economy in human history. No other economy has ever grown as fast for as long as China's has done.

Quite reasonably, people tend to extrapolate the past into the future. The people who are doing that have not paid attention to China's demographic fundamentals. China is about to face a perfect demographic storm which is going to make much more difficult the task of rapid economic growth and maintaining social stability.

I'm going to try to show you why. This chart here attempts to show what China's population structure today, the blue and red graphic, will look like compared to China's population structure twenty years from now, the transparent graphic. Because of subreplacement fertility, we can see that in this future China, the China twenty years from now, every age group under fifty years of age is going to be smaller than it is in China today. On the other hand, every age group over fifty is going to be larger, and in some cases much larger, than today.

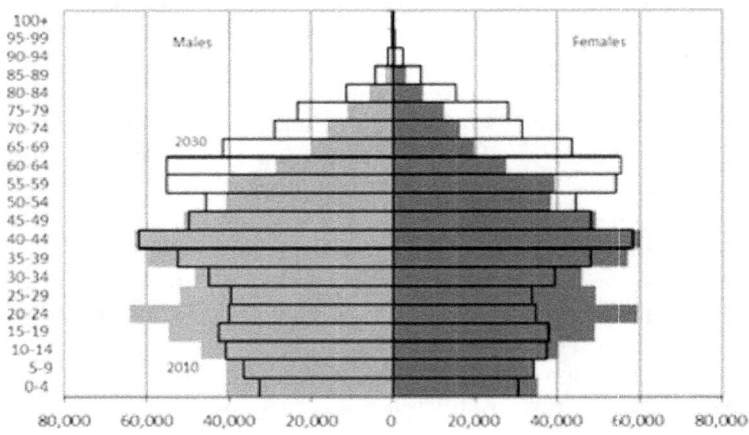

The Shape Of Trouble
Population Structure: China, 2010 vs. 2030

Source: US Census Bureau International Data Base, January 2011

What does that mean? In the period of China's remarkable economic boom, China enjoyed sustained manpower growth, over two percent a year over almost a thirty-year period. Between now and 2030, China's manpower growth is going to be negative. China's working-age population will be smaller in 2030 than it is today.

The composition of that working-age population is going to change radically. In all societies young people, new fresh blood in the labor force, are the people who

No Repeat Performances..

Adult Population 15+ by Age Group: China, 1970-2030 (estimated and projected, thousands)

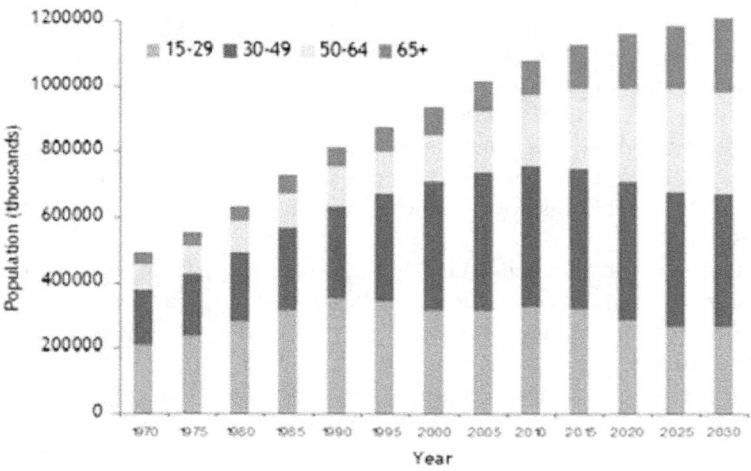

Source: Population Division of the Department of Economic and Social Affairs of the United Nations Secretariat, World Population Prospects: The 2008 Revision, http://esa.un.org/unpp, Wednesday, May 13, 2009; 2:12:34 PM. Note: "medium variant" projections

Beijing Forgot About This Population Explosion...

Estimated and Projected Population Aged 65+: China, 1980-2030

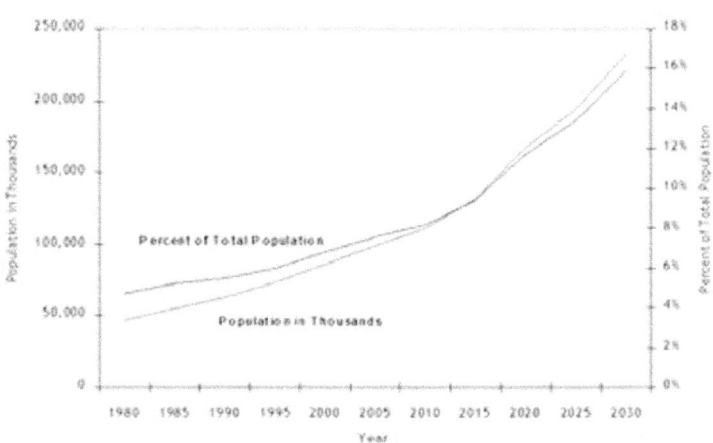

Source: Population Division of the Department of Economic and Social Affairs of the United Nations Secretariat, World Population Prospects: The 2008 Revision, http://esa.un.org/unpp, Wednesday, May 13, 2009; 2:12:34 PM. Note: "medium variant" projections

have the latest skills, the highest educational attainment, the greatest potential for improving productivity. China's young labor force is going to drop by 100 million persons between now and the year 2030. We can see this already; almost all of these people are already born.

On the other hand, there is going to be an enormous growth of people over the age of fifty in this labor pool. This will be the least healthy, the least educated segment of China's working-age population. It's going to be very different, very different input from what we've seen over the past generation. While China's working-age population will shrink, China's population of senior citizens is going to explode. In fact, it's going to be growing at over 3 percent a year between now and the year 2030 [see figure, p. 137]. China is going to be aging at a pace which is almost historically unprecedented.

The only time we've ever seen such a tempo of graying in human history before was in Japan over the past generation, but Japan became gray after it became rich. China is going to have to do it the other way around. The other way around is a whole lot less fun, let me promise you that.

In addition to the manpower squeeze and the old-age boom, China is facing something which is a bit of a science-fictional problem. We have never seen this sort of problem in a modern human society before. This is the extraordinary imbalance between little boys and little girls that has emerged over the course of the one-child policy campaign. In ordinary human societies there are about 105 baby boys for every 100 baby girls. In China today there are about 120 baby boys for every 100 baby girls. Little boys and little girls grow up to be prospective brides and grooms. So what does this mean? What it means, quite simply, is that China is facing a historically unprecedented marriage squeeze in the years ahead.

China: Where The Girls Aren't

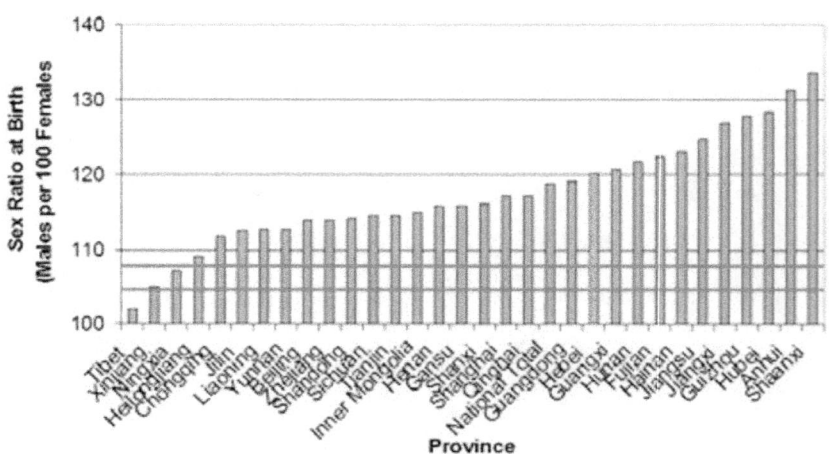

Source: 2005 China One Percent Population Survey.

Up until now, China has been a universal marriage norm society. Almost everybody expects to get married in China. What's going to happen in the years ahead? You can see what this means over here. Take young men in their late thirties. In the recent past only about 5 percent of China's men in their late thirties didn't get married. On current trends, given the marriage squeeze, over a quarter aren't going to be able to get married—for men in their early forties, over 20 percent, going from less than 3 percent up to 20 percent.

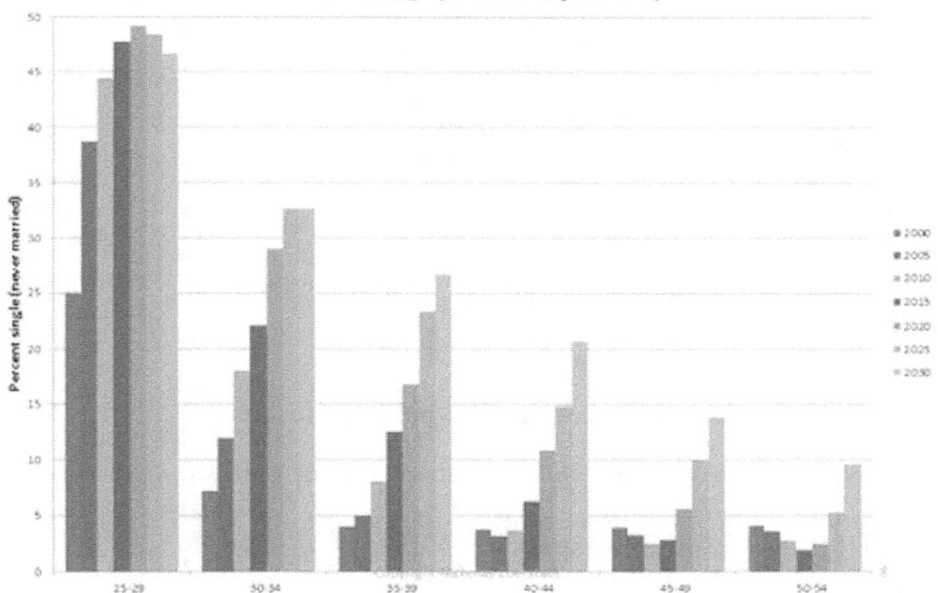

A Growing Army of Unmarriagable Men
Proportion of never-married males by age group:
China 2000-2030 (projected from Zeng et al. 2008)

What does it mean for a country like China to have a growing army of unmarriable young men in their midst? I don't know. I don't think you can know. We're going to find out in the next twenty years. Stay tuned. I don't think the impact on social stability is going to be zero [see figure, p. 140].

A word or two about Russia. I wish our Russian colleagues were here. I was hoping to discuss this with them, but I'll discuss it with you all. The Kremlin has very ambitious plans for economic rejuvenation. It's going to be very difficult to achieve those plans with Russia's demographic trends. Since the end of Communism, 13 million more people have died than have been born in Russia. Almost three deaths for every two births. Russia is on a path towards continuing depopulation, and its labor force is set to decline by 20 percent over the next two decades [see figure, p. 140].

To make the situation even more challenging, Russia has been experiencing a terrible health crisis. The mortality levels have been going in the wrong direction and are extraordinarily high for an urbanized and literate society.

Just to give you a sense of this health crisis in Russia, I've put up here a schedule, mortality schedule, we might call it, for the Netherlands. I could use the USA or any other developed country to make the same point. As we know, death rates rise

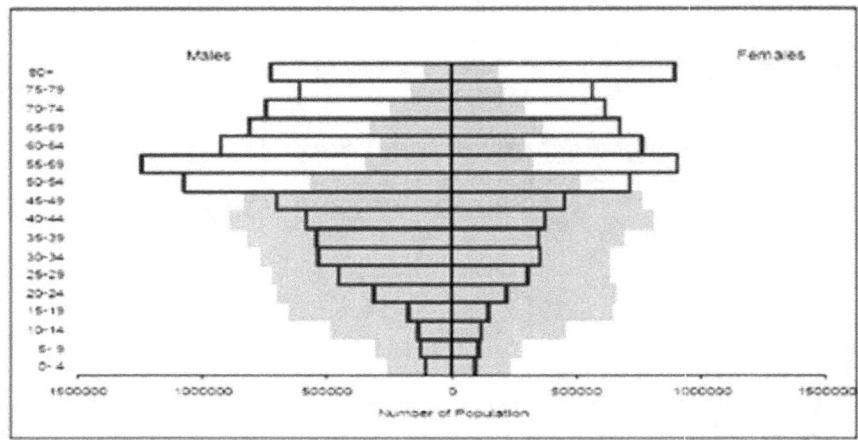

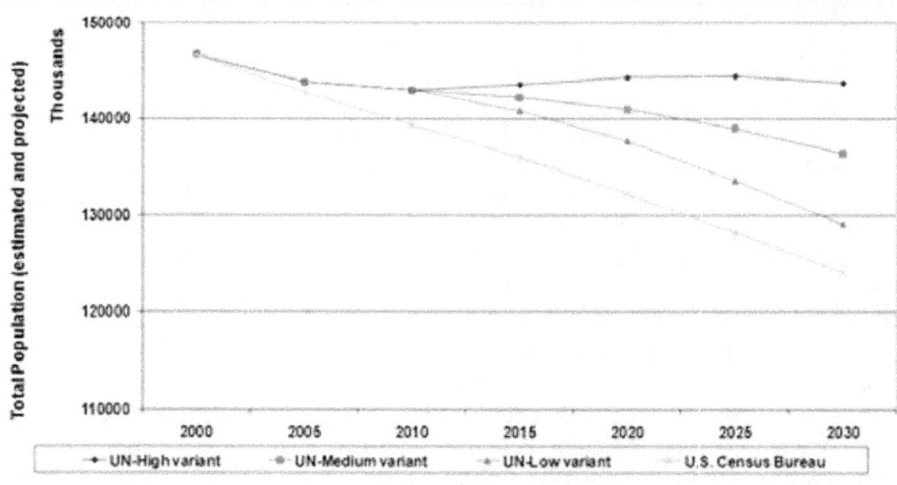

for men as they head from age thirty to age sixty, but what about the death rates of thirty-year-old men in other countries? Well, if we look at Russia's thirty-year-old men, their death rates today are about the same as death rates for fifty-eight-year-old men in the Netherlands. This gives you a sense of just how fragile the health of the Russian population is. This phenomenon has to be addressed if Russia is going to find the economic success its people want for the future.

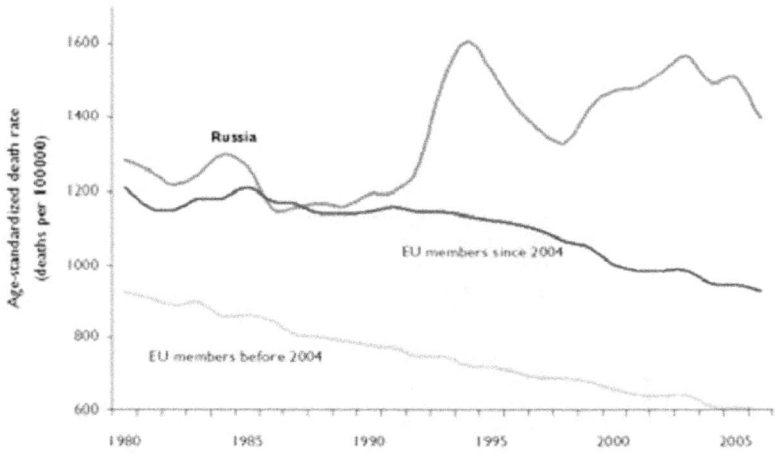

Difficult, But Not Impossible

Death rates from all causes, 1980–2006: Russia vs. EU (males plus females)

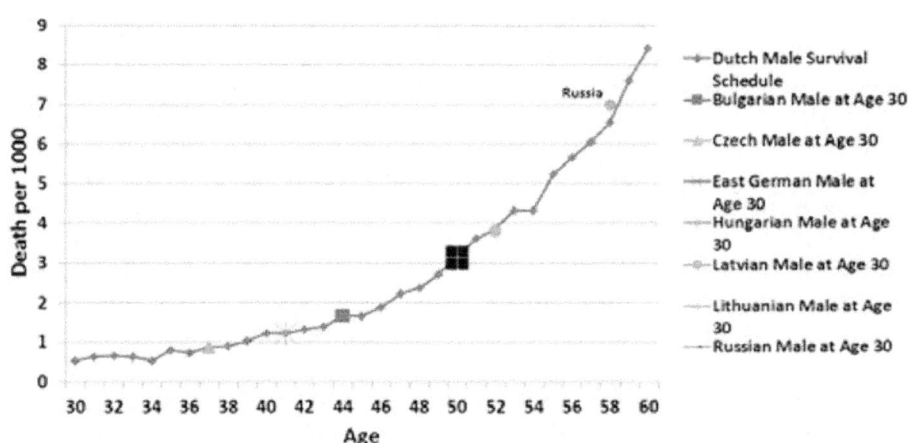

30 Is The New 58...In Russia (2008)

Mortality At Age 30 for Men In Selected Post-Socialist Countries Compared With The Dutch Male Mortality Schedule

India is another rising power. India's demographic prospects look quite promising. India is an example of what demographers talk about as a so-called demographic dividend. Over the next twenty years India's working-age population is set to grow much more rapidly than the total population, meaning a relative increase in labor force, potentially greater savings, potentially greater investment, and by this chain of logic, potentially faster economic growth.

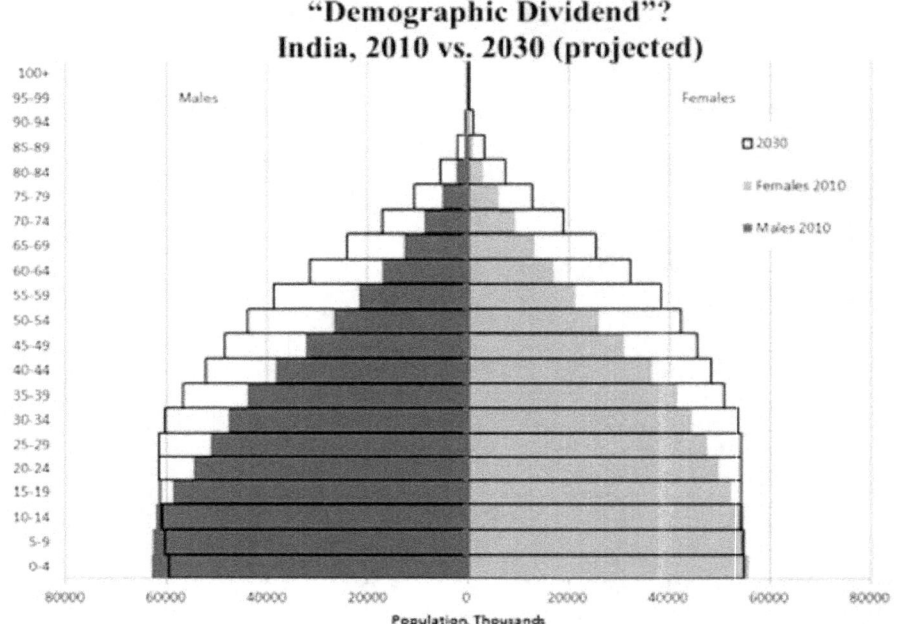

Source: US Census Bureau International Data Base

If we look at the particulars of India's situation, however, there are some issues that can't be avoided. India has enormous regional diversity, as I'm sure you all know. Part of this is demographic diversity. In northern India, in the Gangetic area and out to the west, women in India are having an average of four or five children per lifetime, whereas down in the south, in the area that used to be called the Madras Presidency, women are having two or fewer children per lifetime—an enormous difference.

This is creating two different Indias. Two different Indias are being born today. In the north there will be an India whose population structure is similar to many traditional lower-income countries, in the south, a population structure much more like Western Europe or some of the developed countries. But there is a problem here. To oversimplify, southern India is the jobs and growth factory for India and northern India is the baby factory for India. The babies that are being produced in the north do not have the educational attainment and skills which will be needed by the jobs factory in the south. All of the people that I know from India are geniuses. They're PhDs, scientists, MDs, and there are millions and millions of them.

Projected Population Structure for North India, 2025

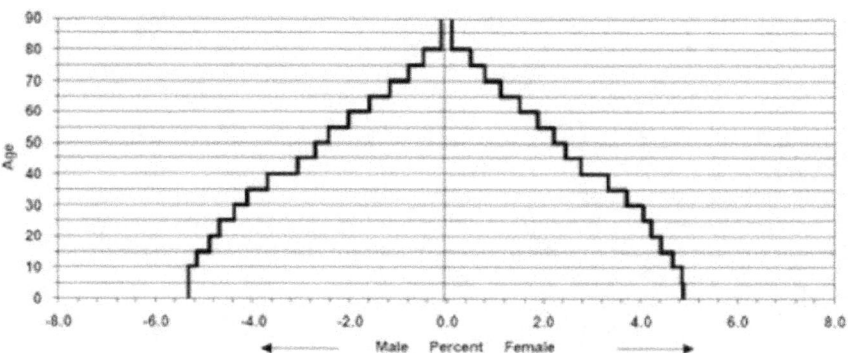

Source: Bhat, P.N. Mari, "Demographic scenario, 2025." Institute of Economic Growth, Delhi, Figure 5. Available online at http://planningcommission.nic.in/reports/sereport/ser/vision2025/demogra.pdf accessed May 2005.

Projected Population Structure for South India, 2025

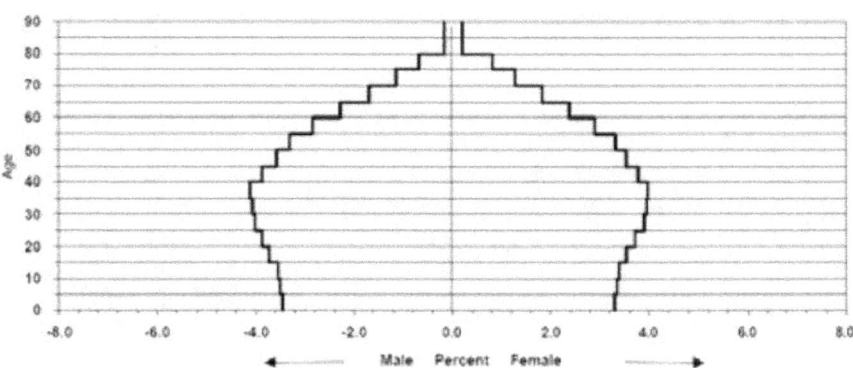

Source: Bhat, P.N. Mari, "Demographic scenario, 2025." Institute of Economic Growth, Delhi, Figure 6. Available online at http://planningcommission.nic.in/reports/sereport/ser/vision2025/demogra.pdf accessed May 2005.

The problem, however, is that there are a billion people, roughly speaking, in India's working-age population, and hundreds of millions of them have never been to school at all. Let me show you graphically what I mean. This is a slide showing China's educational attainment over time [see figure, p. 144]. You don't need to

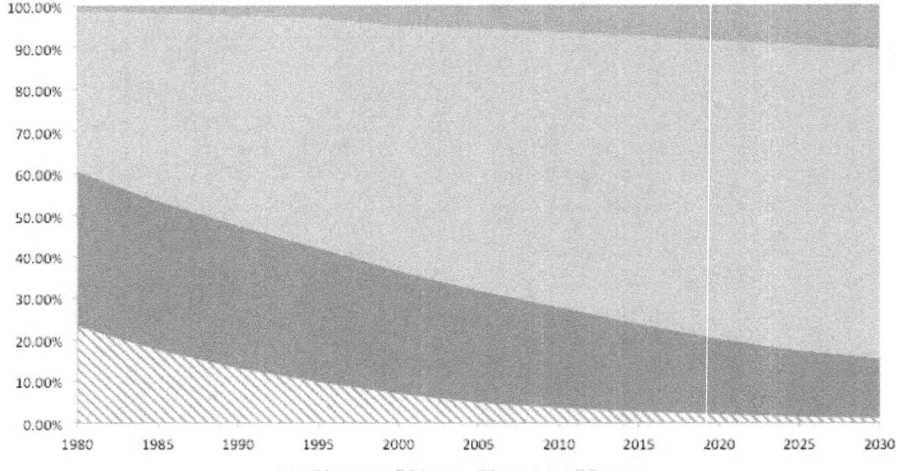

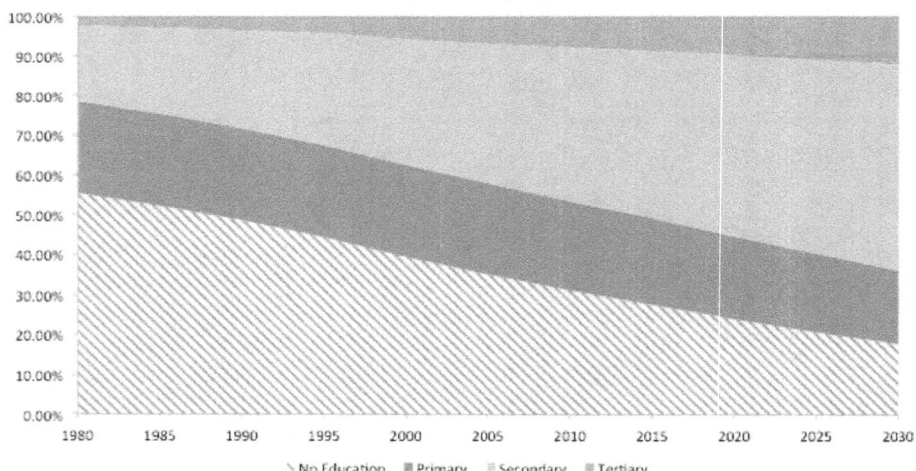

pay a great deal of attention to it. Just look at the little [striped] segment at the bottom. That's the proportion of the Chinese workforce that has never been to school from 1980 to today, projected out to the future. Just look at the share of the slide that [striped] portion takes up. I'm going to show you India's corresponding shares next. Do you see the difference? Can we go back to the previous slide, please? And now forward to India. Let's stay there. Here we are. India in 2030 will have about the same share of persons never in school in their labor force that China had fifty years earlier. This will be the challenge for India's economic rise and also to some degree for social stability.

Just a word about Japan. I don't generally say that demography is destiny, but Japan's birth trends have an immense bearing on the prospects for the future. Today the number of births in Japan is barely a third as great as it was a little over sixty years ago. Japan is on track to have only 25 percent as many births in the year 2047 as it had a hundred years earlier.

This obviously constrains not only military manpower, but many other things. I'm using the example of France to illustrate trends generally through Europe. I'm not trying to pick on France in particular. I had to select a country, so I closed my eyes.

Europe's prospects can be seen in one sense by this divergent set of lines [see figure, p. 146]. Europe has enjoyed an extraordinary health explosion over the past two generations. All of that health dividend and then some has been translated into retirement and vacation. If Europe is going to move towards a more sustained future of prosperity, European populations are going to have to have conversations among themselves about how to rearrange work, government, life, so that more of Europe's health dividend can be unlocked as value for its people. That, of course, has a bearing on defense budgets and many other things as well.

Now to the United States. America is a very strange country. We don't do things that we're supposed to do. We're an affluent country, and affluent countries in the

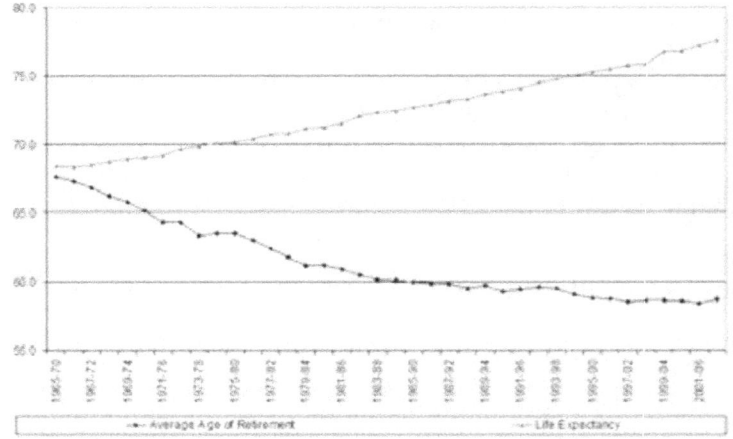

world as a whole are supposed to age rapidly and stagnate demographically, but as you can see, the United States is on pace to continue to grow moderately.

Its labor force is set to expand. It is set to be a much more youthful society than some others. Part of the reason is that America is open to immigration. Some of the immigrants who come to the United States are even legal, but in addition to this, the United States has a peculiarly high birthrate. You can see this by comparison to Europe.

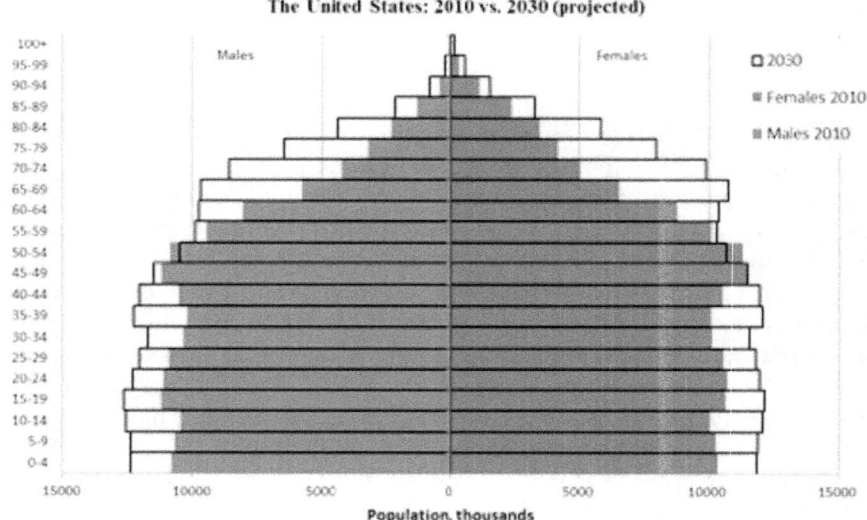

The United States birthrate went down in the 1970s, but then a funny thing happened on the way to depopulation. The United States birthrate went up to about replacement, unlike almost anyplace else in the rich world. What this means, among other things, is that the U.S. is set to account for a more or less steady proportion of the world's total population, even as Western Europe's share declines, and as Russia's share declines, and—if we were to have Japan here—as Japan's share declines [see figure, p. 148].

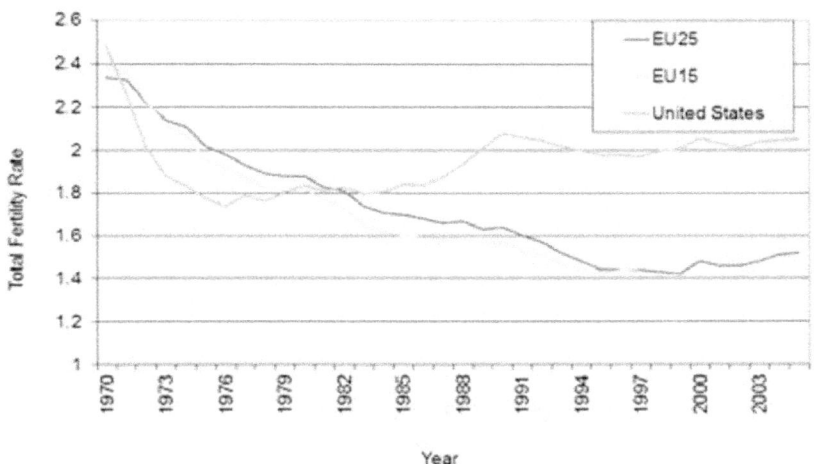

Americans Are Different
Total Fertility Rates: EU25 and EU15 v. United States, 1970-2005

Sources: Eurostat and Martin, Joyce A. et. al. "Births: Final Data for 2005." National Vital Statistics Reports, Volume 56, Number 6, December 5, 2007.

This also raises a challenge. I'll try to show you the challenge in the next couple of minutes. It's a challenge that I call the demographic divergence within the U.S. alliance system. This slightly messy graphic tries to show what's happening with the so-called median age of populations in the U.S. and in some of America's key treaty allies [see figure, p. 148].

Median age is the halfway mark in a society, bisecting between the older and the younger. So right now the median age in the United States is about thirty-six, which means that about half of our population is older than thirty-six and half younger. You see that the United States is aging much more slowly than all of our treaty allies.

You will also see that the share of people sixty-five years of age and older is rising in the United States, but not nearly as quickly as for our treaty allies [see figure, p. 149]. Their pension burdens, their claims—health claims—from older citizens are presumably going to be increasing much more dramatically over the years ahead.

While the working-age population of the United States is slated to continue to rise, the working-age population of many of our treaty allies is slated to decline, or to grow very slowly [see figure, p. 149]. This is also true for the demographic group most relevant to military manpower, which is to say trained people between the ages of fifteen and twenty-four, people who have a high school education or better.

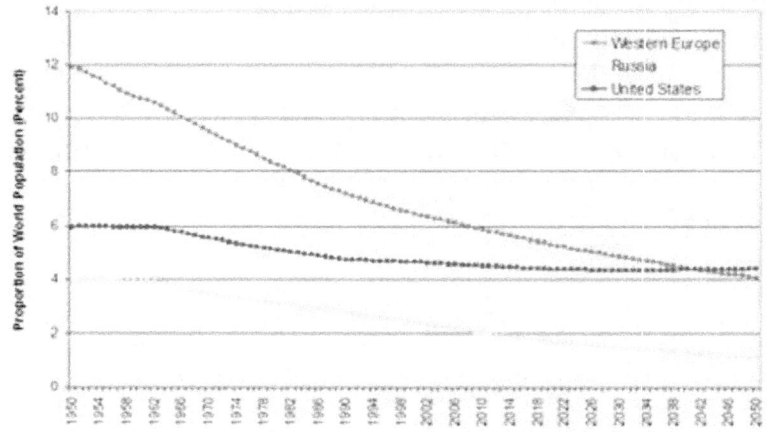

Source: US Census Bureau, International Data Base, http://www.census.gov/cgi-bin/ipc/agggen.html, accessed 10/30/2008.
Copyright Nicholas Eberstadt

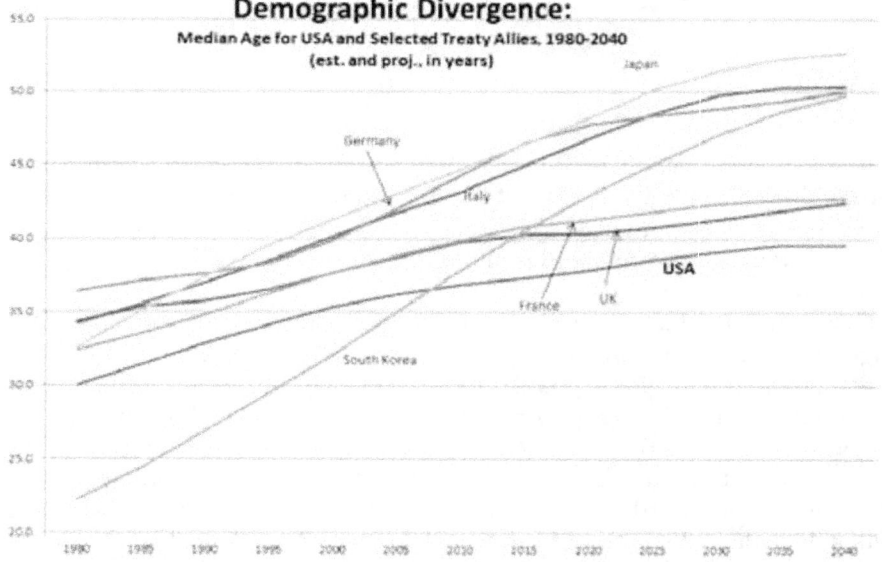

Source: US Census IDB, available at http://www.census.gov/population/international/data/idb/informationGateway.php

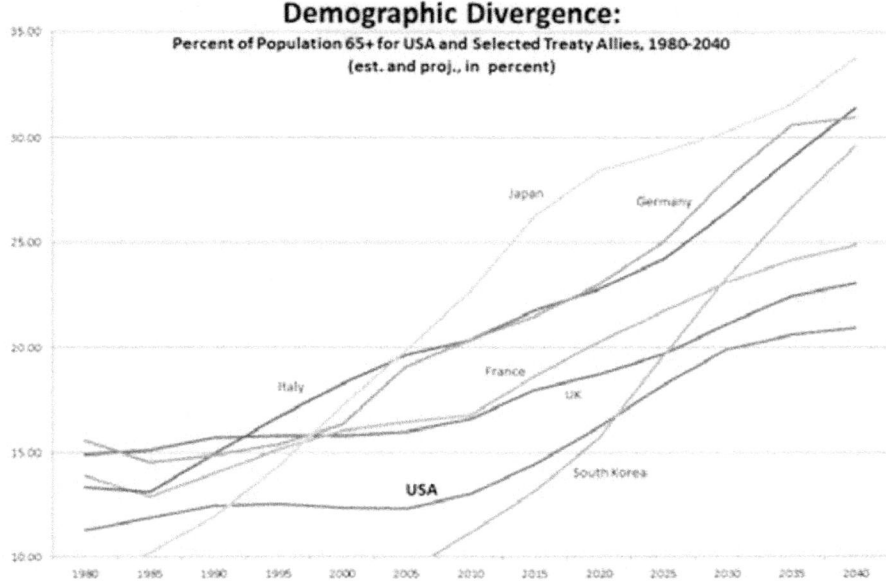

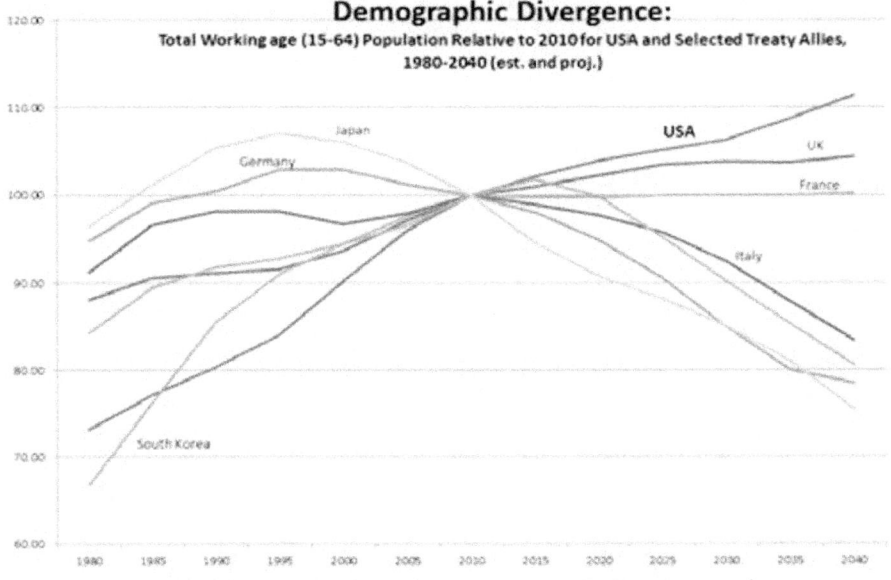

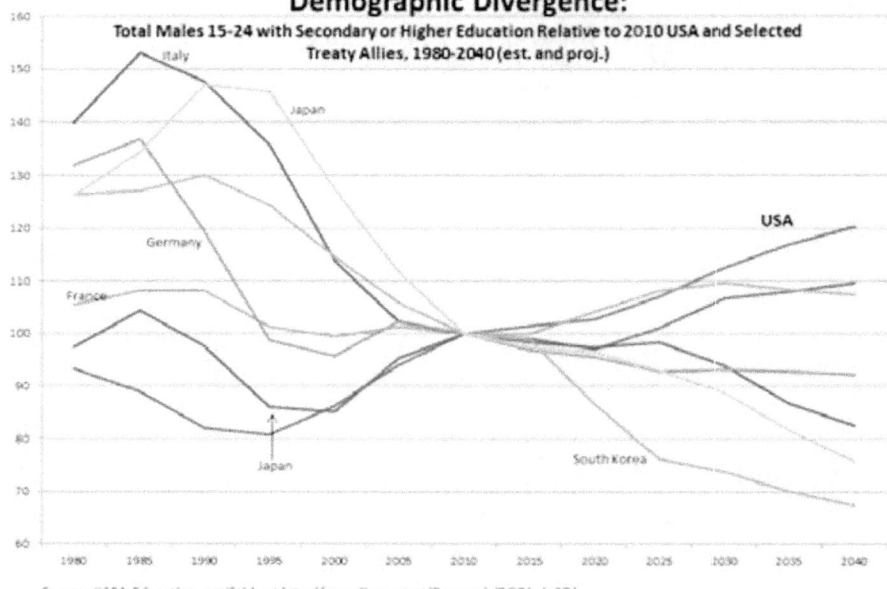

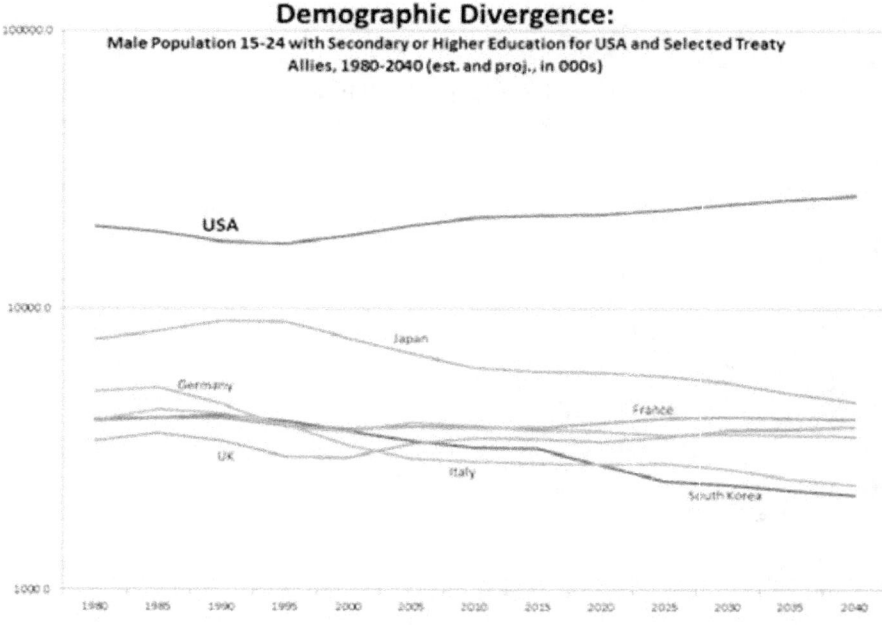

Again, you can see that from the 1990s to the indefinite future this demographic group is going to be increasing in the United States, but in some of the other treaty allies that we have, it's going to be declining, declining quite dramatically. Now, this has to have an impact on capabilities, absolute capabilities and relative capabilities for ensuring international security. It's something we need to think about, I believe, very carefully.

This is another way of showing the divergence between the U.S. and some of America's military treaty allies with respect to young trained male manpower. I've put this on a logarithmic scale, so this is ten times as high as down here, and this is ten times as high as there [see figure, p. 150].

Let me show you some other countries [and] what their young, trained manpower looks like. Here's India, here's Indonesia, the Philippines, Iran, Vietnam. We could have chosen other countries as well. I selected these somewhat arbitrarily. You see the very different trends. Can we go back to the previous slide? And forward. See what I mean?

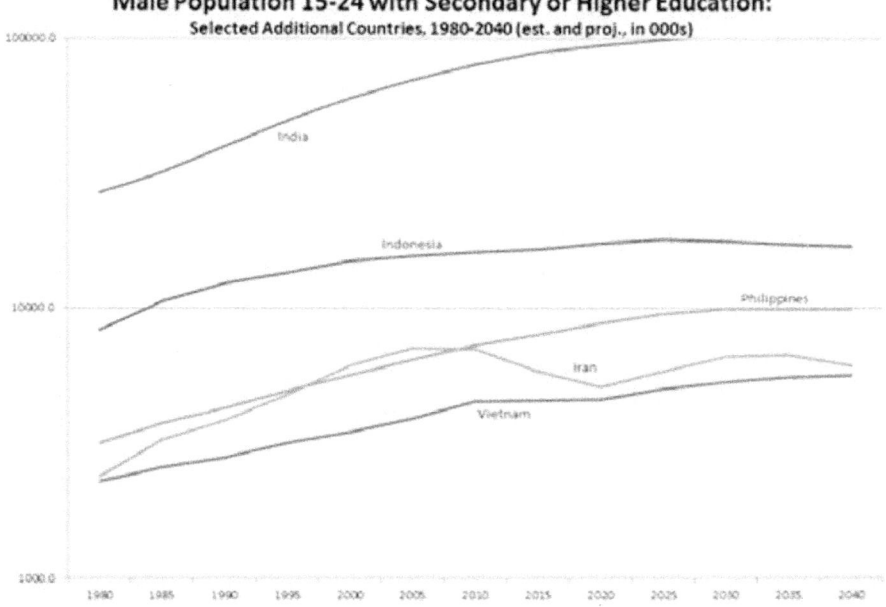

India is on track, interestingly enough, to have more highly trained young manpower than China just ten years from now [see figure, p. 152]. This crossover point may be a time of particular significance. If we look at the trained working-age population, we see similar general trends with stagnation, growth in the case of some allies, decline in the case of some others.

In 1980 India and Japan had about the same number of trained working-age people. By the end of this graphic India will have roughly ten times as many trained men and women of working age as Japan. Big changes are under way in some of these other countries as well [see figure, p. 152].

The question that I pose, and I can't answer it, unfortunately, is whether it will be possible in the next two decades or three decades to include more friends, more partnerships, more alliances, more affinity, working relationships in the equation

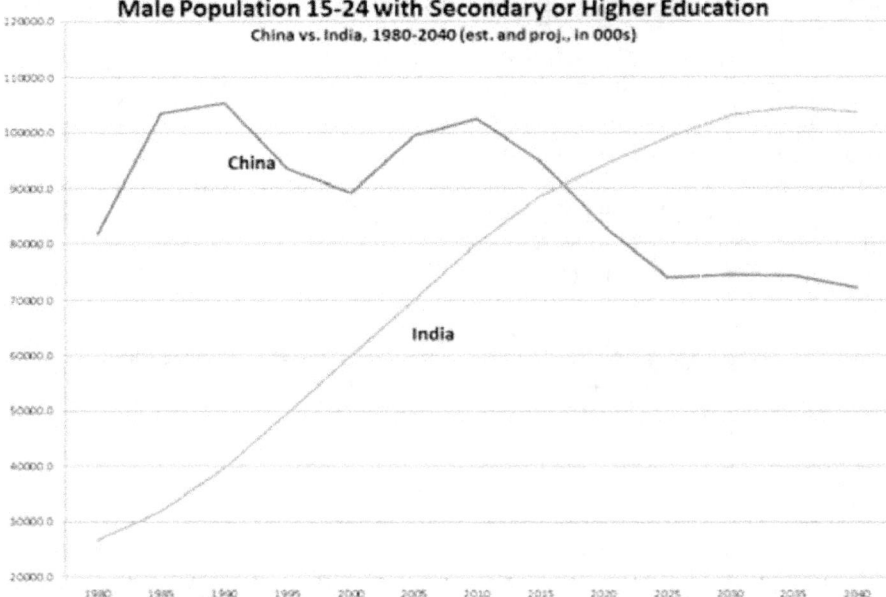

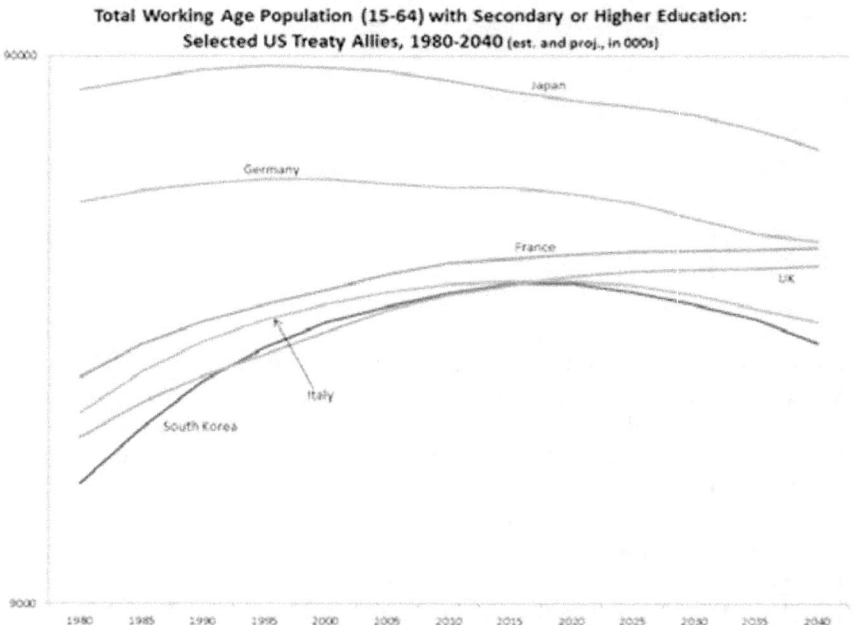

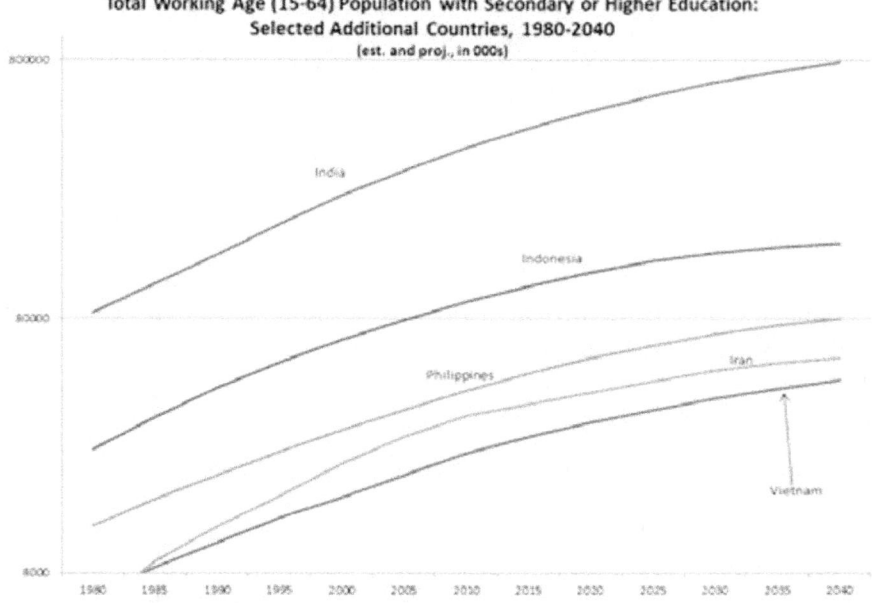

that maintains international economic security, international social and political security.

It's not a question of leaving old friends. It's a question of making new friends and increasing the partnership that makes for prosperity and security in the years ahead. Thank you very much for listening to me. I'm happy to discuss anything that you would like to in the next few minutes.

Admiral Jonathan Greenert, United States:

Doctor, I wonder, looking at India on a previous graphic, an early graphic, I took away that there was a divergence in the number of educated folks if you look to the south. What I'm taking away here is with a subtle change in the behavior, if you will, of the way India educates or decides to collaborate with its regions, this graphic could go way up high to the right; am I interpreting this right, and what that might portend?

Dr. Nicholas Eberstadt:

Absolutely, absolutely. India's future educational profile is not set in stone. It's an open chapter that has yet to be written. There are some promising signs portending today. India's government has recently promulgated rules that will require all children under the age of fourteen to go through school. This has not been the case up until now. What this, of course, will mean is that twenty or thirty years from now a much more educated young population can be on the rise throughout India.

The flip side, the problem, is that people in their twenties who have not been through school are almost sure to remain illiterate for their working-age lives. There have been many attempts all around the world to have adult education programs, many different approaches to this in different countries. They've almost all been failures, because apart from exceptional people, it seems to be really difficult to teach people to read and write once they've reached adulthood.

It may be possible to circumvent some of the illiteracy problem with iPhones, or whatever the future version of iPhones will be, or some sort of iPhone with the technologies, but for the most part it's an enormous loss of human potential and human welfare. We can see the future for the young being perhaps much more auspicious, but twenty-year-olds today in India will be fifty-year-olds in 2040. They will be going through their working-age careers.

Rear Admiral Bradley Gehrke, United States:

Your population projections on China, do those assume a one-child policy? If China started to selectively modify its one-child policy, what if it goes to a two-child policy or three-child policy?

Dr. Nicholas Eberstadt:

That's a very good question. The projections I used here come from the United Nations Population Division and the U.S. Census Bureau. They don't copy each other's homework, but they come out with very similar assessments. They don't explicitly make any assumptions about the one-child policy and its viability into the future. They presume that China's future birth trends will head slightly up.

China is far below replacement at the moment. They assume that China will head towards higher but still below-replacement fertility. Here's the question: What would happen if some sort of political change occurred, maybe with the new leadership in China next year [2012], and the program were scrapped, or I suppose the polite way would be to say "revisited"? What would happen if it were thrown out?

Many people in China's political leadership seem to fear that China would go back to having four or five births per woman. In reality, the likelihood is that there wouldn't be too much of an increase. I'll try to explain why. In cities like Beijing and Shanghai, Tianjin, the metropolises of ten million or more people, the current birth level is under one baby per woman per lifetime. In those cities people aren't even using their current quotas from the one-child policy.

So if the one-child policy were scrapped in the big cities, I don't think we'd see very much of a change, because there has been such a radical transformation of mentality. The question is what would happen in the countryside. China has been undertaking some limited but very informative experimentation in that regard. In one province, for example, a number of counties have been offered a new permission. People, farmers, with only one child are given permission to have a second one. In those counties, the results have astonished demographers because almost a majority of the people who were offered the chance to have a second child turned it down. We cannot tell if this is a general phenomenon for all of the rest of China— China is a very huge, diverse nation, of couse—but it suggests it may have been a radical transformation in mentality regarding family in China during the one-child period. If, for some reason, there was a big upsurge in children, that would affect births and, of course, labor force, but it would not affect labor force for another fifteen years because those babies would have to grow up. So for the time period we are looking at, even a radical change in birthrates in China would not affect this tableau too much.

Captain Nazih Jbaily, Lebanon:

We didn't see that the Arab world is included in your study. We know that the growth may affect the security of the world, especially because of the uprisings that are going on now, especially because in the Arab world you have a five-to-ten-children policy, and even a four-wives policy.

Dr. Nicholas Eberstadt:

Thank you, Captain. One of the most fascinating things that I've had the pleasure of working on in this past year, homework that I haven't yet published, concerns precisely this, what I call the other revolution in the greater ummah, not just in the Arab world, but in the Muslim world more generally.

Very quietly and much to my surprise there has been a transformation of birth patterns in Muslim-majority areas. If we look at the whole postwar period, six of the ten countries with the biggest drops in births are Muslim-majority countries: Libya, Tunisia, Algeria, Kuwait, Maldives, Oman. Nowadays there is a growing number of Muslim-majority countries with below-replacement birthrates, including Algeria, Tunisia, Iran, of all places, and your own Lebanon.

This quiet transformation, I think, is going to play out in very important ways over the next generation. Of course, one of the consequences of the birth drop is to create what we might call a youth bulge or a youth quake, kind of like the increase in the proportion of young people in the United States in the 1960s.

It's no coincidence, I don't think, that we saw this big increase in the share of young people in the United States in the '60s, and the '60s were a time of big change in the U.S. We see this happening, or in process, in a number of the Arab societies now. They've coincided with some of the revolutions of this past year. We see it under way in Iran as well. We're going to see it under way in the future in places like Yemen and in places like Pakistan. So stay tuned.

Admiral Manuel Rebollo García, Spain:

Thank you for your very interesting briefing. I would like to know if you can say a couple of words about the population trend in a very interesting area from my point of view, going south of the border of the USA to Cape Horn.

Dr. Nicholas Eberstadt:

Sure. Again, in Latin America and the Caribbean we've seen this same demographic trend of lower birthrates transforming the environment. It differs from country to country, of course. In Mexico, for example, birthrates are still slightly above replacement, but they've been heading down very steadily.

In Brazil they're strikingly below replacement. Brazil's society is going to be aging very quickly over the next two decades, and that's going to bring big questions for Brazil with its pension policies and with some of its other social welfare policies. Chile, Argentina, and Uruguay are at or below replacement. Some other societies are also perhaps surprisingly in this low-birth category. El Salvador, for example, is now at or below replacement.

With the exceptions of the countries on Hispaniola, with the exception of Haiti and Dominican Republic, almost all of the Caribbean is below replacement. The birthrates in the Caribbean are now lower than in the United States. Thirty years ago, one would have been astonished to hear such things. That, of course, affects manpower and availability of young persons for military service and many other things.

10

Panel Discussion Three
Maritime Security, Evolving Demands, Adaptive Partnership

Moderated by
Admiral Edmundo González Robles, Chile

Panel Members:
Rear Admiral Bernt Grimstvedt, Norway
Admiral José Santiago Valdés Álvarez, Mexico
Captain Igor Schvede, Estonia
Vice Admiral Enrique Larrañga Martin, Chile
Admiral Masahiko Sugimoto, Japan

Admiral Edmundo González Robles, Chile:

Thank you. Professor Culora; Admiral Greenert, U.S. CNO; Rear Admiral Christenson, President of the U.S. Naval War College; dear colleagues and friends; ladies and gentlemen, I am very happy to be back in Newport, especially for the great honor of being invited again to act as a panel moderator, as I did during the last ISS.

Today's panel topic is based on maritime security, evolving demands, adaptive partnership. This week we participate in interesting and thoughtful discussions relating to different threats in our sphere of action. We have to consider the way we face those threats in our respective areas of responsibility. In this context, the many navies here represented have had leading roles in the cooperation and integration activities required to neutralize those threats.

We can conclude that these transnational problems are independent of the capabilities of any of our institutions. The present panel of discussion relates to our vision of the future. Although our navies have played a leading role in the globalization process, mainly by ensuring free maritime commerce over the last three decades, new scenarios and situations require us to reevaluate and reformulate the role of the navies in our current environment.

Undoubtedly, information technology has facilitated connectivity and influenced the way people live, change in behavior, and the manner in which humans communicate. This situation has increased dependency on new technologies. Not very long ago, when we were still young officers, the war room meetings and the ways we related to each other or to our friends were very different from what happens now.

Today we have an overwhelming influence of media and communications. BlackBerries, iPhones, the Internet, and computers, to mention a few, have made us absolutely dependent on technology. Every day we see people walking on the streets, talking, apparently alone, but connected by a tiny telephone to someone.

Even more, we can appreciate the increasing desperation when you do not have a signal, or the Internet is down, or we cannot know in real time what is happening in activities for which we are in some way or other responsible. Right now I can see many of you playing or sending messages with your smartphones or tablets in a covert way.

The great dependency is what makes us vulnerable—the high level of activities in the world could not be sustained without the fundamental use of information technologies. Could you imagine coordinating the thousands of flights to and from the airports of Washington, D.C., or controlling the hundreds of ships and containers near Hamburg without the current information equipment?

Cyber attacks against information systems are new threats resulting from a variety of causes and motivations. Facing these threats is not easy. Equally challenging is mitigating their consequences. It is not enough to install the best antivirus or the latest modern firewall. We have to do more than that. These threats constitute a challenge to current and future generations.

Another significant aspect of the globalization process is the prominent role of free and good trade. However, it has also facilitated free and bad trade. I am specifically talking about narcotics or drug situations that threaten the development and life of our most precious possession, our kids and young people, who for different reasons feel tempted to consume drugs, seeking to find the element they think will allow them to pursue and reach a higher degree of happiness. As we all know here, these kinds of unlawful substances only degrade our societies in the worst possible way.

The maritime environment by its very nature, as we all know, provides multiple means for this type of illegal commerce, and we can only partially control it by open and efficient cooperation among all the navies and coast guards here present. Drug traffickers who are smart, ambitious, and unscrupulous use our seas as the main illegal means of transportation, creating the most innovative and sometimes unpredictable devices to carry their lethal products to more attractive and profitable markets.

They use their profits to hire engineering experts from all over the world to develop new ways to trade their products. We are facing immoral, smart, and creative people who will continue to evolve as circumstances, their resources, and their creativity allow them to the detriment of our societies.

On the other hand, it is a fact that our world is experiencing real climatic changes, altering our ecosystem dramatically through floods, earthquakes, tsunamis, tornados, heavy storms, and droughts, among others. Examples of this are the humanitarian catastrophes in Africa; earthquakes in Chile, Haiti, New Zealand, and Japan; tsunamis in Indonesia, Japan, and Chile; and the many hurricanes in the Caribbean Sea that have made our citizens turn to us for protection.

We know, as sailors, that the primary mission of our navies and military forces is to defend the state as a whole. But, we also must be able to protect people and mitigate the negative effects of these natural phenomena which are occurring with greater intensity and frequency.

In this sense, I would like to take this opportunity to sincerely thank the United States Navy for the immediate and efficient support it gave us as a country in Chile after the devastating earthquake and tsunami that occurred on 27 February in my country last year, and for the recent search for victims in the air force accident on Robinson Crusoe Island last September. It supported our efforts in oceanographic surveys and search operations with naval devices and divers, respectively. Thanks again to the former CNO and [my] friend, Admiral Gary Roughead, and to the current U.S. Navy leader, Admiral Greenert. I wish you the best, Jonathan. It is not a simple task, but count on us.

Likewise, global warming is melting vast ice surfaces, opening new navigation routes and maritime communication lines. I am referring to the new Northwest Passage in the Arctic Sea connecting the Atlantic and Pacific Ocean. While this presents new opportunities and a viable alternative for maritime commerce, it also affects important ecological reserves.

Even though the naval forces were not created for this purpose, we must ask, Can we avoid the responsibility of giving support to the community? My inner conviction is no. After this brief introduction I will leave the work to our distinguished panelists, who will analyze all these topics, pose important questions, and provide conclusions with the purpose of highlighting these new threats and situations. Thanks to this International Seapower Symposium, we now can explain, study, prevent, and hopefully identify new approaches and joint solutions to reduce these kinds of threats.

In order to be well prepared and motivated to participate in the next FIFA (soccer) World Cup, Brazil 2014, I will use for time control the same procedure as I did when I was invited to act as moderator at the last ISS, and in the same way as my colleague and friend, Admiral Aziz from Malaysia, copied me two days ago, with some minor differences.

As you can see in the present video slide, this is only an example of a good goal by Chile against the World Cup champion Brazil. Mainly for motivation. However, to be brutally honest, this video was captured many years ago, but we are very confident that some day we'll achieve this dream again.

Each speaker will have fifteen minutes to share the vision in accordance with the topics already mentioned. For a good panel time distribution, and we are very tight for that, and to leave on schedule for the next activities of this ISS, I will show the original FIFA cards: the yellow one when you have only one minute left, and the red one when your time is out. I hope there will be no need to use my whistle, if someone attempts to exceed the assigned time of presentation, like a FIFA official. [Whistle.]

Well, now I will introduce your distinguished panelists one by one. First, from Norway, Rear Admiral Bernt Grimstvedt—it's correct, the pronunciation?—chief of the Royal Norwegian Navy, with the panel topic "Changing Sea Routes and Maritime Infrastructure." Rear Admiral Grimstvedt joined his navy in 1977, and his operational career specialization and command have primarily been oriented to the Coastal Arterial Branch Weapons Systems. He has completed many staff courses, and since 15 June 2011 he is the current chief of the Royal Norwegian Navy. Please, everyone, give a warm welcome to Rear Admiral Grimstvedt.

Rear Admiral Bernt Grimstvedt, Norway:

I'd like to thank the U.S. Navy for hosting such a great event. It's my third time as a delegate, and I'm even more convinced than ever that this is a symposium that has a great future. So once again, thank you very much.

I also noticed yesterday the name of Alfred Thayer Mahan is getting a renaissance. I tell my army colleagues at our Joint Staff College that they teach too much

Clausewitz and too little Mahan. First of all, thank you very much for having the opportunity to address this distinguished audience on the topic "Changing Sea Routes and Maritime Infrastructure in the Arctic Region."

This part of the world is currently undergoing rapid changes. It is mainly due to climate change and implications of global warming, and a result of this is the possibility for new sea routes, and in addition the increased oil and gas activity and exploration of other minerals will, in total, probably result in significantly increased maritime traffic, both from Asia to Europe and America and to destinations along the routes.

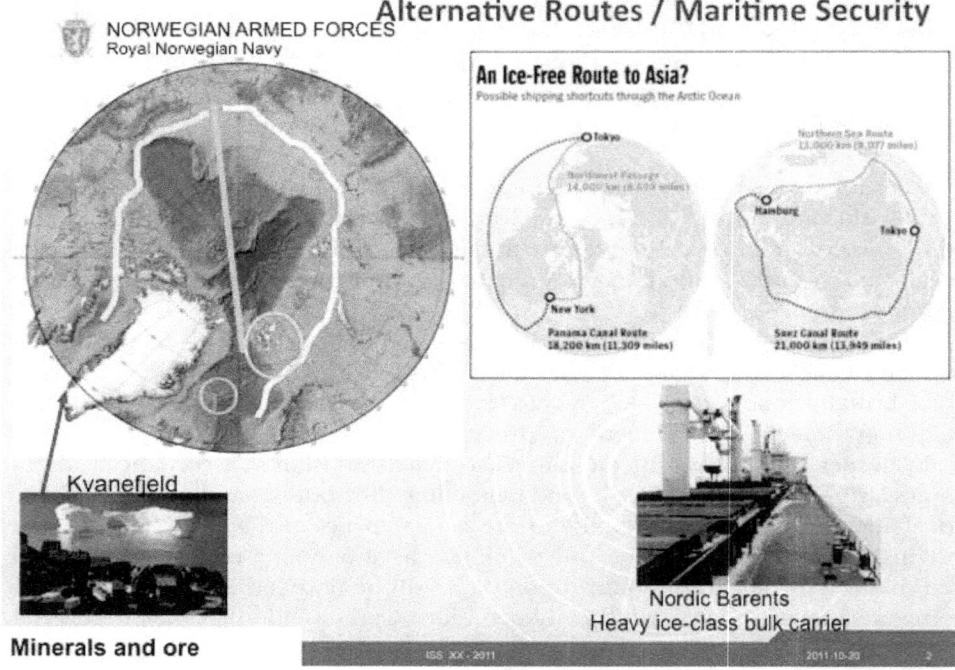

In theory, there are three possible transpolar routes. These are the Northeast Passage for the Northern Sea Route off the Siberian coast from the Bering Strait to the Barents Sea, the Northwest Passage from Alaska to Canada to Davis Strait, and finally the transpolar route.

My presentation will mainly cover the Northeast Passage, because this route is where the maritime activity has the greatest potential in the short and medium forecasts. The Arctic region is a very tough one. Polar conditions can be very unpredictible throughout the year. In addition, it has an extremely small population, which results in lack of all types of infrastructure. Hence, there are major challenges to all kinds of safe human activities, yet there are obvious reasons for maritime use of these waters. The distance from Tokyo to Hamburg is 8,000 kilometers shorter via the Northeast Passage than through the Indian Ocean. For any shipowner operating in transcontinental traffic, this represents a great potential in terms of saved time and money.

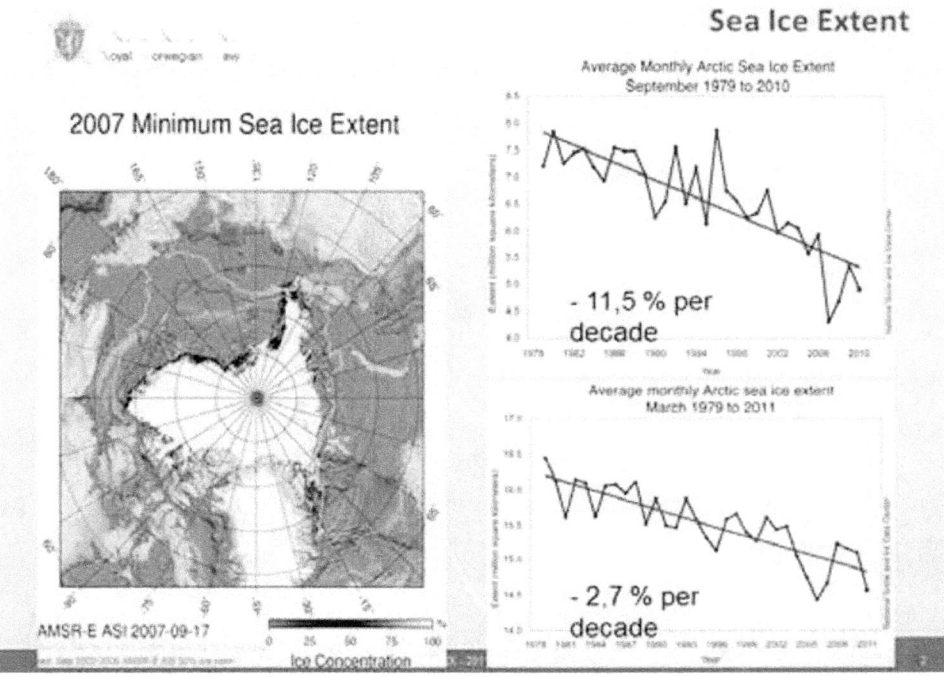

As I already have mentioned, one major factor is the rapid decline of the ice extent in the Arctic. The decline is accelerating and going faster than expected. There's especially little ice observed in the period between July and September, and the amount of ice which is more than one year old is also rapidly declining. The ice has also moved towards the north tip of Greenland and around the Canadian islands.

The development goes faster than current climate models predict, which means that safe maritime operations might be available earlier than we even expect today. This slide shows the predicted ice extent decline in the years to come with current models, while the red line here shows the absurd decline.

As you can see, we are even below the expected annual differences or variations from year to year, and we are now on a record-low level of ice extent. There are three major models explaining why the ice is declining. It's the change in the normal atmospheric situation, it's increase in the Arctic Sea temperature, and changes in normal wind patterns. The geophysics in the Arctic is extremely complicated and not fully understood. Reliable models are difficult to create, and many nations are carrying out comprehensive research activity in the region. There are also other issues that have to be taken into consideration. There are currently a number of unresolved issues in the region. Let me mention the most important ones. Who owns the Arctic, if anyone? What is the real potential for exploitation of natural resources? The determination of the outer limitation of the continental shelf and the right of navigational freedom? Nations are already preparing their positions for resolving these issues. There are a lot of high-level activities going on, and Norway is a key player.

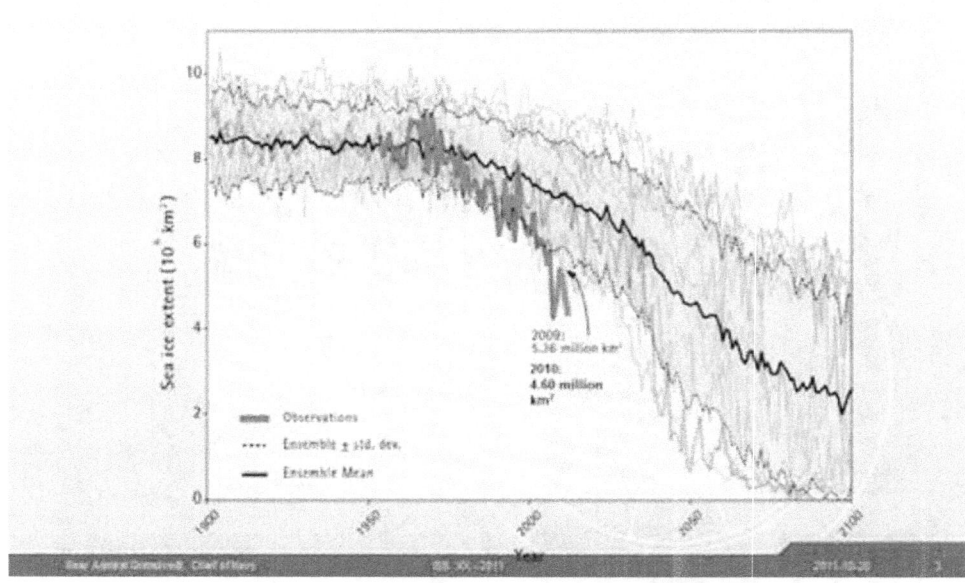

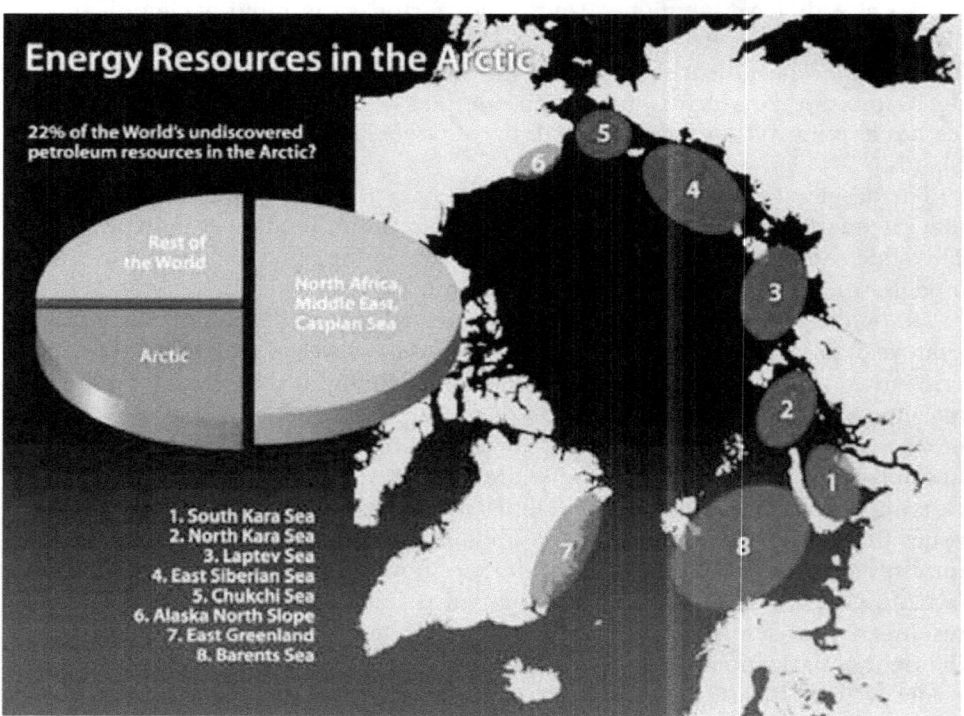

The Arctic is a promising region for exportational oil and gas and valuable resources. Some claim that as much as 25 percent of the world's undiscovered oil and gas resources are located in the Arctic. Offshore fields are currently concentrated in the Barents Sea; however, it is expected that oil and gas activity in the region will increase. This will include both onshore and offshore exploration and transport to markets through pipelines and by ship.

This slide shows the current transport routes. The next slide shows the expected situation in 2020 [see figure, p. 164]. As you can see, there is a large expansion expected of transport of oil and gas in the region. Now, to what extent the remaining unresolved issues will provide a delay in the overall maritime activities in the Arctic is difficult to predict. This issue is not a showstopper for civil merchant activity.

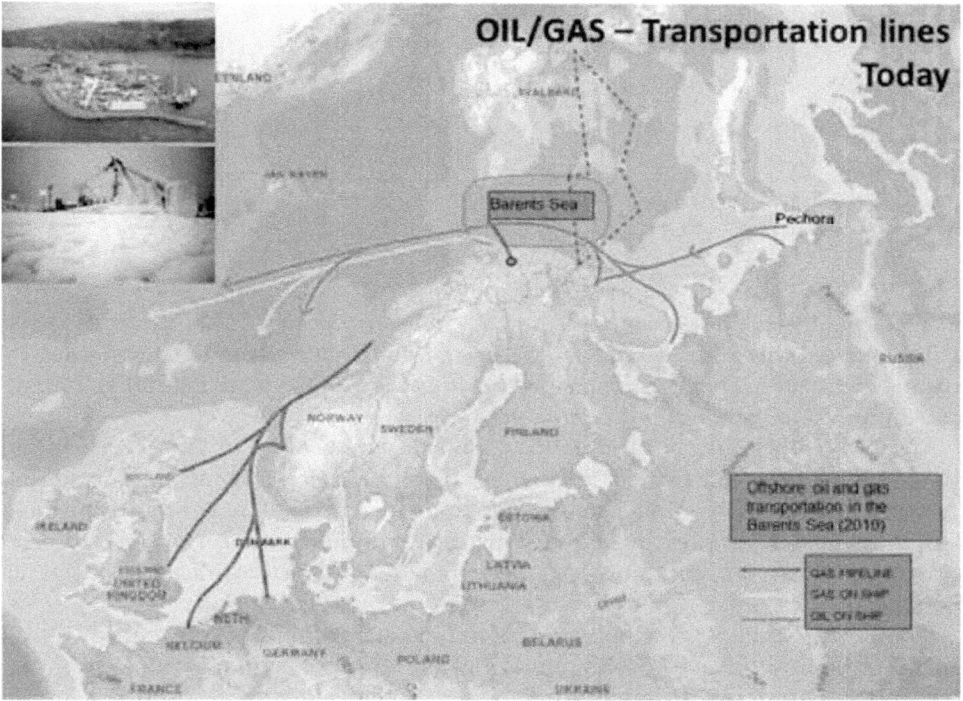

There is a general positive development, and it's my view that all questions will find a satisfactory solution. Now, since we are naval colleagues, I would also like to mention the military activity in the Norwegian area of interest. The Norwegian Navy, and especially our coast guard, operates continuously in the Barents Sea and in the waters around Spitsbergen Islands.

The Russian Northern Fleet has its main base in the Murmansk area, and its main exercise fields in eastern Barents Sea. We do not see military activity in the Arctic as an obstacle to civil merchant traffic. On the contrary, Arctic navies can provide additional search and rescue capabilities in a scarcely populated area. As the *Maxim Gorky* accident shows, the potential for major disaster is real when ships meet ice.

This accident took place in 1989 where, fortunately, there was a large Norwegian Coast Guard vessel just a couple of hours from the *Maxim Gorky*. You could imagine

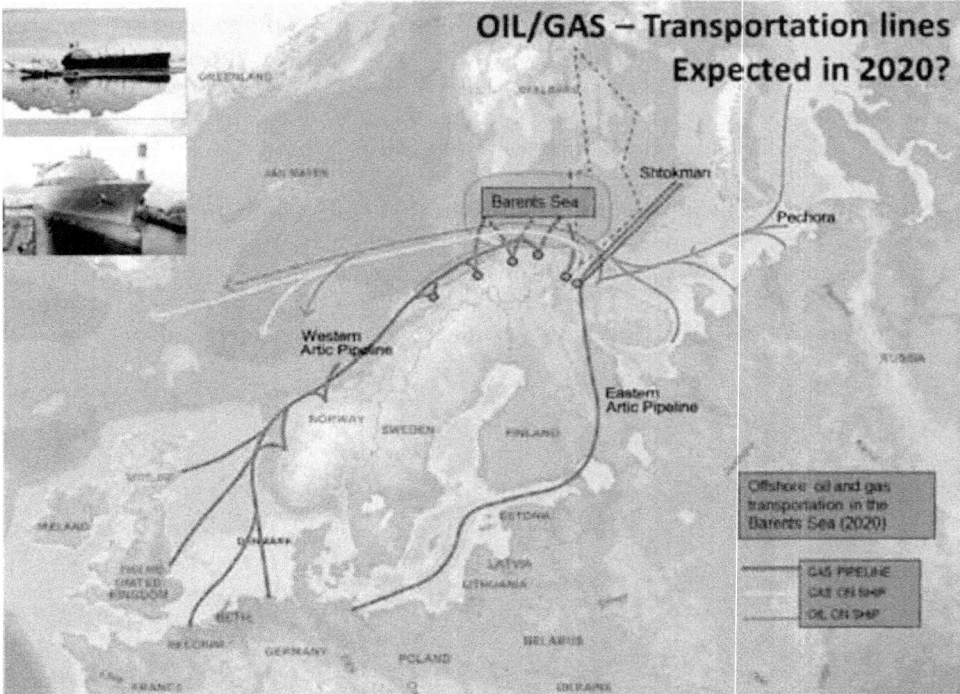

what potential this accident could have had when you have seawater temperatures around zero, elderly people not properly clothed. We managed to take all on board, four hundred to five hundred people on the coast guard vessel.

What is really going on now, more or less, as we speak? The first international agreement made exclusively for the Arctic region was signed at the ministerial meeting in Nuuk, Greenland, on 12 May this year [2011]. The agreement, which deals with search and rescue, and aeronautical and maritime vessels and passengers, is also the first international agreement made under the auspices of the Arctic Council.

The Arctic Council is now planning another international agreement for introduction which will deal with oil pollution in the Arctic. The main emphasis of the agreement is to develop swift and efficient measures when accidents occur in the harsh Arctic region and to ensure as much as possible proper search and rescue operations. This is done by the closest states, where the member states commit themselves to nominate certain national institutions in each state that will have full discretion in the field of search and rescue in the area. These national institutions are not only bound to take efficient measures, but also to notify other relevant national institutions when appropriate.

Russia is also planning nine rescue centers along the North Sea passage. These centers will provide a full-spectrum rescue service, like search and rescue helicopters, firefighters, and vessel traffic control. Russia will also have a fleet of heavy icebreakers that provide assistance. Of the current fleet of six vessels, two have nuclear propulsion. This fleet is, however, aging, and six new vessels are under planning, three nuclear and three conventional.

Arctic SAR agreement signed May 2011

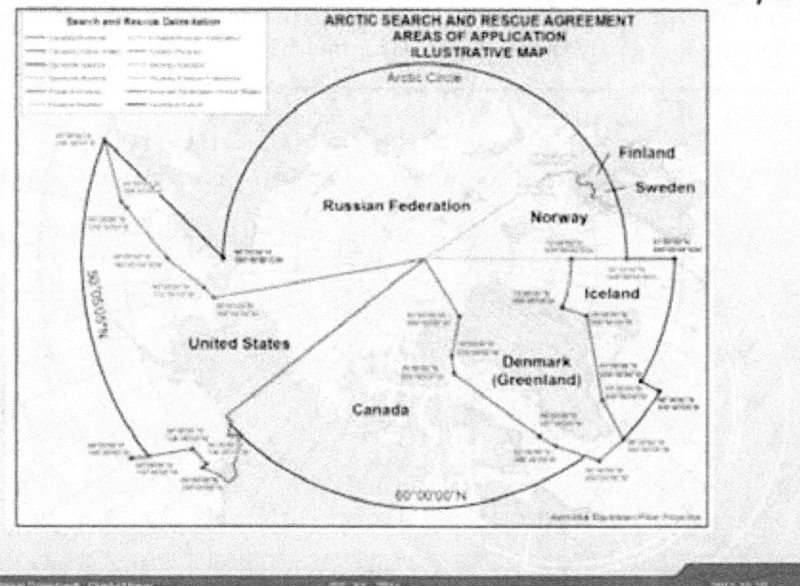

Planned Integrated "Rescue Centers"

Russia is also investigating in detail the navigational challenges in the east part of the Northeast Passage. These waters are very shallow, and large vessels, type Suezmax, are forced to go even further north on this part of the route. This increases the risk of hitting ice with increased [risk] potential for the vessel, crew, cargo, and the extremely vulnerable environment.

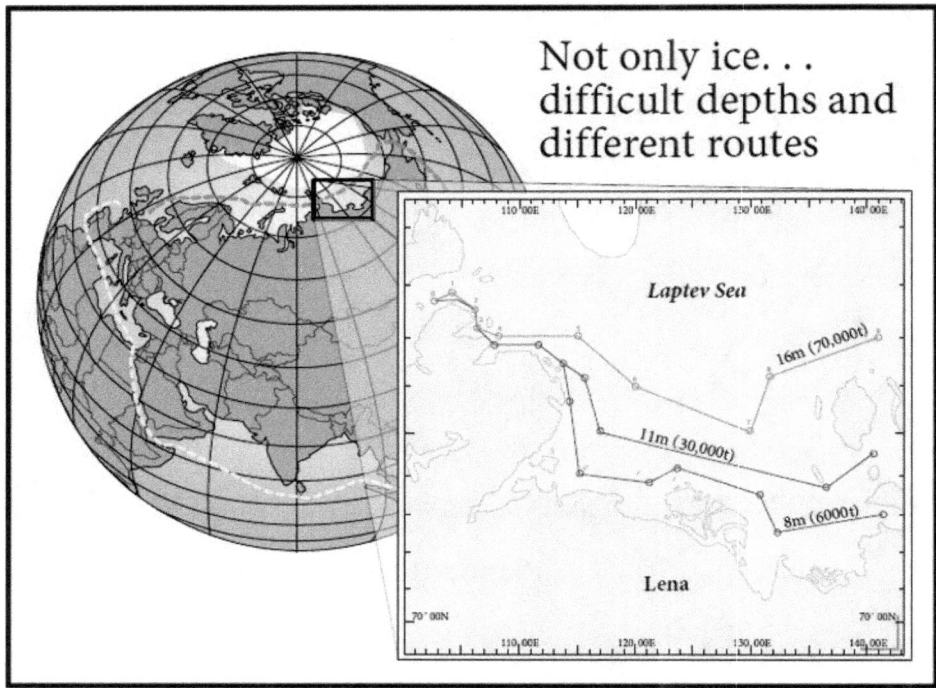

Two thousand eleven has been a breaking year for merchant traffic in the Northeast Passage. This includes both transient traffic and destination traffic. However, the number of ships is very limited compared to the normal route through the Suez Channel. We expect about fifteen ships in full transit traffic this season. The vessels have to be ice class and need icebreaker escort and permission from Russian authorities.

Let's have a look at some of the vessels that operate in this traffic. First one is called the *Nordic Barents*, which left Kirken's, in northern Norway, with iron ore for Asia. The next one is the fleet belonging to the Novatec Company, which has specialized in gas condensate cargo. One of the Novatec company's vessels is the *Vladimir Tikhonov*, which is the largest vessel up to now that has been sailing from west to east. As you can see, this is a very large vessel, 162 tons deadweight.

Since the ice has declined so much, they could follow at least on the eastern part of the passage a kind of transpolar route. But the Arctic will always be a challenging area. So-called ice-free waters will never be 100 percent ice-free. Insurance premiums, coastal state regulation, violating just-in-time demands from customers, and other factors might result in hesitation for maritime business when it comes to major use of polar routes.

Nordic Barents

- Left Kirkenes 4 Sep 2010 enroute for Asia
- First non-russian through the Northern Sea Route
- Carried 41 000 tons of iron ore concentrate jernmalmkonsentrat
- Has "1A Super" ice class, required bu Russian authorities
- Escorted by nuclear icebreakers from Rosatomflot
- Saved 8 days compared with Suez and an additional 10-15 days compared to the "pirate free" route around Africa.

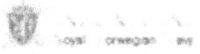

NOVATEC

- Novatec have 6 shipments with a total of 420 000 tons of gas condensate
    - The Perseverance (Aug)
    - STI Heritage (Aug)
    - Marilee (Aug)
    - Vladimir Tikhonov (Aug)
    - Panamax (Sep)
    - Panamax (Oct)

In 2006 there was a survey among a number of shipping companies. The answers are interesting. The container segment, as you can see here, seems little interested, while the general cargo [segment] is more optimistic. The reason for this is, of course, that the container traffic relies heavily on the just-in-time principle. You can't come in January with the Christmas presents.

To sum up, as mentioned on this slide, the Northwest Passage will, according to our estimates, not be a major route in the foreseeable future. The Northeast Passage, however, has a greater potential. The established route has been in use for several decades, although mainly for destinational traffic.

Northwest passage

- Irrelevant for European traffic – no savings.
- Gives shorter distance between Asia and the US Eastern Seaboard, but there are othermore attractive options
- Only 2 completely ice free days in 2009
- The shipping season will at best be measured in weeks within the foreseeable future. Does not allow for the necessary infrastructure investments (escort icebreakers, staging ports etc.)
- Presently no escort icebreaker service

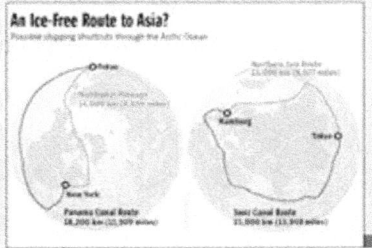

Northeast Passage

– Well prepared for transit traffic
– Regulations still requires ship with high ice-class (minimum ICE-1A)
– Cost of icebreaker support reduce profitability

Concluding Remarks

- The extent and thickness of sea ice in the Arctic has diminished significantly in recent years.
  - This trend is expected to continue until the Arctic is predominantly seasonal ice
  - The timing for this to evolve is extremely uncertain,– The immediate future, during the transition, will be particularly variable, uncertain and challenging
- Even in this future seasonal ice scenario, Arctic shipping will face considerable obstacles
  - Variable ice conditions
  - Logistical support, Search & Rescue
  - Bureaucracy

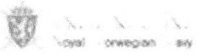

Concluding remarks

- Primarily ships with high economic advantage or with no alternative will be attracted to the Arctic
  - Routine transit shipping is still some years into the future
  - Destinational voyages will dominate and increase (resources & re-supply)
  - increased tourism, alterations in fishing patterns, and changes in community re-supply may further raise activity levels

Russia has some advantages. It has established an ice pilot, icebreaker service. It has a dedicated administration and national regulations covering all aspects of northern sea route shipping. It is now preparing routes that can include ships with a draft of more than twelve meters.

Maritime traffic in the Arctic will increase, maybe even faster than we expect today. The main factor is to predict the decline of the ice extent; the necessity of an up-to-date maritime domain awareness engagement will have to follow accordingly. The circumpolar nations will have to establish an infrastructure, both shore-based and through a modern support vessel fleet, in order to guarantee, at least to a certain level, reliable routes during the season.

However, commercial interests will dominate the shipowner's decision if and when to establish a regular operation. My estimate is that we still will have to wait a number of years before we see big volumes of merchant traffic in the polar basin, but it is probably only a matter of time. Thank you for your attention.

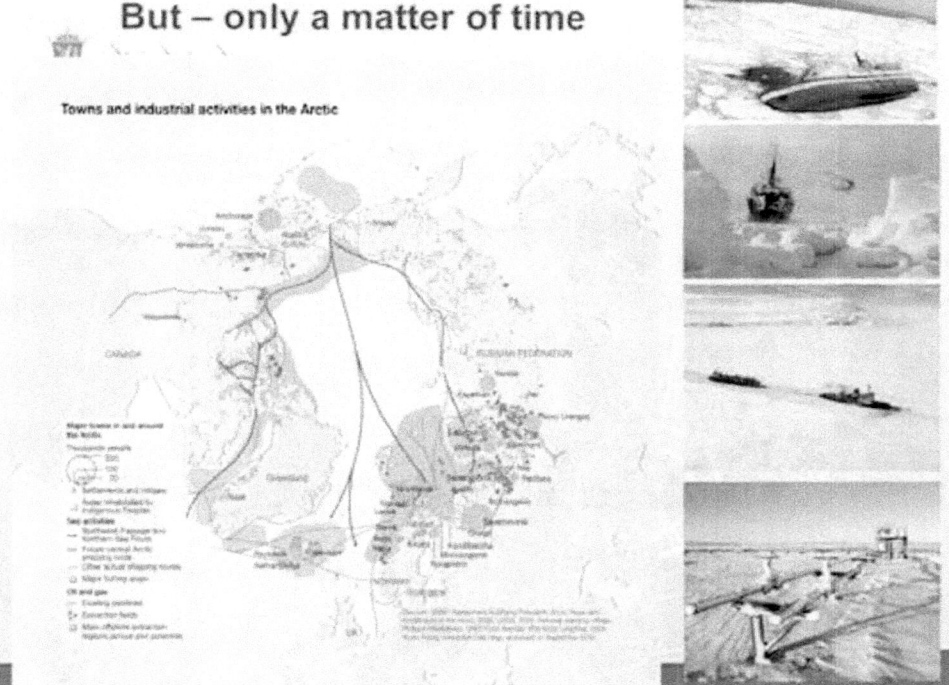

Admiral Edmundo González Robles, Chile:

Thank you, Rear Admiral Grimstvedt. Three minutes inside here, no problem. Well, our next speaker is from Mexico, Admiral José Valdés, with the topic "Trafficking, Sophisticated and Deadly." Admiral Valdés joined his navy in 1965, and his operational career has many seagoing experiences.

He was the commanding officer of two mine hunters, DM05 and 806, also commanding the auxiliary oil tanker *Tlaxcala* and the coast guard cutter *Pedro Sáinz de Barenda*. His career, along with his vast operational and command experience, has included a superb educational background. To mention only a few, he attended the Center of Naval Studies of National Defense in Spain and the U.S. Defense University.

He also has completed many staff courses and was promoted to admiral in 2008. Earlier this year he assumed his current position as the Mexican Navy Chief of Staff. Please, everybody, a round of applause welcoming Admiral Valdés. Admiral Valdés will give us his presentation in Spanish, so get ready to use your headsets.

Admiral José Santiago Valdés Álvarez, Mexico:

Admiral Greenert and Admiral Christenson, esteemed colleagues, the Ministry of the Navy of Mexico is very pleased to greet you and is honored to join you in this international forum to present to you the conclusions regarding trafficking, not only in Mexico, but in the international context.

We hope very much that the strategies and the policies that Mexico has adopted will be of interest to you and, more than that, might be useful to you as you study your own national context in the manner in which it may lend itself to the best strategy to fight drugs.

INTRODUCTION

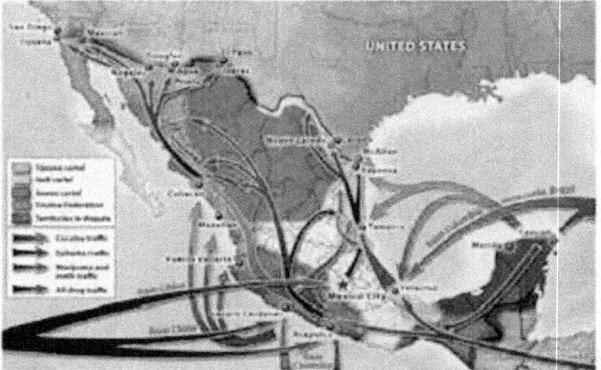

Clearly the fight against drug trafficking has much to do with the national legal framework that exists, the dynamics of consumption and production, the actual measures that the countries of the region may have adopted to fight narco-trafficking, and the tendencies of the criminal gangs themselves.

We have a great number of asymmetric threats in the region that grow apace with globalization. They grow apace with the lack of control, the porosity of the frontiers of the borders, and the many adverse measures that bear on social conditions that

INTRODUCTION

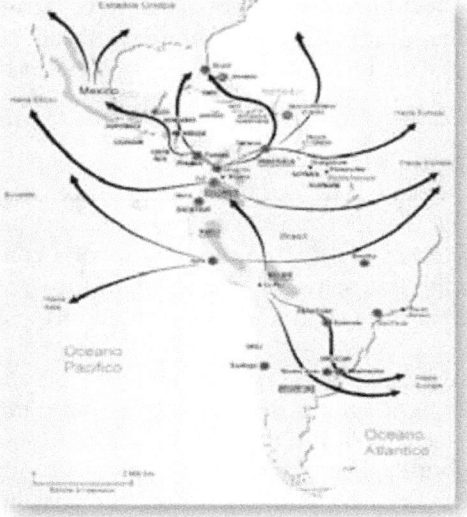

The Region face asymmetric threats, expanded and strengthened by:

- Globalization
- Trade and cultural exchanges
- Control deficiency
- Porosity of borders

INTRODUCTION

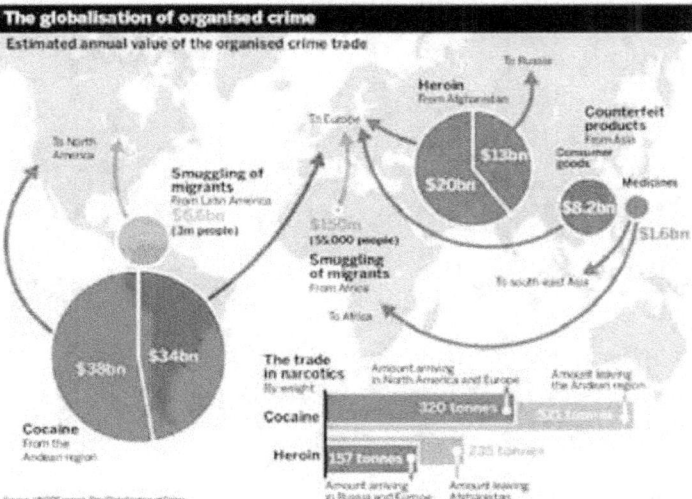

at a regional level serve as a breeding ground for a great spate of illegal activities, all of which are a great challenge to the state, with a capital S.

Among these I would mention the transnational organized crime phenomenon, which is a tremendous threat to our national and international security; the drug trafficking, particularly with regard to marijuana, cocaine, and chemical precursors that are sent to Africa and Asia, among others; also, certainly, the illegal arms trade that flows north to south, into Mexico; and health issues that can suddenly lead to a pandemic and that can affect the whole world because of globalization yet again.

There is also, last but not least, the threat of terrorism and the recognition that the country could at any time be the target for terrorist activity, or a platform for such terrorist activities or an organization of terrorist activities that may be planned to be carried out elsewhere.

With all of this in mind, the country has put its best heads together and decided that two fundamental elements must be present at any strategy. Illegal trafficking, trafficking in humans and drugs and in arms, comes from the social conditions, and these, of course, are what enable the traffickers to threaten the security of a country, inasmuch as they have the means to avail themselves of ever-more sophisticated technological weapons and have, of course, the greed and determination to use them.

From 2006 we decided to review the strategies of the navy of Mexico such that we could be directly linked to the broader fight against drugs, for one, and crime, in general, that could affect the internal security of the country. It is in that sense that naval operations have increased and our capacity for detection, identification, and interception of suspicious activities has been revamped all along the coastline of Mexico.

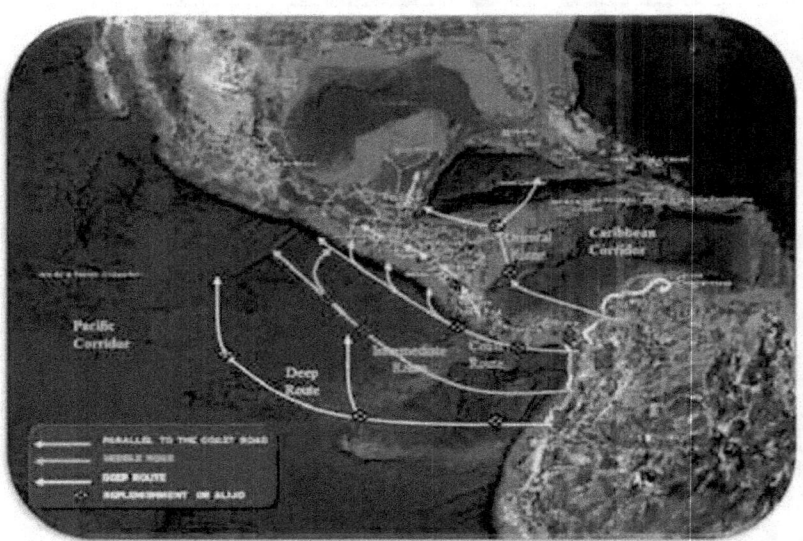

We also look to see what maritime traffic is, and we see particularly the use of semisubmersibles, of fishing boats and cargo containers that are all used for drug trafficking and other trafficking as well. Containers, particularly, as you can imagine, are very, very useful for the traffickers. The means employed for smuggling chemical precursors generally use the three routes along the Pacific.

There's the coastal route that hugs the coastline of Central America and the south of Mexico; [the] intermediate line that jumps off the coast of Colombia and goes away from the exclusive economic zone of Central America, although it can sometimes come closer to Central America or to the Mexican coast; and then there is the route farther south that launches from Ecuador and Peru. It goes through the Galápagos Islands and then aims further north to the exclusive economic zone further up, although it is aimed at the south of the country of Mexico, as you can see here. We see that what leaves Colombia and then goes to Honduras and Belize, that describes the land route that, again, aims at Mexico.

These chemical precursors are used for synthetic drugs or designer drugs. We know that phenylacetic acid and its derivatives are the main ones. Busan, Korea; Yokohama, Japan; Singapore, Chiwan; and Hong Kong are some of the major [destinations]. They first come to Manzanillo and Lázaro Cárdenas, as an intermediate port from which they go to the Asians. Pseudoephedrine and all of the ephedrine groups go to Altamira, and Veracruz, along the Gulf of Mexico. That's what we've seen.

Here are the statistics. Here is how the pie graph breaks down. From 2006 to 2010 we see 53.70 tons of cocaine, 13 percent in go-fast, 28 percent in fishing [boats], SPSS [self-propelled semisubmersibles] 10 percent, and the rest [49%] in cargo containers. It must be highlighted that most of the containers carrying cocaine gave us a total of 23 tons.

STATISTICS

SEIZURES OF COCAINE FROM 2006-2010

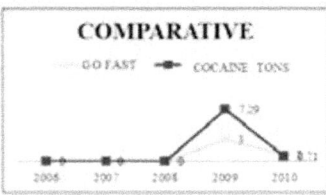
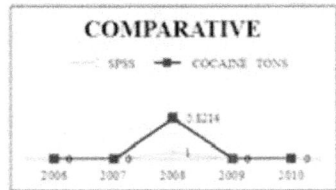

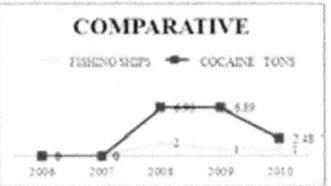
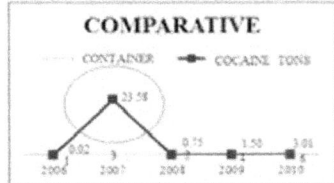

SOURCE: SEMAR

But, from 2008 to 2010, what we saw is that the traditional gangs shifted their MOs [modi operandi] and changed the amounts that were being sent, and they were then sending, in fact, less than half a ton or about half a ton per shipment. Almost five hundred tons of chemical precursors were sent, most of which is ephedrine, pseudoephedrine, and 94 percent phenylacetic acid. The chemical precursors analysis also shows that phenylacetic acid increased in 2010.

STATISTICS

SEIZURES OF CHEMICAL PRECURSORS MADE BY SEMAR 2006-2010

449.46 TONS. of CHEMICAL PRECURSORS

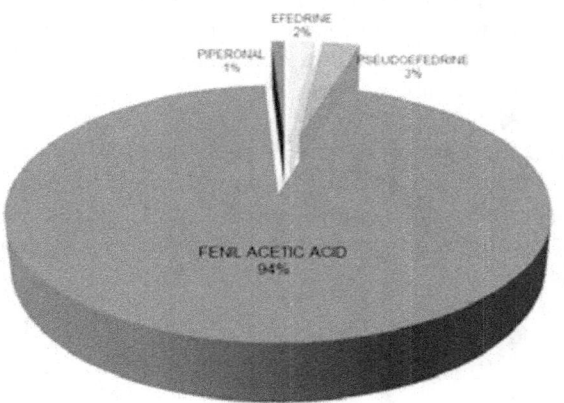

SOURCE: SEMAR

STATISTICS

SEIZURES OF CHEMICAL PRECURSORS FROM 2006 TO 2010

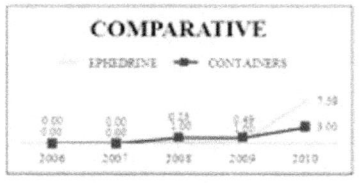
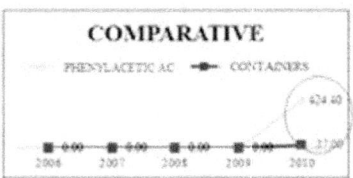
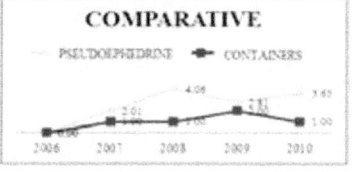
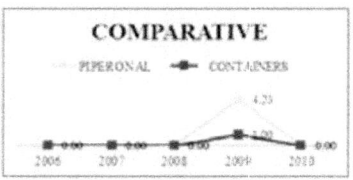

SOURCE: SEMAR

Over these last years, as we've also seen, associated violence has been devastating. Thirty-four thousand deaths, at a minimum, have been noted in Mexico, generally as a result of intergang warfare—frankly, a turf war, fighting for their share of the retail going up to the United States.

STATISTICS

The number of deaths related to drug trafficking has been on the rise, having surpassed the 34,000 deaths during current federal administration, most of them were criminals.

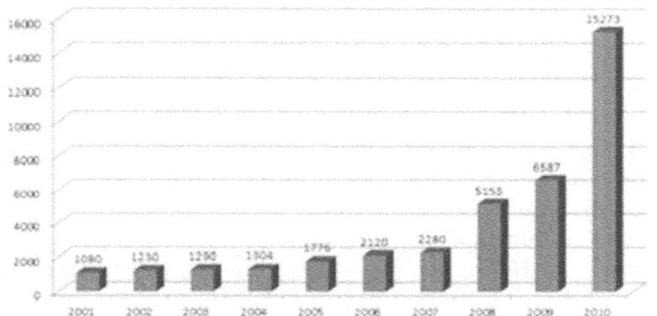

(Source: Moloeznik 2009, Poiré 2011 and www.justiceinmexico.org)

STATISTICS

Firearms Trafficking Corridors and Planned ATF Gunrunner Team Locations Along the Southwest Border

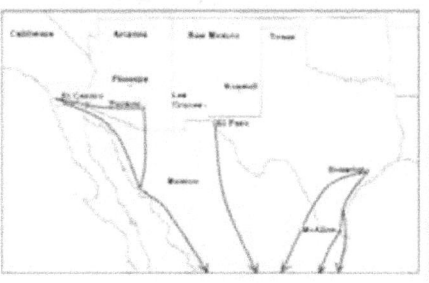

- Weapons used by trafficking are becoming more lethal
- Most were purchased in the US and introduced to Mexico illegally

The use of weapons and the MOs of these gangs are ever more savage. One hundred thousand portable and semi-portable weapons, most of which come from the United States, are now widespread. The Mexican Navy has therefore faced this, paying particular attention to the promotion and protection of human rights.

Our country is a signatory to human rights conventions, and in March of 2011 the Mexican Navy signed a collaboration agreement with the National Commission for Human Rights in order to have our naval personnel better aware of what is entailed in respecting human rights.

We also decided to set up directives for the Mexican Navy in the use of force by naval operations that are based on the Code of Conduct for Law Enforcement Officials as issued by the United Nations. So it is the entire series of international legal instruments of which we are very much aware and [we] try our very best in our training and in our operations to remain cognizant of these important provisions.

Following the 9/11 attacks, we know that the United States very much tightened its border controls. This naturally affected the drug cartels, which sought alternative routes into the American market, with the immense demand for drugs that exists therein. Mexico, therefore, implemented a national policy sustaining the prevention and control of such demand in our country, eradication of drugs, and better interinstitutional, interagency cooperation.

We also looked very hard at what we could do actually in terms of intercepting the onslaught of these shipments, particularly tracing the go-fast routes offshore in the Caribbean and in the Pacific. We have had numbers of operations on both of these fronts and have carried out numbers of operations together with the U.S. Navy and the U.S. Coast Guard.

CURRENT SITUATION

TRACE GRAPH OF GO FAST OFFSHORE

Trends:

- Decreased traces to southern Mexico, increased traces to Guatemala and Central America

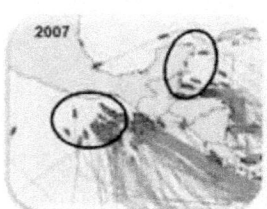 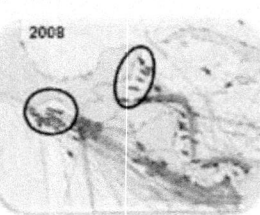

- Decreased traces to Mexican Caribbean, increased traces to Belize and Honduras

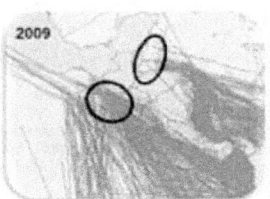 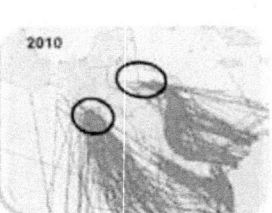

Source: JIATF-S

There have been a number of incidents therefore in both of those coastlines, and we've intercepted great numbers of attempted deliveries to Honduras, Nicaragua, and a number of other Central American countries. There is, of course, also the question of acquired vessels, some of which—I have a picture of one here that was acquired in Brownsville. You can see from this graph where some of them go out. They are loaded with cocaine in secret compartments, and then go into the Mexican Pacific area. This one was forty nautical miles south of El Salvador when we caught wind of it. This one, the *Juan Alejandro,* had been a recent acquisition and, in fact, it had never carried out fishing operations when we looked into it. When we took a harder look at how the vessel was structured, we realized it was being used to smuggle much of these substances.

CURRENT SITUATION

Acquired boat in Brownsville, Tx.

Juan Alejandro Route

Then you have the leisure boats that are used. You have *Daylight* and the *Fiona* yacht, pictured here [see figure, p. 180]. More recently we see, again, an evolution of how these drug cartels are evolving. They're diversifying their activities, both in terms of methods of production as well as in terms of the transportation of these.

They also engage, as we know, in kidnapping, extortion, assaults, forgery, and all kinds of additional illicit activity, piracy amongst them. We all recognize, alas, that they engage in ever more savage, more violent actions and tremendous defiance to authority.

We have witnessed over the last years, as I hinted earlier, how much they rely on technology. There is the use of semisubmersibles. These have increasing capacities. They can sink up to three meters of depth. They have night vision as well as day vision. This naturally means, for our side of the divide, much greater effort in terms of money and manpower.

CURRENT SITUACION
OTHER MEANS USED FOR SMUGGLING

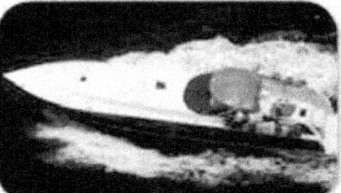 

Yatch "Daylight" sighted at 800 NM SW of Acapulco, Gro. in October 2009   Yatch "Fiona" sunk at 183 MN NNW of Clarion Island in October 2009

Sailing boat "Allende" seized in June 2010

Recently, June 2009, in the port of Progreso in the Yucatán peninsula, the Mexican Navy seized 194 kilos of cocaine that had been hidden in frozen sharks. These were coming from Costa Rica. They will use anything. This shows a level of sophistication that is very hard to detect.

CURRENT SITUATION

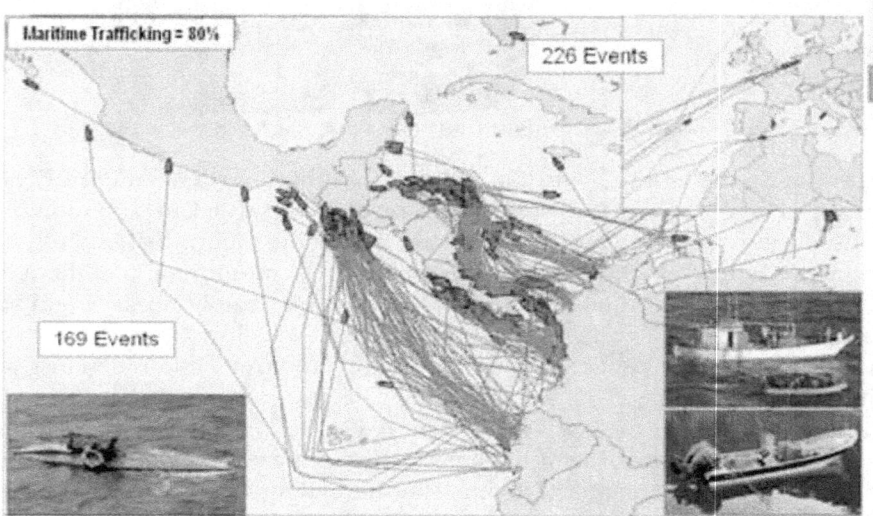

Source: Data from Jan – Aug. 2010, JIATF-S

Thirty-eight countries have been involved here, in Europe, in Africa, in the Middle East. There are links between the Italian Mafias and the criminal Mexican gangs. They use Italy as a go-between point, where the Italian Mafia sends the drugs on to Africa and other places. They basically serve as a bridge. The use of Central America as conduits, of course, has had a tremendous impact on the social, economic, and military situations there. Drug smuggling being very, very great along our southern border; there are agreements that have been ascribed to in order to buttress the situation. We also know from our Central American neighbors that Mexican cartels, however, are not limited to there. They are as far down as Chile, Paraguay, Argentina, and elsewhere in South America. International cooperation, therefore, is imperative.

There is no question that in order to successfully tackle this deadly threat there has to be more than simply the letter of international cooperation. There has to be a very live spirit and determination to make it real. The magnitude of the phenomenon has to be based on a very real sense of shared responsibility, a burden sharing that is rooted in a global vision, not only bilaterally but multilaterally, regionally, however we want to slice it.

We are all in this together. It is the well-being of our world that is at stake. The three heads of state of government of North America got together in Aspen at one point. We have the SPP [Security and Prosperity Partnership] agreement that was set up in order to defend North America from external threats, prevent and fight domestic threats, and to work more closely along our shared borders.

The SPP on the maritime front means our having two main goals in sight—to improve our port security, identifying threats, vulnerability, and risk on the one hand, and on the other to develop and implement a common plan aimed at protecting our legal maritime activities.

With that in mind, the Mexican Navy, together with the Armed Forces of the United States, including, of course, the Navy, set up the North American Maritime Security Initiative, its acronym, NAMSI, setting up common standards of operation between our two countries aimed at achieving a higher degree of efficiency of maritime operations and stricter compliance with the Law of the Sea provisions.

Last August, Canada joined in through the Canada Command, and that now means that the whole of North America is on board, as it were, in this regard. To conclude, most of the maritime cocaine shipments arrive in Central America by road; that continues to be the case. From there, they move on through Mexico. Synthetic drugs and chemical precursors are now being shipped alternatively as they're moving through Central American countries.

The transnational organized crime groups are changing how they operate, depending on what is found to be most useful. They use leisure crafts and sport boats, but the submersibles and other boats, of course, are very useful, too. This represents an enormous threat, which, in turn, we believe will require ever-closer collaborative links and more, really intense attention to this tremendous scourge.

This is a common problem. As I said earlier, it must be viewed as one which can only be fought together, one which must be fought equally with full respect and awareness of human rights and the ambit of national and international law. Thank you very much indeed.

Admiral Edmundo González Robles, Chile:

Thank you very much, Admiral Valdés. Our next speaker is from Estonia, Captain Igor Schvede, with the panel topic "Threats to Information Sharing." Captain Schvede, one of the youngest CNOs in this room, started his career in the Soviet Navy in 1986 and graduated from the Russian Naval Academy in 1993, then that same year joined the reestablished Estonian Navy.

His operational career has many seagoing experiences. He was the commanding officer of ENS *Ahti* and ENS *Sulev* and also squadron commander of their mine countermeasure units. He attended the U.S. Naval Staff College in 1996 and currently is attending the Naval Command College, the class of 2012.

Since 15 June 2011 he is the current Commander of the Estonian Navy. Please, everyone, give a warm welcome to Captain Schvede.

Captain Igor Schvede, Estonia:

Admiral Greenert, Admiral Christenson, distinguished heads of the navies and coast guards, ladies and gentlemen, good morning. Admiral Greenert, thank you very much for organizing this remarkable event, for giving me the opportunity to participate in this great panel and to present the topic of cyber defense. That is relatively new to all of us and has direct and practical significance to my country.

The aim of this short presentation is to raise your awareness of cyber defense and highlight the relevance of this issue for the maritime domain, and more specifically, for maritime information sharing. In our professional and everyday lives we are increasingly relying on personal computers, smartphones, and Internet. The threat caused by the abuse of quickly developing interdependent network of information technology is changing rapidly.

Over the last two decades hacking has evolved from activity largely viewed as a nuisance to a serious, large-scale, criminal enterprise. It has now entered into an even more dangerous phase, one in which an attack on the network can amount to a terrorist strike, espionage, or an act of war.

I will follow with a few examples. Among the long history of malicious software epidemics, very few can claim sustained worldwide infiltration of millions of infected machines. Frightening is Conficker's potential to do harm. In the best case, it may be used as a sustained and profitable platform for massive Internet fraud and threat. In the worst case, Conficker could be turned into a powerful offensive weapon for performing concerted information warfare attacks that could disrupt not just countries, but the Internet itself. Remarkable is the fact that the developers of Conficker and their aims are still publicly unknown. Because of the ubiquitous nature of cyberspace, we have witnessed increases in the deliberate infiltration of computer networks in an effort to gain intelligence.

A number of attacks have infiltrated the government and security departments of many of our countries. Security specialists have warned of the increasing threat of attacks that can actually destroy equipment. Malicious code, itself, cannot cause a physical effect, but rather can be used to sabotage or assist a system's suicide.

Stuxnet, the first-known example of a computer worm designed to target major infrastructure facilities, was unleashed in 2010 and has infected computers at Iran's nuclear power station. Its release caused the European Network and Information Security Agency to note that it represented a paradigm shift in threats to critical infrastructure as it targeted supervisory control and data acquisition (SCADA) systems.

In April 2007 Estonia saw Web sites belonging to governmental departments, Internet providers, and banks under siege from sustained cyber attacks. The culprits were a widespread network of botnets preprogrammed to launch distributed denial of service attacks.

 ## Disruptive attacks / Estonia 2007

- DDoS attacks against:
  - Governmental websites and services
  - Banks, news portals, etc.
- Attack force formed by politically motivated individuals- "*Hacktivism*".
- Social networks used for coordination of attacks.
- Attack tools and knowledge controlled by few, used by many.

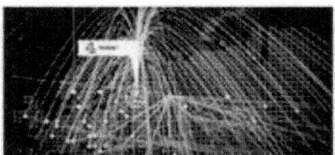

These massive attacks resulted in government officials being unable to access their e-mails, citizens unable to use their debit cards and banking accounts, and some government Web sites being defaced with pro-Soviet propaganda.

The fact that social networks and forums were used to coordinate attacks of individuals and easily distribute the necessary tools was a new development called by many "hacktivism." This coordination was conducted by using Russian Web sites, but there was no hard evidence linking any of the governments to the cyber attackers.

This slide shows the distribution of attackers' IPs [Internet protocols], in one of the networks that was attacked. IPs are from different points across the Internet, and it illustrates the difficulties in finding those responsible for cyber attacks. The military attacks against Georgia in 2008 were supported by a massive cyber campaign. Remarkable about that case is that actions in cyber domain were well coordinated and synchronized with activities in the ground, air, and maritime domains.

The politically motivated cyber attacks against Estonia and Georgia created a national debate, which has propelled the concept of cyber warfare into a major foreign policy issue and national security problem. The cyber domain is very different from land, sea, air, and outer space. Cyber is the military environment's first entirely man-made domain, and it touches every geographic region and operational realm. Unlike the physical word, the amorphous cyber domain has no clear geographic areas in which commanders can operate, and even attributing military or domestic jurisdiction poses a significant challenge. It is ubiquitous, ready to use, virtually free of boundaries, and open to almost everyone who can afford the necessary infrastructure.

Operating in cyberspace presents a number of challenges. The attribution problem is the biggest obstacle for creating a set of rules surrounding behavior in cyberspace. The role nonmilitary actors, such as cyber mercenaries, cyber privateers, and cyber vigilantes, will play in future cyber defense and their roles in cyber conflicts—this needs to be addressed.

The differentiation between cyber criminals, cyber terrorists, cyber warfare, and espionage is difficult, as they all use many of the same tools, and attacks are launched from the same platform. One of the main challenges facing the international community is establishing global norms for cyber engagements that could avoid some serious international tension in the future.

Nations that employ cyber warfare capability should be aware about the possible consequences. As our ability to defend our networks grows, we need consensus on the right way to address specific threats. We must not let differences between jurisdictions create a weak spot for attackers to exploit. Establishment of any level of control over the Internet should be considered in relation to personal privacy in cyberspace.

We are also facing a number of technical questions. How do we develop international awareness in cyberspace? What sensors do you use? Can we provide advanced warning of impending cyber attacks? How do you fuse the information, and how do you display it in an understandable format to operators?

Modern naval equipment is loaded with computerization. Our reliance on information systems is growing rapidly, as well as a wider interconnection between the military systems and the Internet. Maritime domain awareness is the prerequisite of maritime security and depends on surveillance and information sharing by our international community.

With increasingly overlapping activities, with so many risks and threats hiding among regular businesses, maritime surveillance is becoming more and more a necessity which requires the exchange of information with all stakeholders. As trade volumes and maritime congestion increase at key destinations and choke points, pressure is growing to take advantage of technology now available for a more active approach to maritime traffic control in the interest of safety, security, and efficiency.

Tailored communications and information systems become less affordable and suitable. Civil and military technology are tending to converge. The technologies to support collaboration, information discovery, and exchange across multiple classification domains are often commercial off-the-shelf (COTS)–based service-oriented, loosely coupled federation of systems connected over the Internet. The described environment provides a potentially attractive target for adversaries seeking to exploit vulnerabilities for criminal or harmful intent.

If not properly protected, maritime information systems are open to attacks that intend to collect, destroy, and change critical information inside systems, as well as [cause] system disruption or destruction. Maritime situational awareness and understanding are essential to success, but depend on the resilience of the relevant information systems.

The culture ought to be changed. We cannot afford to do things the old way. We have to have up-to-date technology. Our adversaries will exploit any weakness in even slightly old technology. We have to provide robust intelligence and counterintelligence, maintain qualified people, establish uniform policies and practices, introduce training and awareness.

People should be aware of the problem of cyber attacks and have training to deal with them. We should develop cyber defense partnerships with industry. It will optimize a shared effort. As protecting from cyber attacks is an exceptionally complex mission, it requires interagency coordination.

The difficulty in delineating which governmental agency has authority and jurisdiction over a particular cyber incident should be addressed. Nations must stand [up] security guards, but they must also forge links with like-minded countries and elaborate international law enforcement agreements.

To enhance the capability, cooperation, and information sharing among NATO, NATO nations, and partners in cyber defense, the NATO [Cooperative] Cyber Defence Centre of Excellence (CCDCOE) was activated in Estonia in May 2008. The center is a source of expertise in the field of cooperative cyber defense. The center accumulates, creates, and disseminates knowledge in related matters.

The Centre of Excellence now hosts one of the most advanced cyber defense research centers. The center conducts research in legal and policy, concepts and strategy, and technical areas. The center has taken a NATO-orientated interdisciplinary approach to its focus areas. The work of the center is based on extensive information exchange, and cooperation with NATO and NATO states, as well as academia and the private sector. The center holds technical courses to bring together and train computer and network computer specialists.

The cyber dimensional warfare has exposed us to ever-increasing threats. It is rapidly transforming many aspects of military affairs, international relations, and national economies. These changes are going to require us not only to rethink tactics but redesign equipment, as cyber threats are transnational and developing appropriate responses in a world of such dynamic threats requires effective international cooperation. Thank you very much.

Admiral Edmundo González Robles, Chile:

Thank you, Captain Schvede. Our next panelist is from Chile, Vice Admiral Enrique Larrañaga, head of the Chilean Coast Guard, with the final topic, "Disaster Response Experience."

Vice Admiral Larrañaga entered the Chilean Naval Academy in 1973. He is specialized in general staff and navigation systems. Among other staff instruction, he graduated from the Joint Staff Course of the French Armed Forces in 1998. During his more than fourteen years of seagoing experience, he has served in many ships from the Chilean Navy and was the commanding officer of the fast missile boat LM *Chipana*, the transport ship TS *Aquiles*, and our famous tall ship TS *Esmeralda*.

Since June 2009 he assumed the head of the Chilean Coast Guard, named Directemar. Admiral, you have the floor, and do not forget that you still belong to the Chilean Navy for the purpose of controlling your time. Please give him a round of applause.

Vice Admiral Enrique Larrañaga Martin, Chile:

Thank you, Admiral. Admiral Greenert, U.S. Chief of Naval Operations; Rear Admiral John Christenson, President of the U.S. Naval War College; distinguished heads of the navies and coast guards; ladies and gentlemen: first of all, I would like to thank you on behalf of the Chilean Navy for the opportunity to share the experience obtained from the earthquake and subsequent tsunami that hit our coast on 27 February 2010.

As I only have fifteen minutes, and considering the serious warnings made by the panel moderator, that in my case could represent more than just showing me a red card or blowing the whistle, I will do my best to point out the aspects I consider relevant.

My presentation will unfold as follows: First of all, I will refer to the characteristics of the earthquake; then I will provide details on the earthquake's main consequences as well as those caused by the subsequent tsunami. I will also mention the assistance provided by the navy in the affected regions, concluding with a summary of the lessons learned.

As you may well know, Chile is located in the Pacific basin, in an area where we experience permanent seismic activity due to the convergence between the Nazca and South American plates. We are one of the most seismic countries in the world, experiencing frequent tremors of different intensites.

On 27 February 2010 at 0334 hours the country was hit by an earthquake that reached a magnitude of 8.8 on the Richter scale, lasting almost three minutes. The epicenter was located twenty kilometers off the coast, which generated, a few minutes later, a tsunami that reached various ports and coastal facilities.

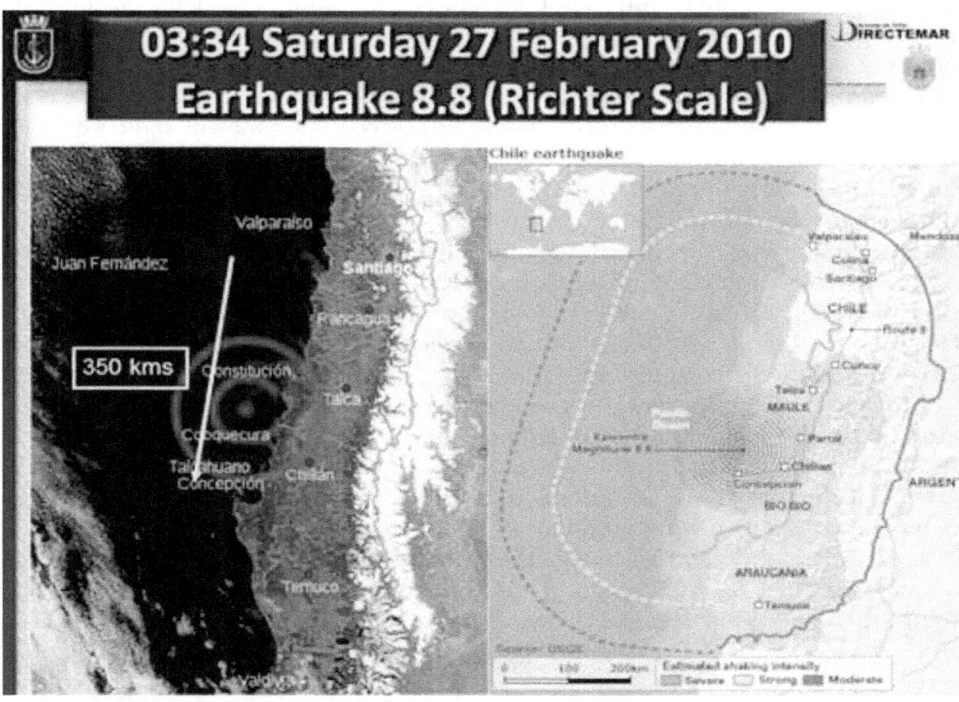

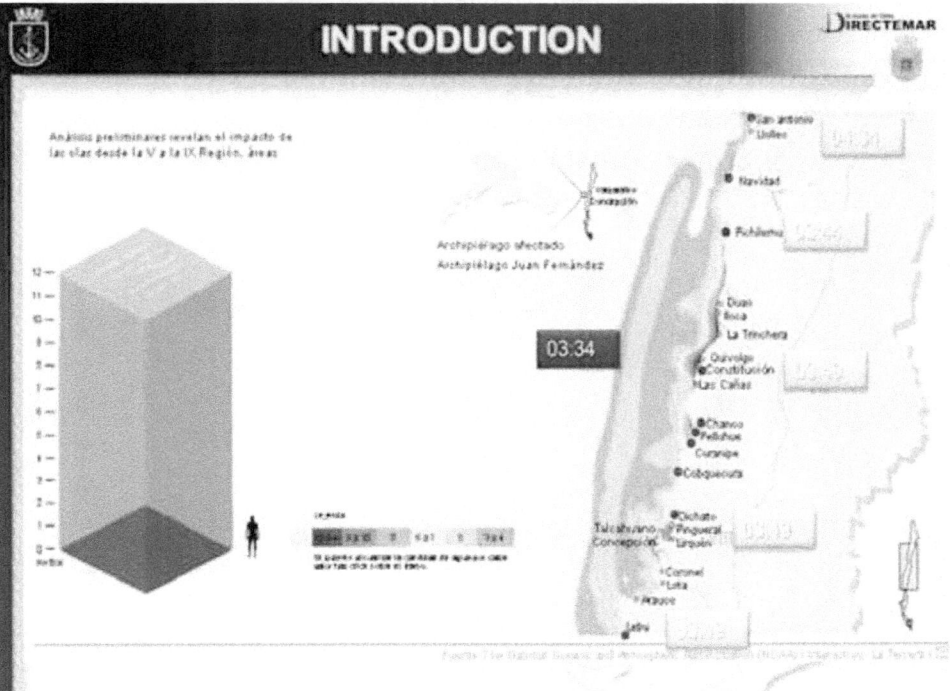

The earthquake covered the country's central area, where the largest number of people live. Nearly six million people were involved in the earthquake, which represents 34 percent of the country's population. Fifteen minutes after the earthquake the first tsunami waves reached the coastline. These ranged from three to fourteen meters in height, depending on the geographical areas affected.

An important fact that reveals the seismic intensity is the impact of the earthquake on our coastline. The earth's crust was displaced three meters to the west and significant variations to the subsoil elevations were generated, changing the topography of the coast and ports. This has demanded intensive hydrographical work to update the relevant cartography.

Having described the characteristics of the earthquake and tsunami, I will now explain its consequences. First of all, the electric power went out in all the central areas, together with the total loss of communications, landlines and cell phones. This caused a high level of misinformation and the inability to correctly assess the damages and the real magnitude of the disaster.

With the first light of dawn, it was possible to assess the damage caused by the earthquake and tsunami. As a consequence of the earthquake, hundreds of buildings were destroyed, such as homes, public buildings, hospitals, schools. Bridges, roads, and highways were also destroyed, which obstructed the movement of vehicles and consequently the possibility of providing further assistance.

Moreover, due to the devastating effects, mainly of the tsunami, all coves located between the cities of Valparaíso and Talcahuano were seriously damaged. Most of them were completely destroyed, as you can see here in the slides. Our ports also suffered the effects of the tsunami. Hundreds of small- and medium-sized ships were pushed inland. At the same time two of the most important ports, Valparaíso and Talcahuano, had to temporarily stop their operations so as to have a real view of the damages.

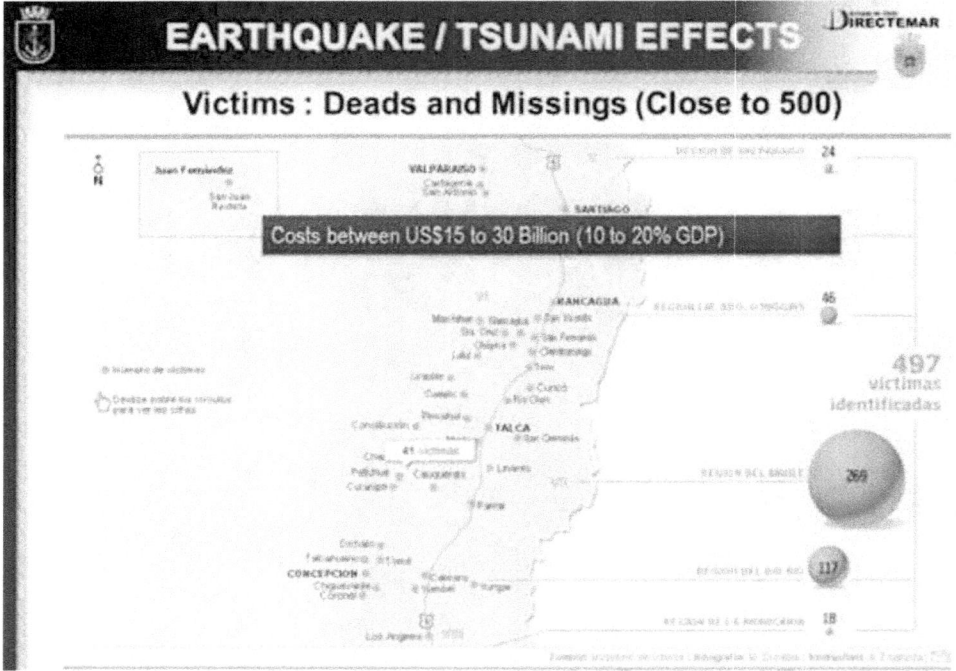

The operations of the berthing sites that did not suffer damage were gradually restored in order to carry on with maritime trade activities. In terms of human lives, this disaster left nearly 500 fatalities and missing people, 156 of them due to the tsunami. In the economic area, the cost of the appraised damages was between $15 and $30 billion, which corresponds to 20 percent of the gross domestic product of Chile.

The navy also suffered significantly the effects of this incident. Our main naval base and naval shipyard are located in Talcahuano, one of the regions that was most affected by this catastrophe. The naval base was badly damaged, and the shipyard was virtually destroyed by the effects of the tsunami.

The estimated cost of the damages reached $600 million, which is very close to the annual budget of the navy. The ships that were under repair were also damaged, some of them to a great extent, as you will see in the following slides.

Here we can see a missile boat and a floating dock that were moved on top of one of the piers. At the same time the merchant ship *Laurel*, which was being repaired on a dry dock, was ejected from the dock, being left above one of the facilities nearby. The scientific ship *Cabo de Hornos*, which was due to be [christened] on that day, grounded in the coastline, fortunately with minor damages only.

The shipyard's repair dock was completely damaged, as in its interior two floating docks were sunk, together with other ships that were tossed by the waves. Additionally, piers were severely damaged; hence, ships were unable to berth. Luckily, eleven ships of the navy that were in Talcahuano departed immediately after the earthquake, following the institutional doctrine. Therefore, they were not affected by the tsunami.

Some of the captain of the port's offices, which are under the maritime authority command, were also severely affected. In the slide you can see the captain of the port's office at Constitución and the house of the personnel which disappeared due to the tsunami.

Assistance provided by the navy: forty-eight hours after the catastrophe the Chilean government made a first assessment of the situation, and the results were alarming. More than five hundred thousand houses had been destroyed, and 1.5 million people were isolated with no water, electricity, or food. Almost a thousand vessels had run aground, about 700 people had died or were missing, and supermarkets were being looted in the cities most severely affected by the catastrophe. Faced with this scenario, the government declared a state of disaster in six of the fifteen administrative regions of Chile and requested the assistance of the armed forces through the Joint Command in the efforts to respond to the emergency. The Chilean Navy undertook two tasks. The first one was the reconstruction of its main naval base and shipyard, which had been heavily damaged. I would like to point out that the base has been recovered to an important extent and that our shipyard, ASMAR [the Chilean shipbuilding and ship-repair company], is 80 percent operational at this time.

The second task was the assistance provided to the community, for which the navy deployed marine troops in the area of Talcahuano to enforce the curfew imposed by the government and to provide protection for the safe arrival and distribution of the aid coming from the center of the country.

Similarly, a logistics train comprising surface ships and helicopters was set up on 1 March to provide assistance to the seventeen coves that were isolated. The distribution of supplies and essentials was performed in coordination with the regional

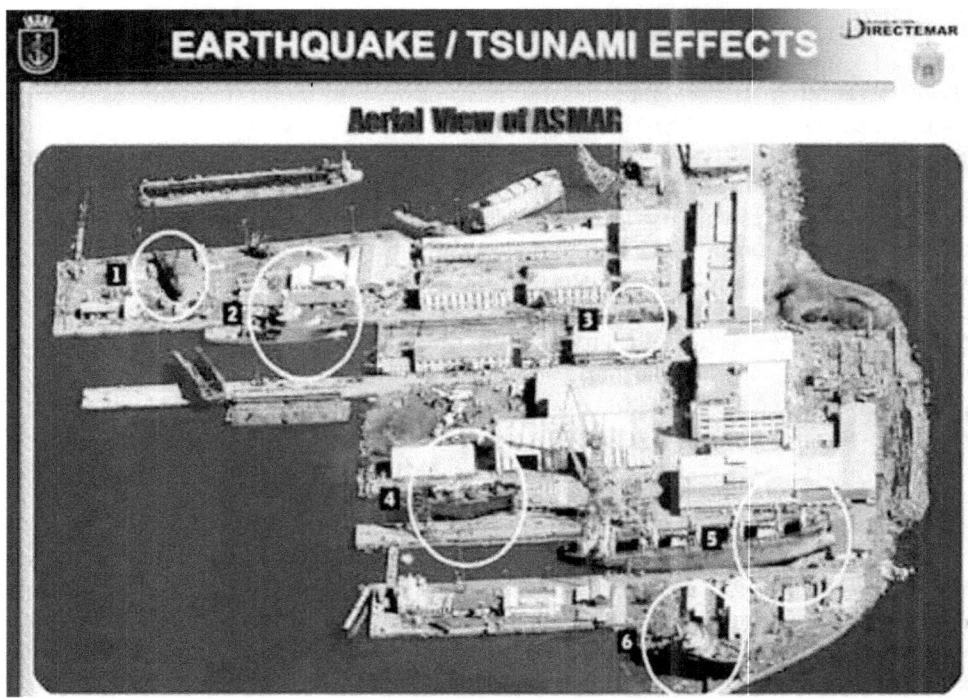

authorities. Fourteen ships were deployed to provide all supplies required by these isolated communities until the land infrastructure was restored. Health care and emergency medical assistance were provided as well.

It is very important to mention the work of the navy in two of the areas most severely affected by the catastrophe, Talcahuano and Juan Fernández archipelago. Both communities have always had special ties with the Chilean Navy. The main naval base is situated in Talcahuano, and Juan Fernández, consisting of several islands, has always relied heavily on the assistance provided by the navy.

This is why the commander in chief of the Chilean Navy decided to organize a special task force to contribute to their reconstruction, allocating a significant amount of personnel and resources to that end. Through this effort, the restoration of the basic services and a great deal of the reconstruction work were completed.

The support provided by the navy, apart from that above-mentioned regarding coves, also involved the assistance in the removal of debris, the construction of emergency housing and schools, the transportation of relatives, and the restoration of basic services, such as water, electricity, and gas. This is still being done in the case of the Juan Fernández archipelago. In a nutshell, immediately following the disaster, the navy deployed all of its resources to assist the community. During the first twenty-two days, it deployed twenty-three ships and more than five thousand personnel, and transported more than three thousand tons of supplies to the cut-off areas.

After this brief description of the tasks performed, I will now share with you the lessons we learned from this experience. From a broad perspective, the most important lessons are in the following: Nobody is ever fully prepared to face an event of such a magnitude. However, emergency preparedness always contributes to reduce significantly the potential effects of a catastrophe.

Communications are essential. In spite of being generally quite efficient, modern systems are not sufficiently robust to stand the demands in emergencies of this kind. People were desperate to get in touch with their relatives, and as a result, the reduced capacity of the cell phone network was overloaded. Most of the people that died and went missing due to the tsunami lived inland and were vacationing on the coast. This is why it is important to educate and prepare inhabitants of inland areas and make them able to react the same way as people who live on the coast.

Under extreme situations, like the 2010 earthquake, an initial shortage of basic supplies is very likely, leaving the police force overwhelmed. Therefore, it is important to assess the situation diligently, to declare a state of emergency when necessary, and to employ every single resource required to maintain order and protect the population.

The national emergency plan that involves the government and the armed forces proved to be effective. Eleven days after the earthquake and tsunami, a new president took office, and this change of government did not disrupt or cause any disruption in the activities to maintain support and order.

Our naval doctrine was highly effective. In spite of the fact that most of our personnel were on holiday, they rushed to board their ships, which set sail with no official order, preventing elements of great importance to our navy from being damaged.

When faced with a situation like the one described, prior to authorizing the use of ports, it is imperative to probe the existing depths to identify any potential variations. Depth reductions of up to two meters were detected in this case, and had this work not been done, major inconveniences might have arisen.

Every single effort made to increase the preparedness for this type of emergency and to enhance the procedures established to work jointly with safety and emergency agencies are the best contribution to protect our citizens.

To conclude, I would like to share a final thought. The engagement of the navy in situations of this nature will be increasingly necessary, demanded, and judged. The capabilities required to assist the population must be prepared, organized and trained for the navy to be as efficient as it is today in other roles we deem more important for it to fulfill.

This concludes my presentation. Thank you very much for your kind attention.

Admiral Edmundo González Robles, Chile:

Finally, from Japan, my friend Admiral Masahiko Sugimoto with the panel topic "Naval Force Resilience and Disaster Response." Admiral Sugimoto graduated from the National Defense Academy in Japan in 1974. He has served as a surface warfare officer throughout his entire career.

His long sea duty includes commanding officer of the destroyer *Haruyuki*, Commander of Escort Flotilla 3, Commander of Training Squadron, and Commander of Fleet Submarine Force. Admiral Sugimoto was the Commander in Chief of the Self-Defense Fleet between 2009 and '10 and became the thirtieth Chief of the Maritime Staff of the Japan Maritime Self-Defense Force in July 2010. Please, everyone, give a warm welcome to Admiral Sugimoto.

Admiral Masahiko Sugimoto, Japan:

Admiral, thank you for that kind introduction. Admirals, fellow officers, and ladies and gentlemen, I am Admiral Sugimoto, Chief of Maritime Staff, Japan Maritime Self-Defense Force [JMSDF]. First of all, on behalf of the Japanese nation, I would like to extend our sincere appreciation for your support during the east Japan great earthquake. It's also a great pleasure that I am given a chance to speak in front of all of you. Admiral Greenert, Admiral Christenson, thank you very much for this wonderful opportunity.

The Japan Maritime Self-Defense Force has conducted various overseas operations, such as activity in the great east Japan earthquake and international activities in [response to] the 2004 Indian Ocean earthquake and tsunami.

I would like to talk about naval force resilience and disaster relief response. The contents are shown on the screen. The first part is about Japan Maritime Self-Defense Force's activities in support of the great east Japan earthquake rescue, recovery, and reconstruction.

To begin with, I will introduce an overview of the disaster. The Tohoku region earthquake struck at 1446 on 11 March 2011. It was an unprecedented earthquake. The Richter scale was 9.0. This quake generated a huge tsunami with a maximum 18.3-meter wave crashing ashore and causing immense harm.

 ## Brief Overview of the disaster (1/2)

For the peace and Stability

Tohoku Region earthquake	
Date	Friday, 11. MARCH, 2011 1446i
Hypocenter	ESE130km off Oga peninsula, Depth 24km
Richter Scale	M 9.0
Tsunami	Maximum Height 18.3m (Reached to the place 37.9m)
Human	Dead 15,823 Missing 3,884 Injured 5,942
Damage House	Completely 118,621 Half 181,687 Partial 601,868
Refugee	73,249 (max.386,739)

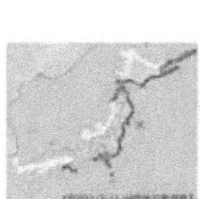

Seismic Intensity Map   Tsunami   Tsunami Effect

Approximately 16,000 people died. Approximately 4,000 people are still missing, and approximately nine hundred thousand houses were destroyed. This tsunami caused a nuclear disaster in Fukushima's number one nuclear power plant as well. The current condition of each reactor is shown on the screen. The screen shows the characteristics of the disaster and the Self-Defense Force's [JSDF's] response.

Brief Overview of the disaster (2/2)

Nuclear Disaster in Fukushima NPS No.1

History ECCS: Emergency Core Cooling System

11, MARCH 1446i	All Reactor: Shut down automatically after the quake.
1527i	Tsunami Crashed Ashore
1542i	Loss of A/C power, Inability of water injection of the ECCS
12, MARCH 1536i	Hydrogen Explosion in NPR1
14, MARCH 1101i	Hydrogen Explosion in NPR3
15, MARCH 0610i	Hydrogen Explosion in NPR2
0614i	Hydrogen Explosion in NPR4

Current Condition

	Unit1	Unit2	Unit3	Unit4
Reactor	Cooling by Fresh water			
Spent Fuel Pool	Circulation Cooling by Fresh Water			
Drainage from the Turbine Building	Moving to other building			NONE

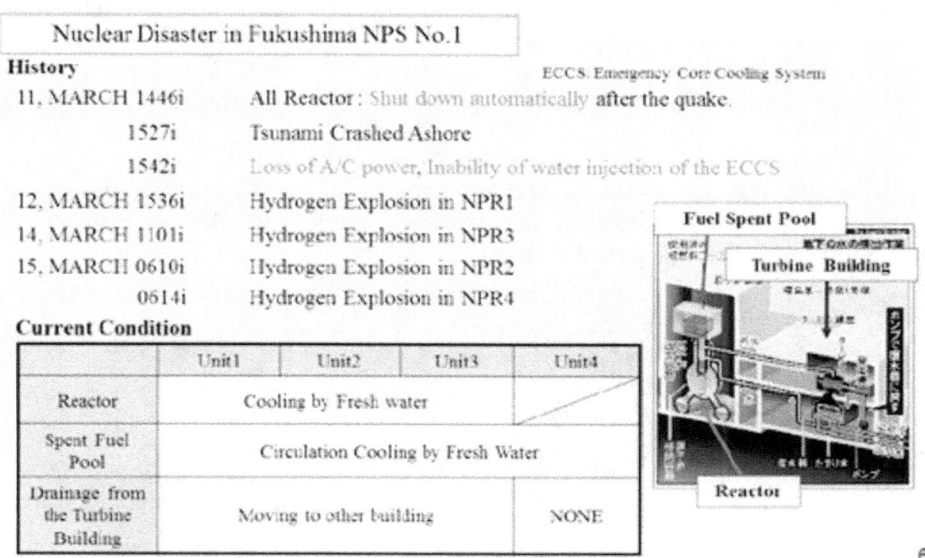

The characteristic of this disaster is an unprecedented earthquake, causing a huge tsunami that crashed into the broad area from the Kanto region to the Tohoku region. The characteristic of the Self-Defense Force operations is that the JMSDF conducted two operations, respond to quake and respond to the nuclear disaster.

Overview of JSDF Activities (1/3)

4 Apr 2011

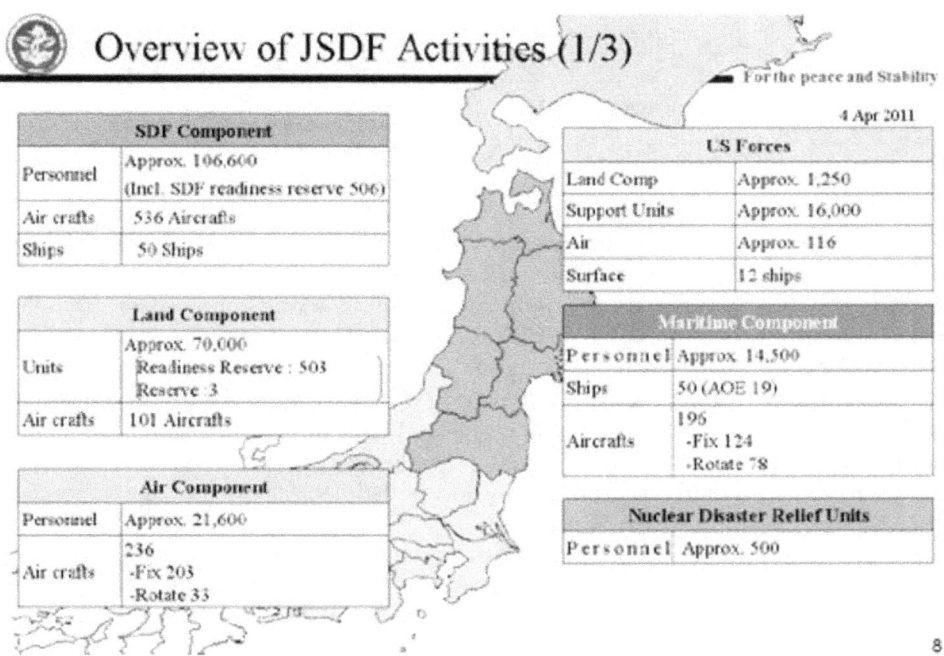

SDF Component	
Personnel	Approx. 106,600 (Incl. SDF readiness reserve 506)
Air crafts	536 Aircrafts
Ships	50 Ships

Land Component	
Units	Approx. 70,000 Readiness Reserve : 503 Reserve : 3
Air crafts	101 Aircrafts

Air Component	
Personnel	Approx. 21,600
Air crafts	236 -Fix 203 -Rotate 33

US Forces	
Land Comp	Approx. 1,250
Support Units	Approx. 16,000
Air	Approx. 116
Surface	12 ships

Maritime Component	
Personnel	Approx. 14,500
Ships	50 (AOE 19)
Aircrafts	196 -Fix 124 -Rotate 78

Nuclear Disaster Relief Units	
Personnel	Approx. 500

The screen shows Japan's Self-Defense Force activity on 4 April. Not only JMSDF but U.S. Joint Support Force conducted this operation, TOMADACHI, for the support of Japan. The screen shows activities conducted by JMSDF units, the engagement in disaster relief operations along the coast of northeastern Japan. The Pacific Fleet of the United States Navy also kindly conducted Operation TOMADACHI. We also conducted search and rescue operations and livelihood support operations in the isolated areas.

In support of the nuclear disaster relief operation, JMSDF conducted support operations for water spraying and the water supply mission. The international community supported us through not only providing aid and supplies, but also activities by the international disaster relief team.

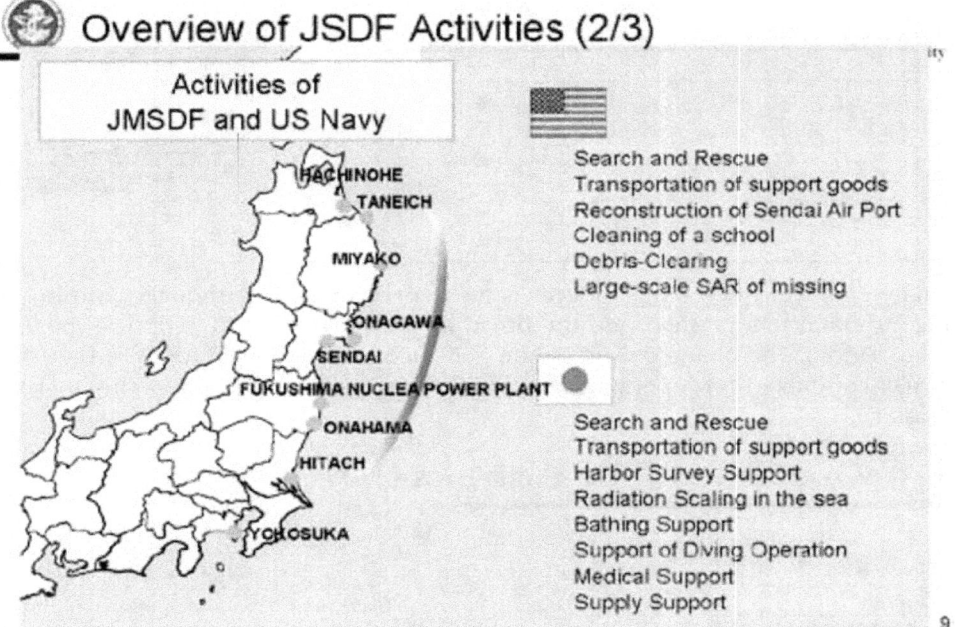

Among the countries providing us support, the U.S. forces were the first to react. A lot of U.S. Navy units, such as *Ronald Reagan* Strike Group, suspended their original missions and commenced the support operations along the disaster area. We realize the significance of the Japan-U.S. alliance, and we successfully demonstrated the fruit of cooperative efforts between our two navies.

Next I will discuss the utility of the navy and what we have so far learned through our HA/DR activities in the earthquake region. First I will explain the utility of the navy on the shore when the infrastructure facilities were damaged. Civil airports were damaged, and many roads were cut off when the great east Japan earthquake struck Japan.

The air force bases and their aircraft were damaged by the earthquake and the tsunami. However, while functions of ground bases were damaged, the JMSDF demonstrated flexibility and sustainability, core naval force characteristics, in a

Overview of JSDF Activities (3/3)

Response to the earthquake

	Land Component	Maritime Component	Air Component
Current OPS	Livelihood support Transportation Reconstruction Recovery of bodies	Search and Rescue Livelihood Support for isolated area – Transportation – Shower operation – Medical support	Livelihood support – Transportation – Reconstruction Recovery of Air Base

Nuclear Disaster Relief OPS

	Land Component	Maritime Component	Air Component
Current OPS	Water-spraying Decontamination Evacuation of residents	Support for Water-spraying Water Supply	Support for Water-spraying Reconnaissance

full-fledged manner. This is a fusion of the navy's function in an environment other than warfare, which demonstrates the great utility of the navy.

[The] naval characteristic of diversity was also shown, as was the case in the relief operations during the Indonesian-Sumatra earthquake. JMSDF contributed various kinds of activity in order to fulfill the diverse needs in the case of disaster response.

[The] naval characteristic of versatility functioned effectively during these activities. For example, the LCAC [air-cushion landing craft] is generally used in amphibious operations. However, it contributed to transportation of personnel, materials of huge amounts, and landing of support vehicles. Especially noteworthy was its utility regarding "barrier free" transportation for the old and the sick.

In addition, rescue ships and minesweepers, which usually engage in search and rescue operations and minesweeping operations, were quite useful in port clearance operations and search and rescue operations for those missing. The high-end equipment which we have procured to fight and win various kinds of battles showed its versatility and was adapted to a variety of activities and the successful performance of the mission. This adaptation cannot be achieved by tanks or fighters. Only the navy can do it.

Finally, I will show you some insights to the establishment of the maritime security through humanitarian assistance and disaster relief operations, which is to adapt itself in various operational circumstances.

The world situation has changed in the last decade, and the naval operational concept has also changed according to the global situation. As time has changed, the naval operational concept has changed as well, from battles on the blue water to ones in the littoral waters. Now our mission has expanded and diversified to a symmetric warfare, like the war on terror, and to gray-zone activities.

We previously considered sea lanes of communication [SLOCs] as lines. However, it is clear that securing the safety of SLOCs in a unified and standardized manner is difficult, due to the difference of security situation, threat, and the capabilities of coastal navies in each region. Therefore, we think it is more practical to divide our

Transformation of naval operation concept
For the peace and Stability

1980s Cold War, response to world war Wartime

Battle on the open sea

1990s Post Cold War, response to regional conflicts
    1991 Detachment of main sweepers to Gulf of Persia
    1992 Cambodia PKO
    1999 International Disaster Relief Activities of Turkish earthquake

Battle on the coast

2000s Response to establishment and maintenance of global security
    (Transnational threat (terrorism, piracy, natural disaster))
    2001 Refueling activity etc.
    2002 East Timor PKO
    2005 International Disaster Relief Activities of Sumatra
    2009 Anti-piracy Activity

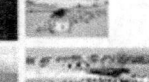

Asymmetry Warfare
+
Activities in peacetime

Peacetime

 Peace time efforts for Maritime Security
For the peace and Stability

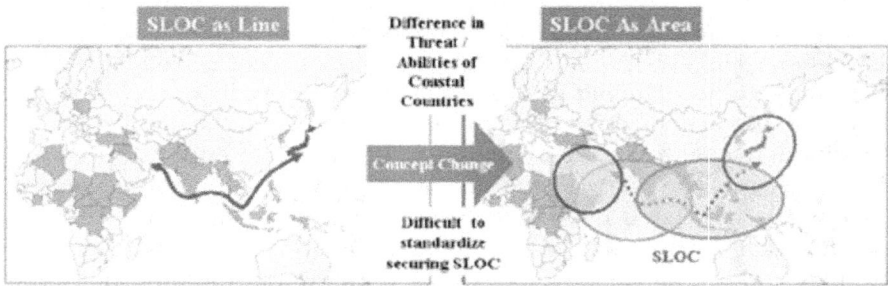

Up until now, when we thought of securing the safety of maritime routes, we thought in terms of "lines," as in Sea Lines of Communication (SLOC). However, it is clear that securing the safety of maritime routes in a uniform and standardized manner would be difficult due to differing situations and threats in various maritime regions, and the differences in capabilities of various littoral states. Instead, it may be more practical to divide up SLOCs into several maritime regions, or "areas," **in order to come up with measures to ensure maritime security in relation to each area's specific circumstances.**
Statement by Mr. Toshimi KITAZAWA, Minister of Defense of Japan, at The 9th IISS Asia Security Summit (The Shangri-La Dialogue)

SLOCs into several regions or areas in order to draft measures to ensure maritime security in relation to each area's specific security environment. Therefore, JMSDF divides SLOCs reaching from Japan to the Middle East into four areas based on the security situation in each region.

Next is an introduction of our effort in the Asia-Pacific region as part of the peacetime engagement of the navy. JMSDF approaches the activity regarding peace-time engagement in the framework of ARF [ASEAN Regional Forum], WPNS [Western

Peacetime Engagement of Navy (Efforts in Asia-Pacific region)

For the peace and Stability

ASEAN Region Forum

ARF-EWG
- HA/DR
- Maritime Security
- Military Medicine [Japan Malaysia Co-Chair]
- Response to terrorism
- Peace Keeping Operation

Information Sharing
Work Shop
Seminar
Promotion of
Joint Exercise

Bilateral
- ARF-DIREX [Japan-Philippine Co-hosted]
- ARF-VDR

Western Pacific Naval Symposium

Efforts regarding Maritime security, Enforcement of interoperability regarding operations etc. MOOTW etc. including HA/DR
⇒Seeking multinational cooperation in new field etc. Approach to wide and complex issue

Seminar etc.
- WPNS Symposium
- Short Study Program
  【JMSDF Hosted】
  (Educate lesson of HA/DR Activities)
- Seminar of Maritime Security
- Establishment of SOP

Joint exercise
- Multinational Training on the water
- Submarine Rescue Training in West-Pacific
  【Next JMSDF Hosted】
- HA/DR Table Top Exercise (TTX)

Pacific Naval Symposium], and so forth, in the Asia-Pacific region. JMSDF conducts joint exercises, such as ARF DiREx [Disaster Relief Exercises]. JMSDF holds a short-term exchange program and various seminars and HA/DR exercises. Also, it actively makes an effort to share lessons learned in the peacetime engagement, such as HA/DR.

Peacetime engagement is one of the most important measures to contribute to the regional and global maritime security. Conducting these activities will enhance the military exchange and promote the cooperation between participating navies. In particular, cooperative activities with the same purpose and in the same area are full of possibilities that spin off regional stability by materializing regional confidence building and mutual understanding.

Therefore, we think that outreach activities at the global level that only the navy can embody as peacetime engagement is significant. Through the cooperation with other navies of the world, we will conduct proactive engagement towards the maritime security, which we have been conducting.

We think that the JMSDF should promote partnership among navies which are facing common issues in peacetime and contribute to the improvement of free and open maritime security by taking a leadership role based on the cooperation with the U.S. Navy in order to respond to changing security environments.

This picture shows a dog I named Kongo Maru. Security dogs usually engage in guarding a base. However, he was deployed to a devastated area as an HA/DR dog to achieve a mission in the time of the great east Japan earthquake. Unfortunately, he died because of disease soon after he returned to his home base. Thus, naval versatility means not only the equipment on vessels. I would like to conclude my presentation. Thank you for your attention.

Admiral Edmundo González Robles, Chile:

Thank you, Admiral Sugimoto. I think we have a short time for maybe a couple of questions. I would like to offer the questions to the distinguished military. If there's any question, please raise your hand.

Mr. David Titley, United States:

Admiral Grimstvedt, thank you for your presentation on the Arctic. Sir, talk about the sea lanes and resource competition. Are there any things in the Arctic that, as we go to these conferences, maybe we should be thinking about from your perspective that are not normally discussed? What are we missing, if anything? Thank you, sir.

Admiral Edmundo González Robles, Chile:

I would like to complement your question to Admiral Grimstvedt with [another]: how will these changes affect, or not, the future building of merchant ships that will use those routes?

Rear Admiral Bernt Grimstvedt, Norway:

What are we missing? Of course, that's a difficult question to answer in a very short way. Let me mention something. I think at least what we have not discussed in detail, but what we fear in my country, is the migration of the fishery stocks as a result of changes in the seawater temperature.

There are huge economic interests related to the fisheries up north. We do not know really what impact it will have on the fishery stocks, but that is obviously one area. Another thing is, of course, if we foresee an accelerating increase in the temperature in these areas, what will that do to the infrastructure? The land-based infrastructure, at least in Siberia, especially, is based on the permafrost. Is that the right English word for it? If you get a meltdown of the permafrost, it would also have impacts.

Of course, there's the political climate. What is achievable during a period where you still have disputed areas or unresolved issues could also be something that we do not foresee the full consequence of. As I mentioned in my presentation, I think that we have reason to be optimistic relating to establishing a sound political climate. That is probably the most important thing.

Admiral Edmundo González Robles, Chile:

Thank you, Admiral. How is it going to affect the future of shipbuilders and merchant ships, must be ice class or not?

Rear Admiral Bernt Grimstvedt, Norway:

That means the ship will be more expensive and, of course, that will have to be withdrawn from the benefit you gain from saving fuel and time, insurance premium, more expensive ships, and, of course, it's the bottom line. Is it a red number or black number on the bottom line? That will obviously be the final decision point for the shipowners.

Admiral Edmundo González Robles, Chile:

Thanks. An extra question, please?

Vice Admiral Paul Maddison, Canada:

My question is for Admirals Larrañaga and Sugimoto. Listening to your excellent presentations brought back very real memories of how the world reacted, first, in shock [to] the scale of the disasters in your two countries, which then transitioned quickly into great admiration for the way in which you displayed leadership, national will, and great resilience in overcoming the incredible challenges that these disasters presented to you.

In listening to your presentations and for this audience, I can understand why you focused on the responses of your navies to the natural disasters, but I'm sure that your armies and your air forces were also involved. I'm wondering whether you can comment on the degree to which there was integrated joint planning and execution in response, and whether there are lessons that you have learned from that response that you will apply in the event that this happens again.

Admiral Sugimoto, Japan:

Thank you very much for your question. Let me respond. First of all, not only the JMSDF but also ground force and air/ground force—in total, one hundred thousand people were deployed to respond to that disaster. Furthermore, from the United States Army and Air Force and Marine Corps, all of them also participated in disaster recovery.

In particular for the JMSDF, the response to the earthquake and rescue of humans have to be done within seventy-two hours. This is the criteria learned from my experience. Within this seventy-two hours, how fast you can deploy your forces and be engaged in the rescue operation, this is the major point. So air, ground, and sea forces all have the system to deploy the forces.

After that period, from the United States, there are all kinds of support provided to us. We have a U.S.-Japan [alliance], both Air Force and ground Marine Corps, all seven [Japanese and U.S. armed forces] were involved in this kind of operation. We thought this is a very difficult endeavor. However, the JMSDF, for instance, since 1952, more than fifty-five years, [has had] a joint exercise done with U.S. Navy. Based on that foundation, the joint integration of U.S. and Japan forces was able to fully perform in executing the joint operations. The same applies to JGSDF [Japan Ground Self-Defense Force] and, as I said, JASDF [Japan Air Self-Defense Force].

In terms of lessons, I think in terms of information sharing, in terms of emergency, both ground as well as the air and the Marine Corps of the U.S. forces, I'm sure there's some room for improvement, because all seven forces—how are we going to incorporate all these seven forces into one system and one information network?

In terms of protocol and communication and also the Internet communication, we would have to do further research and do more exercise operations jointly.

Vice Admiral Enrique Larrañaga, Chile:

In fact, sir, the Chilean Armed Forces jointly undertook rescue and recovery missions. When I made my presentation, I focused only on the work conducted by the navy, but the work was not limited thereto.

I want to point out that we have a national emergency plan that provides for the centralization of decision making at a particular agency where we have the convergence of deputies and delegates from the armed forces, from law enforcement, and from fire departments. This national center assesses the situation, and then through the joint staff, in the case of the armed forces, determines the type of support that is needed to offer response and solution to the problems that arise. We also had a great deal of international support, mainly from the United States, that swiftly responded to our situation. We also received a great deal of support from Japan, which offered significant assistance.

Our organization should be self-sufficient to face this type of emergency. After the disaster, we conducted a series of meetings to improve dated procedures, to develop updated protocols, and the navy plays a very important role here, because we have under our responsibility the hydrographic and oceanographic service of the navy, which is responsible for evaluating the potential for tsunamis. We give this information to the information center, which then disseminates it throughout the country.

We improved our communication protocols with this center, and we also improved and updated our communication equipment, and we reinforced our naval and maritime networks. We were able, as a result, to have better communication, if any such emergency would arise again.

Admiral Edmundo González Robles, Chile:

Thank you so much. We are just on time. Just allow me to give some reflections or final conclusions to this discussion panel. Taking into account the vision of each distinguished speaker on this panel, related to evolving demands and adaptive partnerships under the maritime security scenario, I think we must conclude that the key challenges to confront the wide nature of threats that all maritime nations face now and in the near future are [as follows].

First, as we say, when we train our units at sea we must follow a sequence from the very basic to the advanced naval activities. I mean, we must then walk and finally run. That said, I am convinced that it's a milestone in order to improve our adaptive partnership to start by increasing our interoperability based on common procedures, communication systems, and a common doctrine.

Second, with the basic interoperability established, next we need to set up a framework of flexibility in our operations. We are all very skilled in our core war-fighting competencies; however, we must continue to strive to apply those competencies effectively in many nonconventional missions, such as disaster relief, counter–illicit trafficking, cyber attacks, and many others in which we can apply our capacities, providing the nature of flexibility of all naval forces.

Third, and finally, we need to continue to strengthen international cooperation and trust among all maritime countries in order to establish and develop flexible mechanisms in which our opportunities and synergy must be fully oriented to be used against the current and new threats present in the maritime environment.

The world is changing, and the threats out there using our seas are evolving. That's why we need to be able to adjust our navigation track while sailing towards a safer and sheltered port. This consideration is crucial if we want to provide our people and future generations a better place to live and a safer maritime environment. Thank you so much.

What I would like to do now is, again, invite Admiral John Christenson back up to the podium to close the forum.

11

Closing Remarks

Admiral John N. Christenson, U.S. Navy
President, U.S. Naval War College

Admiral Jonathan W. Greenert, U.S. Navy
Chief of Naval Operations

Admiral John Christenson, United States:

Thank you. As you all have now experienced, the International Seapower Symposium plays a unique and important role in naval affairs. You, the leaders of the world's navies and coast guards, have come together to think together and to build ever-stronger relationships. We have listened to each other's thoughts and concerns. We are continuing to learn from each other's different experiences and viewpoints. I observed it during the symposium. Our exchanges have been forthright and friendly.

When you envision and then execute an event of this magnitude, a tremendous amount of support is required. It is not possible to speak aloud all the names of those who executed the planning and preparation, but I will recognize their effort and thank them all.

To our ambassador, Mary Ann Peters, our provost and dean of faculty, thank you for leading our distinguished academic faculty and committing their support to this symposium. Captain Russ—"Gladys," to his medium-attack buddies—Knight my deputy and chief of staff, thank you to the team you led from the front.

Thank you to Captain Jim Harland and our naval officers who have been working on the planning of this event for the last twelve months while also holding down jobs, families, and living many miles from Newport. Naval Station Newport, in particular the Officers' Club, thank you for the great food, the receptions and the lunches here at the college. Thank you, shipmate Professor Tom Culora, our master of ceremonies. You, my artist, aviator, physicist, and intellectual friend, did a perfect job of keeping us on time and treating everyone so well. Special thanks to all the attachés and escort officers who made sure that each of the delegates got to the right place at the right time.

Thank you, Captain Scott Seaberger from CNO staff in Washington, and my classmate Professor Mike Sherlock, who together made this symposium happen. Thank you to our panelists and speakers, specifically Mr. Carmel, whose remarks are available in hard copy now back in the command center. They will also be included on your CD of the symposium.

Finally, and most of all, thank you to Admiral Greenert, our CNO. CNO, may the rest of your tour be as successful as you have made ISS XX in your first month leading our navy. So thank you all again for your participation in the Twentieth International Seapower Symposium. We came here to make our nations and the world a better place through the enlightened employment of our home away from home, the sea.

We look forward to your next visit to Newport and to the Naval War College. It is now my pleasure to invite CNO Admiral Greenert back to the stage for his final address to us all.

Admiral Jonathan Greenert, United States:

That was a pretty good summary for thanking folks. You're getting everything very organized. I do realize that between you all and that lunch is me. That's a tenuous place to be for a crowd like this.

Distinguished guests, thank you again. Thanks to the War College staff led by our President for putting this together. Listen, measured by all means that I do anyway, this was a success. People say you got to put the right topics together, make sure the food is decent, and get the right people in the room and let it go and things will happen. I think we pretty much saw that here.

Collectively, I think you all did great. I really didn't know what to expect. You can't expect things when you bring a symposium together, but I saw some great things come out. Individually, I had the opportunity to meet with many of you. That was really a privilege and honor, not to mention even [talking] in groups with all of you. Thank you for that.

I would also like to thank you on behalf of the Newport Chamber of Commerce, for your spouses who did their part out there to enhance our economy here in the New England area. Way to go.

Please let me close with three items here. Insights from the regional breakouts—I'll show you some pieces. These are not all insightful, as much, because there is much thinking yet to be done. These are a collection of observations from what we saw our folks put together for us, in my opinion, and some, I'd say, key takeaways from the panels.

From the regional breakout groups I took three things away, really, key matters—interoperability, maritime security, and assets. With regard to interoperability, it's clear it's not just about equipment. You can't just deliver stuff and say, "This is really cool, look at all it provides," and say, "We're good to go." That just won't work. We need to understand that it's about the people as well. It's more about the people. For example, it was clear that symposiums—or symposia, as you look at it—like this, although this is a broad scale, but those regional symposia are really starting to reap fruit. People are moving out. You all are moving out in a very deliberate way. It is clear that exercises and operations together build confidence. Clearly it builds trust. The panels made that clear to me.

Personnel exchange at sea and ashore, liaison officers at every opportunity—let's face it, that's a good investment. I learned a lot from that. We look at it sometimes as a nagging thing. Nobody likes to give up a staff officer. But if you put your best staff officer, I learned, over somewhere else, you reap fruit two, three times on that.

So we need to develop a common, what I would call a standard, operating procedure. If that is too specific, then maybe standard concept of operations where we can, maybe in piracy and maybe—as we saw today, what I wrote down on the panel this morning, because it happened so fast, the response needs to be so fast for disasters—maybe we can get a concept of operations for HA/DR.

I think we need to increase cooperative efforts. That's always good. We have just seen success in so many areas, examples from today's panel. Rather than list all the exercises—there's many of them—what we have found, and it was stated over and over again by heads of the coast guard, heads of the navy, that is exercises lay the groundwork for recovery from natural disasters.

The second area, maritime security: I think increasing multilateralism, it's kind of a mandate that we need to pursue. That is easier said than done. We are all products, or we are all sometimes victims, of a political process and policies that don't really lay forward easily for multilateralism.

I'd say if we seek and pursue the issues that resonate with our countries and even with the politics associated, we'd be well paid back for that effort. A good example clearly is antipiracy. We talked about that quite a bit.

Maritime security or maritime intercept, we talked a little about that. We touched on it. On a case-by-case basis, weapons of mass destruction or counter-drug [operations], as an example, might be something we could push forward in that regard. I think we need to unleash, as much as possible, our people, probably more in tier one on chat, on e-mail, on information sharing, because they will take off with it. We need to provide the means among them to do that, and I think that might be a more cost-effective manner. Maybe we can talk about that in future venues and see where we may do that.

With regard to assets, what I got was you have to match the assets to the mission. Don't just send stuff forward. Send stuff that fits in and that resonates. We have to listen. Those that provide, listen to what folks may need, rather than just sending things.

When I think about the symposium overall, a couple of things from last night. I think the dance award clearly goes to Matthieu and Ernie Borsboom, the first couple of the Royal Netherlands Navy, and my congratulations to you. Nobody cut a rug like them.

Now, sometime in the future—you know, these panelists, they have to work hard. It's not easy. We took a lot of video last night. You probably aren't aware of it, so those of you on the dance floor, we may have to use this video in the future for leverage if we don't get the right response from some of our panel requests. Professor Tom, you know you are armed, and you are now dangerous with that.

My takeaways overall—interdependencies. Clearly it's not about the fact that, [as] we learned from Steve Carmel, our economies are truly interdependent. We learned today how interdependent the cyber domain makes us, and every production chain out there is interdependent. Disruption in one part of the world is going to impact many.

This interdependency and the changing demographics, as we learned this morning, in our maritime nation are going to have a huge influence and importance in our maritime security in the future. Many countries, part of this symposium, were up on those screens this morning and on day one on that panel study.

Second takeaway, again, partnerships. It's a key concept. Engaging as soon as you can in a mission, getting everybody engaged as soon as you can saves you so much time. We are so much more efficient later on, and things are rapidly changing and turning over at such a rapid pace, it's hard to pull somebody else in. Building partnerships sooner pays dividends.

Relations, it's a key element to achieving the goals in the common interest. We heard, I think, again and again, that military-to-military interaction and relationships can have a great leverage, particularly in a disaster. I think the Naval Command College, the Staff College, those students, those kids that are at the O5, O4, maybe O6 level, building those relationships, they can be able to send the e-mail, pick up the phone and get things done, such as a port clearance and aircraft clearance. You know, anything from search and rescue. It will go very far.

We've heard from Chile; we've heard from Japan. We found out in Katrina and Haiti, all of us that worked in those operations, those personal relationships can make all the difference. People, in time, will make all the difference. So in short, personal interactions are really a big part of the overall success.

Those are my three real takeaways there. We'll continue to develop them. We'll continue to imbed them. I urge you to feed those back, your takeaways back, either through direct e-mail to me, direct to the War College, or as you send your candidates and delegates to future games or future courses here as need be.

So as I said in my welcome remarks, we need to develop approaches that can help us share capabilities to the best comon level that makes sense, I think. Share technology and, again, to the best common level that makes sense, share approaches to work together at every means possible. That will make us better in maritime security, and it will get us the prosperity that we talked about, that we have up here today.

Before I close, I hope to see many of you next year. We will be celebrating the two hundredth commemoration of the War of 1812. The War of 1812 for our navy really was our rebirth. We were born in 1775. We were reborn in the War of 1812. The things that we wear, the things that we say, our command structure, and actually the tenets and the foundation of our maritime strategy really were born during this period.

So I hope to see as many of you as possible. I know some of you have already committed, and that's wonderful. We hope to see as many as possible next year. On behalf of my navy, on behalf of my secretary, I want to thank you again for an enlightening experience for myself. I have so much to do as a result of it. It's a little bit clearer where I want to go. Please travel safely. I look forward to seeing all of you so much during my tenure. Thanks again.

APPENDIX

List of Delegates

Albania

RADM Kudret Çela

Algeria

MG Malek Necib
CAPT Zinedine Banat

Angola

ADM Augusto da Silva Cunha
RADM João Maria Ferreira

Antigua and Barbuda

LT Elroy Skerritt

Argentina

ADM Oscar Adolfo Arce
ADM Jorge Omar Godoy
CAPT Horacio Nadale

Australia

RADM Trevor Jones
RADM Tim Barrett

Azerbaijan

CDR Natig Askarov
CDR Asad Rustamov

Bahamas

CDRE Roderick Bowe
LCDR Warren Stafford Bain

Bangladesh

VADM Zahir Uddin Ahmed
CDRE Dewan Mujibur Rahman

Belgium

RDML Michel Hofman

Belize

CAPT John Borland

Benin

CAPT Houssou Dénis Gbessemehlan
CDR Vincent Dedo

Bolivia

ADM Hugo Gonzalo Contreras Llanos

Brazil

ADM Julio Soares de Moura Neto
RADM Ricardo Claro
CMDR André Panno Beirão

Brunei

COL Haji Aznan Hajijulaihi
LT COL Saiful Akhmar Shariff

Bulgaria

RADM Plamen Manushev
CAPT Mitko Petev

Cambodia

VADM Tea Vinh
RADM Khun Borin

Cameroon

RADM Jean Mendoua

Canada

VADM Paul Maddison
Mr. Mario Pelletier
Ms. Jody Thomas

Cape Verde

LTC Antonio Duarte Monteiro
MAJ Joao Baptista Tavares

Chile

ADM Edmundo González Robles
VADM Enrique Larrañaga Martin
CAPT Guillermo Diaz

Colombia

VADM Roberto García Márquez

Comoros

Col Djamala-Diny Moissuli

Congo, Republic of the

RADM André Bouagnabea Moundanza
LCDR Brice Ekougoulou Urlin

Côte d'Ivoire

CAPT Djakaridja Konate
LTC Doulaye Sekongo

Croatia

RADM Ante Urlic

Denmark

RADM Finn Hansen

Djibouti

COL Abdourahman Aden Cher

Dominica

ASP Mervyn Pendenque

Dominican Republic

VADM Nicolas Cabrera Arias
CAPT Benny Batista

Ecuador

VADM Jorge Gross Albornoz
Mr. Miguel Santiago Córdova Chehab

Egypt

RADM Aiman Saleh Mohamed Ibrahim
RADM Mohamed Hesham Mostafa Kamel Eissa

El Salvador

CAPT Rafael Armando Guzman

Estonia

CAPT Igor Schvede
CDR Ivo Värk

Finland

RADM Veli-Jukka Pennala
CDR Raimo Pyysalo

France

ADM Bernard Rogel
RDML Frédéric Jubelin

Gambia

CDRE Madani Senghore
LT Adama Trawally

Georgia

MGEN Zaza Gogava
CAPT Besik Shengelia

Germany

VADM Axel Schimpf
CAPT Markus Krause-Traudes

Ghana

RADM Matthew Quashie
CAPT Seth Amoama

Grenada

ASP Osmond Griffith

Guatemala

VADM Manuel Francisco Sosa Batres
CAPT Tyrone Rene Hidalgo Caceres

Guinea

CAPT Zeze Onivogui

Guyana

CDRE Gary Anthony Rodwell Best
CDR Gary Arlington Beaton

Haiti

Commissar Joseph Wagnac

Honduras

CAPT Rigoberto Espinoza Posadas

Iceland

RADM Georg Lárusson
CDR Ásgrímur Lárus Ásgrímsson

India

ADM Nirmal Verma
CDRE Alok Bhatnagar

Indonesia

VADM Laksdya Marsetio
RADM Didit Herdiawan

Ireland

CDRE Mark Mellett
CDR Martin Counihan

Israel

VADM Ram Rutberg
CAPT Ronen Nimni

Italy

ADM Bruno Branciforte
CAPT Gianluigi Reversi

Jamaica

LCDR David Chin Fong

Japan

ADM Masahiko Sugimoto
VADM Kenichi Uchinami

Jordan

BGEN Qasem Tanashat
COL Muhammad Alnairat

Korea, Republic of

RADM Cho Young-Sam

Latvia

CAPT Rimants Štrimaitis

Lebanon

RADM Nazih Mouhamad Zaher Baroudi
CAPT Nazih Jbaily

Liberia

Mr. Dionysius D. Sebwe
LTJG Stephen Mulbah

Lithuania

RADM Kęstutis Macijauskas

Malaysia

ADM Tan Sri Abdul Aziz Jaafar
RADM Abdul Ghani

Maldives

LT COL Ismail Shareef

Malta

BRIG Martin Xuereb
LTC Andrew Mallia

Mauritania

CAPT Isselkou Ould Cheikh El Welly

Mauritius

CP Dhun Iswur Rampersad

Mexico

ADM Carlos Quinto Guillén
ADM José Santiago Valdés Álvarez

Montenegro

VADM Dragan Samardžic
LCDR Igor Vujacic

Morocco

RDML Lahcen Lyamlouli

The Netherlands

VADM Matthieu Borsboom

New Zealand

RADM Tony Jonathan Parr

Nicaragua

RADM Roger Antonio González Díaz
CDR Juan Benjamin Juarez

Nigeria

VADM Ola Sa'ad Ibrahim
CDRE Samson Oluwole Ojediran

Norway

RADM Bernt Grimstvedt
CDRE Henning Amundsen

Oman

CDRE Al-Raisi Rasheed

Pakistan

RADM Waseem Akram
RADM Shafqat Jawed

Panama

COL Luis Ruiz

Papua New Guinea

CAPT Alois Ur Tom

Peru

ADM Jorge de la Puente
RADM Mauro Cacho

Philippines

VADM Alexander Pama
RADM Edmund Tan

Poland

ADM Tomasz Mathea
CAPT Mirosław Draus

Portugal

VADM José Montenegro

Qatar

BG Ali Al-Mannai
BG Mohammad Al-Mohanadi

Romania

VADM Aurel Popa
CAPT Dan Ciocoiu

Russia

ADM Vladimir Sergeyevich Vysotsky
CAPT Alexander Gorelova

St. Kitts and Nevis

LT COL Patrick Wallace

St. Vincent and the Grenadines

LT Deon Henry

São Tomé and Príncipe

CAPT Joao Idalecio

Saudi Arabia

VADM Dakheel Allah Al-Wagdani

Senegal

CAPT Jean Faye
CAPT Oumar Baila Kane

Seychelles

Col Clifford Roseline
Lt Col Michael Rosette

Sierra Leone

CAPT Daniel Saio Mansaray
LT Amara Saeed Kallon

Singapore

RADM Ng Chee Peng

Slovenia

RADM Renato Petrič

South Africa

VADM Johannes Refiloe Mudimu
RADM Robert Higgs

Spain

ADM Manuel Rebollo García

Sri Lanka

RADM Jayanath Colombage
RADM Ruwan Dias
CDR Ruwan Kalubowila

Suriname

LT COL Marino Acton
CPT Delana Guillermo Baal

Sweden

RADM Jan Thörnqvist

Tanzania

Maj Gen Said Shaaban Omar
Col Joachim Endelesi Karia

Thailand

CAPT Graisri Gesorn

Togo

CAPT Ametsipe Yawo Atiogbé
CDR Kossi Mayo

Tonga

CAPT Toni Mavulo Fonokalafi

Trinidad and Tobago

CDR Hiram Amos Mohammed
LCDR Norman Ryan Dindial

Tunisia

CAPT Slaheddine Cherif

Turkey

ADM Emin Murat Bilgel
RADM Serdar Dülger
CAPT Cihat Yayci

Tuvalu

SUPT Talafou Fakaapoga Esekia

Ukraine

ADM Viktor Volodymyrovych Maksymov
CAPT Andriy Ryzhenko

United Arab Emirates

BRIG Ibrahim S. M. Almusharrakh
CAPT Abdulla Al Husain Al Shehhi
CDR Abdulla Sultan Hassan Al Khozaimy

United Kingdom

ADM Sir Mark Stanhope
CDRE Jonathan Handley
CDRE Eric Fraser

United States

The Honorable Ray Mabus
The Honorable Juan M. Garcia III
The Honorable Paul Oostburg Sanz
ADM Jonathan Greenert
ADM Mark Ferguson
ADM Samuel Locklear
ADM Robert Papp
Gen. Joseph Dunford
VADM Jerry Beaman
VADM Manson Brown
VADM David Buss
VADM Kendall Card
VADM Bruce Clingan
VADM Mark Fox
VADM Richard Gallagher
VADM Harry Harris
VADM Joseph Kernan

VADM Bill Landay III
VADM Joe Leidig
VADM Kenneth McCoy
VADM Frank Pandolfe
VADM Robert Parker
VADM Mike Rogers
VADM Brian Salerno
VADM Scott Swift
RADM Robin Braun
RADM Nevin Carr
RADM John Christenson
RADM Phillip Cullom
RADM Steve Eastburg
RADM Bruce Grooms
RADM Arthur Johnson
RADM James Kelly
RADM Kurt Tidd
RADM David Titley
RDML Bradley Gehrke
RDML Paul Grosklags
RDML Robert Hoppa
RDML Terry Kraft
RDML Richard Landolt
RDML Kenneth Norton
RDML Charles Rainey
RDML Joseph Rixey
RDML Doug Venlet
RDML (Sel) Denny Wetherald
AMB Mary Ann Peters
AMB Asif Chaudhry
Mr. Stephen Carmel
Mr. Clookie
Dr. Joseph DiRenzo III
Dr. Nicholas Eberstadt
Dean John Garofano
Mr. Sandy MacIsaac
Ms. Kristen Madison
Mr. Robert Martinage
Dean Vincent Mocini
Mr. Rino Pivirotto
Dean Robert Rubel
Prof. Michael Sherlock
Dr. Paul Speer

Uruguay

RADM Daniel Héctor Núñez
CAPT Juan Carlos Oliver

Vanuatu

SUPT Tari Tamata

Vietnam

RADM Nguyen Viet Nhien

Yemen

BG Ali Ahmed Yahya Rasa'a

www.ingramcontent.com/pod-product-compliance
Lightning Source LLC
Chambersburg PA
CBHW082118230426
43671CB00015B/2732